TEACHING HIS

Related titles:

Richard Bailey and Tony Macfadyen: *Teaching Physical Education 5–11*
Peter Benton and Tim O'Brien: *Special Needs and the Beginning Teacher*
Asher Cashdan and Lyn Overall (eds): *Teaching in Primary Schools*
Sue Cowley: *Starting Teaching*
Christine Farmery: *Teaching Science 3–11*
Duncan Grey: *The Internet in School* (2nd Edition)
Mark O'Hara: *Teaching 3–8*
Janet Kay: *Protecting Children*
Rosalind Millam: *Anti-discriminatory Practice* (2nd Edition)
David Owen and Alison Ryan: *Teaching Geography 3–11*
Carole Sharman, Wendy Cross and Diana Vennis: *Observing Children* (2nd Edition)
Angela Thody, Barbara Gray and Derek Bowden: *The Teacher's Survival Guide*

Reaching the Standard
Series editor: Mark O'Hara

Teaching History 3–11

THE ESSENTIAL GUIDE

Lucy O'Hara and Mark O'Hara

continuum
LONDON · NEW YORK

Continuum

The Tower Building	15 East 26th Street
11 York Road	New York
London SE1 7NX	NY 10010

www.continuumbooks.com

First published 2001
Reprinted 2004

British Library Cataloguing-in-Publication Data

A catalogue record for this book is available from the British Library.

ISBN: 0-8264-5112-8

Designed and typeset by Ben Cracknell Studios
Printed and bound in Great Britain by Biddles Ltd, King's Lynn, Norfolk

Contents

Acknowledgements

We would like to thank friends, colleagues and pupils at St Bede's RC Nursery/ Primary School and Carlton Park Nursery/Infant School for their help in providing some of the exemplar materials with which to illustrate the book, as well as Mrs Ada Collingham for her donation of 1930s artefacts including the cigarette cards. We would also like to thank colleagues at Sheffield Hallam University, particularly Van Gore for his comments on the nature of history as a discipline and Nick Hodge for his constructive and valuable criticisms concerning history and pupils with special educational needs. Finally thanks too to Mrs Holloway for fostering a passion for the past that has lasted for over thirty years and shows no sign of abating yet.

Preface

This book covers the teaching and learning of history and as such makes use of a subject heading which is found in the National Curriculum but not in the Early Learning Goals. Learning in the Foundation Stage is not structured along subject boundaries as it is in the National Curriculum. This difference is based on current understandings of how younger pupils in particular learn and how they do not necessarily make the same subject distinctions with which adults seek to organize teaching and learning. The under-5s curriculum is organized into areas of learning which correspond to, but do not replicate, the subjects in the National Curriculum. In nursery and reception classes activities can offer starting points for learning across a number of areas of learning. Consequently introducing history as a subject in the Foundation Stage is thought inappropriate. It is hard to envisage how the youngest pupils who are coming to terms with concepts like yesterday, today and tomorrow can be asked to deal effectively with much of history as it appears in the current National Curriculum documentation. That said, younger children can be successfully introduced to some early ideas about chronology and the passage of time which will help to lay the foundations for their future learning in history.

Children in the Foundation Stage can be introduced to the following ideas

- there was a past;
- the past was different from the present;
- continuity and change;
- similarities and differences;
- cause and effect;
- there was an order or sequence to the past;
- in many cases (though not all) objects and information from the past remain and can help us to make sense of what things used to be like.

(Edwards and Knight, 1994)

As authors therefore we are faced either with the use of unwieldy qualifications every time the term history is used or the employment of shorthand. As a result, in the interests of readability, the term *history* will be used in those sections of the book not dealing specifically with the Foundation Stage. Readers who are about to embark on school experience with children in the Foundation Stage need to realize that when applying some of the material contained in the book to early years settings, it is more appropriate to utilize the ideas contained in the list above, rather than thinking about history as a distinctive body of knowledge.

Clarification is also necessary in relation to two other areas. First, as many early years settings are outside of the mainstream education system, the contents of the Early Learning Goals are not compulsory in the same way that National Curriculum Programmes of Study are in schools. However, the Early Learning Goals set out the desired learning outcomes for children upon completion of their reception year and those nurseries that are part of mainstream education, as well as reception classes, are expected to be using the Early Learning Goals to structure their work with pupils aged 3–5. Therefore, although the Early Learning Goals have a slightly different status, the term *curriculum* will be used throughout the book to describe the educational provision for all pupils aged between 3 and 11 years of age. Second, the book seeks to address teaching and learning across the Foundation Stage and Key Stages 1 and 2. Once again there is a danger that in our efforts to be inclusive the text will become indigestible. As a result we have opted to use terms like *primary* and *school* as shorthand for those settings where the whole 3–11 age range is represented. In those instances where 3–5 settings are being discussed separately the terms *Foundation Stage*, *nursery* or *reception* will be used.

REFERENCE

Edwards, A. and Knight, P. (1994) *Effective Early Years Education: Teaching Young Children*. Buckingham: Open University Press.

Standards Information

This book is aimed at newly qualified and teacher-training students working in the 3–11 age range. It is intended to be of use to those students and teachers who require non-core, non-specialist history knowledge and those who have a subject specialism in this area of the curriculum. The Standards and requirements for non-core subject knowledge and understanding are set out in DfEE *Circular 4/98*: *Teaching: High Status, High Standards* (DfEE, 1998). However, unlike the core curriculum areas of English, mathematics and science as well as Information and Communications Technology the specific content for history is not yet prescribed. The documentation does, however, make clear that those students and teachers for whom history is a non-core, non-specialist subject need to have a secure subject knowledge equivalent to Level 7 of the National Curriculum (DfEE, 1998, p. 11). As a result non-core, non-specialists may wish to gauge their knowledge, skills and understanding of history against the level description below.

> Pupils make links between their factual knowledge and understanding of the history of Britain and the wider world. They use these links to analyse the relationships between features of a particular period or society, and to analyse reasons for, and results of, events and changes. They explain how and why different historical interpretations have been produced. Pupils show some independence in following lines of enquiry, using their knowledge and understanding to identify, evaluate and use sources of information critically. They sometimes reach substantiated conclusions independently. They select, organize and use relevant information to produce well-structured narratives, descriptions and explanations, making appropriate use of dates and terms.   (QCA, 1999a)

Students and teachers with history as a subject specialism are required to have a secure knowledge of the subject to at least the standard approximating to GCE Advanced Level in those aspects of the subject taught at Key Stages 1 and 2 (DfEE, 1998, p. 11).

All students and newly qualified teachers need to be able to demonstrate that they

- have a detailed knowledge and understanding of the history National Curriculum Programmes of Study and level descriptions across the primary age range (Annex A, Section A, 2di);
- can cope securely with historical questions which pupils raise (Annex A, Section A, 2diii);

- understand the progression from the Early Learning Goals (QCA, 1999b)/Desirable Outcomes for Children's Learning on Entering Compulsory Education to Key Stage 1, the progression from Key Stage 1 to Key Stage 2 and from Key Stage 2 to Key Stage 3 (Annex A, Section A, 2div);
- are aware of, and know how to assess, recent inspection evidence and classroom relevant research on teaching primary pupils in history, and know how to use this to inform and improve teaching (Annex A, Section A, 2dv);
- know pupils' most common misconceptions and mistakes in history (Annex A, Section A, 2dvi);
- have a working knowledge of IT to a standard equivalent to Level 8 in the National Curriculum for pupils and understand the contribution IT makes to history (Annex A, Section A, 2dvii);
- are familiar with history-specific health and safety requirements, where relevant, and plan lessons to avoid potential hazards (Annex A, Section A, 2dviii).

Not only are students and teachers required to demonstrate knowledge and understanding of the subject, they also have to demonstrate the ability to

- plan, teach and manage history in the classroom (Annex A, Section B);
- monitor, assess, record and report on pupils' progress in history (Annex A, Section C);
- fulfil any other professional requirements in relation to history (Annex A, Section D), for example ensuring equality of opportunity and taking responsibility for their own professional development.

Although the structure of the book does not track the order of these requirements, it does address the Standards contained in each of the sections in Annex A (DfEE, 1998). The list below provides the reader with a quick guide to where particular information can be located.

Standards	Chapters
• Knowledge and understanding of history and the history curriculum	1, 2
• Planning, teaching and managing history lessons	3, 4, 5
• Assessing, recording and reporting on history	6
• Fulfilling other professional requirements in relation to history	7, 8, 9

REFERENCES

DfEE (1998) *Circular 4/98: Teaching: High Status, High Standards*. London: Department for Education and Employment.

QCA (1999a) *The National Curriculum: Handbook for Primary Teachers in England*. London:DfEE/ Qualifications and Curriculum Authority.

QCA (1999b) *Early Learning Goals*. London: Qualifications and Curriculum Authority.

Introduction

This book is intended as an introduction to history for newly qualified teachers and teacher training students on 3–11 courses. The book seeks to provide the reader with insights into the nature of the subject and effective ways of planning, teaching and assessing history in primary and foundation settings. It also considers cross-curricular issues that affect teaching and learning in all subjects, such as equality of opportunity and special educational needs (SEN). The book concludes with an evaluation of the role of a history specialist in coordinating history across a whole school. At the end of some of the chapters the reader will find a set of reflective questions intended to reinforce the points made and involve the reader more actively in the subject matter.

Chapter 1 deals with the nature of history as a subject and raises questions about the extent to which it is possible to know how things really happened in the past. It argues that although historical evidence is inevitably incomplete and has to be viewed critically, it is possible for historians to develop increasingly plausible and powerful explanations of past events. The chapter goes on to consider some of the arguments advanced for the teaching of history.

Chapter 2 examines the nature of history in the National Curriculum at Key Stages 1 and 2 and offers suggestions on how aspects of the Early Learning Goals can be used to begin to raise young children's awareness of concepts such as chronology, time and change. The chapter explores the process of history as set out in the 'Knowledge, skills and understanding' component of the Programmes of Study and provides the reader with some examples of history lessons linked to the various study units. The chapter concludes with an overview of the links between history and the wider curriculum involving the cross-curricular skills of literacy and numeracy.

Chapter 3 focuses upon planning and organizing history. It begins by considering the need to ensure continuity and progression in the subject across the 3–11 age range and introduces SCAA's blocked, continuing and linked approaches to planning (SCAA, 1995). The chapter continues by considering development in planning from whole-school long-term plans, through year group and class medium-term planning to short-term planning involving individual history lessons and sessions. Throughout these sections examples taken from across the foundation and primary phases are given. The chapter then considers the relative merits of whole class teaching and group work approaches in history lessons and outlines a number of different approaches to differentiation in history in order to cater for individual needs. The chapter also considers pupil misconceptions in history and suggests strategies for dealing with these. The chapter concludes with guidance on self-evaluation as a mechanism for improving the quality of teaching and learning in history and suggests sources of information and research that can be used to inform history teaching.

Chapter 4 outlines a range of effective teaching and learning strategies in history. The chapter begins by outlining a series of evidence-based approaches to the subject including the use of artefacts, site visits, audio and visual materials, oral work, written documentation and new technologies. The chapter then proceeds to suggest ways in which evidence-based approaches can feed into more creative and imaginative approaches to history and the development of empathy in the subject.

Chapter 5 reviews some of the resources for teaching and learning in history. The chapter takes a broad view of the term resources and includes attention to the learning environment within the classroom, the use of environments and resources beyond the nursery or school and looks at ways of incorporating historical learning into partnerships between home and school.

Chapter 6 deals with the important area of assessment, recording and reporting. Teachers are becoming increasingly accountable for their work. This aspect of their role plays a major part in providing feedback on pupil progress which can be used to target set with children, keeping parents informed about their children's attainment and informing future planning and teaching in history.

Chapter 7 considers the potential for teaching and learning in history to make a positive contribution to the provision of equality of opportunity in the classroom. Not only can the content of the history curriculum be used to challenge stereotypical attitudes and beliefs, the process of historical enquiry can be tailored to underpin an entitlement approach to the curriculum. The chapter examines strategies that teachers can employ in their history teaching to foster fairness, equity and social justice in their classrooms.

Chapter 8 considers the needs of the 20 per cent of pupils with special educational needs in history. These needs range widely and include physical disabilities, learning difficulties and children who might be identified as gifted or talented. The chapter outlines some of the special needs that teachers may encounter and offers suggestions on how the curriculum can be adapted and delivered to support the historical learning of children with special educational needs.

Chapter 9 deals with the role of curriculum coordinator that most teachers now have to take on early in their careers. The chapter outlines the roles and responsibilities of history coordinators and identifies some of the challenges facing coordinators when trying to manage and initiate change in the history curriculum across a school. The chapter takes an inspection report from the Office for Standards in Education (Ofsted) into the teaching and learning of history in a hypothetical school. It uses the history coordinator's responses to the report as a vehicle through which to explore some of the key skills that a history coordinator needs to employ in order to be effective in the role.

REFERENCE

SCAA (1995) *Planning the Curriculum at Key Stages 1 and 2*. London: School Curriculum and Assessment Authority.

History

It is likely that people's understanding of the nature of history will vary widely. For the academic historian, history may be 'an unusual discipline. Its core is hard fact that you cannot get away from and have to learn to master. At the same time you have to be deductive, perceptive and imaginative in the use of that fact' (Carpenter, in QCA, 1999a). For those whose relationship with history is that of occasional consumer, views of the subject may be a product of dimly remembered school lessons, politicians' pronouncements, vague recollections of newspaper articles and television documentaries, personal experience and the transmitted reminiscences and assertions of acquaintances, friends and family. Her Majesty's Inspectors (HMI, 1988) defined history as the study of *everything that has happened*, which, given the incomplete record available, would inevitably be less than the full story but would still be *extremely large and complex*. In this definition the historical record constitutes a body of knowledge and provides the content of the subject. At the same time, the means of gathering, analysing, interpreting and communicating the record constitutes the process of history.

This chapter seeks to explore some of the issues raised by the HMI definition and to discuss reasons why history ought to be a part of the curriculum. It will begin by considering the content of history and the essentially evidence-based nature of the subject. The chapter will outline a range of possible sources before dealing with some of the challenges that evidence from the past presents for historians. Not only may the evidence tend to favour some historical characters ahead of others (history is much more than biographies of famous people), the evidence is not independent of interpretation. The chapter suggests that the facts of history are far from being non-negotiable and that history ought to concern more than just the pasts of powerful, worthy or infamous individuals. It continues by looking at the problems historians can encounter when engaged in the process of history as they attempt to narrate or explain past events. This first section concludes by considering to what extent historians can ever know *how things really were*.

The second part of the chapter considers some of the reasons offered for the inclusion of history in the primary curriculum. The section begins by considering a commonly used argument in support of history, namely that history offers a society a means of avoiding past mistakes. The section then considers the potential educational and economic benefits to be gained from teaching and learning in history. History's intrinsic worth and power to fascinate and motivate forms the third area for consideration and, fourth, the notion of history as a transmitter of *cultural heritages* is discussed. In each of these cases there is much to support history's place as part of the curriculum but the reader will see that none of these claims is unproblematic. While, for example, history can offer insights into contemporary events it does not make historians prophets. The chapter concludes by returning to the work of HMI and attempting to summarize the contribution made by history to children's learning.

The Content of History

The body of knowledge that is history is built on the foundation provided by the available evidence. This historical record can take many forms. While some evidence overtly attempts to tell future generations how things were and who was involved, other evidence may have been intended for a much more contemporary audience. An important source of evidence for historians is documentary evidence. However, while access to documentation of all kinds is an essential part of much historical study, historical evidence is by no means always written evidence. For some historical periods the documentary evidence base may be so small as to result more in intelligent speculation than interpretation of a comprehensive set of contemporary accounts. Historians dealing with ancient cultures and civilizations, for example, may have very little in the way of written or pictorial records and what does exist may concern a tiny proportion of the population. In these cases historians may have only limited archaeological evidence, such as artefacts or geographical features, to help them develop their theories (NCC, 1993). Those engaged in historical study may, therefore, need to employ a wide range of methods of enquiry and investigation and draw on numerous types of evidence.

Historians may seek to understand the past through an examination of visual evidence such as frescos, mosaics, photographs, film, paintings, and sketches. Alternatively where the period being studied is within living memory, they may seek oral evidence and eyewitness accounts of past events and periods. This approach has a long, if chequered, tradition dating back to classical Greece (Warren, 1999). Other historians may glean insights into life in former times by investigating and comparing artefacts. Examples of artefacts of interest to some historians might include coins, stamps, clothing, weapons, toys, tools and utensils. Still other historians may examine whole structures such as houses, churches, transport infrastructure, castles, palaces, factories, shops, vessels or vehicles. Evidence of use to historians may also be obtained by utilizing scientific study such as dendrochronology or geophysical surveys to investigate historical sites in an effort to discover how these locations have been altered by people over time. Medical and scientific evidence may also offer historians information on diet, living conditions, life expectancy, physical appearance and even place of birth. In some instances historians may engage in experimental archaeology, seeking to replicate past technologies as a way of compensating for an absence of hard evidence. Various television documentary series, for example *Mysteries of Lost Empires* (Channel 4, 2000), have covered some of these attempts. Finally, some historians may draw upon comparative studies of current settings and cultures in an attempt to achieve similar understanding relating to past societies.

It is inevitable given the incomplete nature of the historical record that some people will feature more than others. It is simply not possible to study every individual person from the past. Even if the evidence existed, historians would have to be selective if only because the task would otherwise become unmanageable. While history contains stories about individuals, historical evidence tends to favour those with the time and skills to keep a record or, alternatively, with the resources or power to get someone else to do it for them. Historical writing in the nineteenth century and earlier tended to take this dominant form and it has had a powerful and long-lasting impact upon everyday perceptions about the nature of the subject. History is replete with individuals deemed important or significant by historians as a result of their social position, authority, worthy deeds or knavish actions.

Studying the lives of prominent and powerful people from the past and the events surrounding their behaviour is certainly part of history. It is hard to envisage an overview of Ancient Greece that did not mention Alexander the Great or a publication on the Tudor period in Britain that failed to even acknowledge the existence of Henry VIII or Elizabeth I. Members of ruling elites and powerful groups are highly likely to leave *footprints* in the form of pictures, documentation or arte-facts. Furthermore, their access to the levers of power means that their actions may well have a profound impact upon the course of history. Similarly, history may also include accounts of other individuals who were not rulers, but who have also come to be viewed by historians as significant or interesting. However, the individuals on whom historians have detailed evidence were not acting in a vacuum, nor were they the only people taking decisions and making choices that were to affect the future.

Many thousands of people decided to leave rural communities in England in the eighteenth and nineteenth centuries in response to poverty or to take advantage of the new industries growing in the large towns. We remember few of their names yet collectively their decisions had a profound impact upon British history (Thompson, 1963). Similarly, large numbers of Irish people emigrated around the world throughout much of recorded history for reasons that are hotly contested by scholars. Although most of these émigrés are anonymous to historians, their impact has been considerable in many of the countries in which they settled as is illustrated by the power and influence of the Irish–American lobby at certain junctures on aspects of American domestic and foreign policy (O'Brien and O'Brien, 1985).

We all have a history worthy of investigation. History is the story of humanity's past not just the past of a relatively small number of powerful individuals. The stories that history can tell and the analyses that historians develop have characters of every description, ordinary and famous, young and old, male and female, black and white. Although the evidence base is likely to favour some more than others, history is an attempt to increase and improve our understanding of the ideas, beliefs, aspirations, feelings, reactions and decisions of people from all walks of life by examining what they said, wrote, built, made, discovered or destroyed.

The Process of History

Only at its simplest level could history be said to be a body of knowledge or collection of facts that tell us how things really happened in the past. Vikings did attack and invade parts of Britain. There was a world war between 1939 and 1945. Queen Victoria was queen until her death in 1901. We can say with certainty that these and other similar historical statements are true and objective in so far as they are supported by a wealth of documentary evidence and are beyond argument. However, although facts such as those above are important in history, they do not in themselves constitute history. While there are many different potential sources of evidence for historians to draw on there exist problems. A definition of history as a collection of facts about the past is an incomplete definition as it rests on the assumption that there can be certainty about the facts and that they are independent of interpretation or ranking and this is not the case. Documentary evidence, for example, is not always in a form that is immediately understandable or useable by historians. People in the past have recorded many things for many reasons and informing future generations is unlikely to have been a motivating factor in many cases. The documentary historical record is incomplete and subjective. An examination of a postcard from the early part of the twentieth century might constitute a piece of the historical record. Historians could learn about the experiences of a particular individual such as the weather, holiday activities or significant events. It would suggest parallels with today, such as the idea of travelling for a vacation and sending postcards. It might also illustrate differences such as changes in the built environment, modes of transport, holiday destinations, fashion or social norms. But there would also be gaps in the record, things missed out or not seen as worthy of recording given the purpose of the card. The card might raise far more questions than it answered. Historical evidence has to be interpreted not simply presented (Arnold, 2000).

History is an activity as much as it is a body of received knowledge. Uncritical approaches to the notion of history as a collection of facts ignore the problems associated with interpretation at source and secondary interpretation by subsequent historians. Much of the evidence that historians locate and use cannot be regarded as untainted and unadulterated. As history is the study of what people have recorded and left behind, historians have to recognize that people are subjective, they interpret events and evidence and, what is more, people make mistakes. Many of the apparently objective facts that historians work with have already been processed by others; put another way, there can be interpretation at source. Tacitus' account of the revolt of the Iceni and Trinobanti tribes in early Roman Britain is a case in point. Tacitus clearly has a view about the actions of both the Romans and the Britons involved. Recognition, admonition and style of writing are all employed 'to persuade the reader to imitate or to shun the behaviour of the historian's characters' (Warren, 1999). Roman settlers and centurions are referred to as plunderers. Later in his account, phrases such as 'the genius of a savage people leads them always in a quest for plunder' and 'military skill was not the talent of barbarians' leave the reader in little doubt as to where Tacitus stood on the issues (www.britannia.com). At the same time, his word-for-word account of Boudicca's and Suetonius' speeches to their respective armies before the final confrontation are suitably heroic but they beg the question of how he could possibly know what was said in such detail. The reader is left with the strong suspicion that artistic licence has been employed in the service of Tacitus' objective which was to teach moral and political lessons (Warren, 1999).

Clearly then, those giving evidence from the past can be biased. Witnesses from the past may have made conscious decisions about what was significant and should be included in their accounts and what was not important and was therefore omitted. In addition, past chroniclers may also have been influenced unconsciously by the prevailing attitudes and beliefs of the cultures and societies in which they lived. These values and attitudes can also influence the objectivity and reliability of the data available to historians in subtle and not so subtle ways, for example historical sources that hold the inferiority of the Jews or black peoples to be self evident. It is equally possible that when making decisions about what to record mistakes were made. Uncritical examination of the evidence can result in the perpetuation of historical inaccuracy and even myth as historical fact. The portrayal of Vikings with horned helmets in battle or the anachronistic confusion and conflation of the armour worn by medieval knights with Dark Ages warriors are but two examples of inaccuracy and myth.

An English monk who has been told of the destruction of a monastery, the theft of its valuable artefacts and the killing or enslavement of some of his fellow monks at the hands of Viking raiders can hardly be expected to be objective in his reporting of the event. Similarly, as a Christian he may be influenced by different values and beliefs from the pagan perpetrators and this too may colour his account; perhaps he views the Vikings as a punishment sent by God for the sins of the people. Just as important is the fact that our hypothetical monk is reporting second hand, calling into question still further the accuracy of at least parts of his account. Finally, he is unlikely to have known of the artistic, commercial and technical achievements of the culture whose members have just inflicted such damage upon his community, yet the Vikings were explorers, traders, farmers and artists as well as warriors.

Evidence is mounting to suggest Viking settlements in North America hundreds of years before Columbus set sail, they also established vast trading areas that extended far into what is modern day Russia. At the same time, English towns and villages ending with *by* or *thorpe*, local dialects and customs, and the people themselves are testimony to the Vikings as settlers and farmers (www.viking.no/e/heritage/). There is no doubt that the Vikings were responsible for their fair share of destruction and it would be very wrong to seek to portray them as misunderstood tourists of the eighth, ninth and tenth centuries. However, in the context of the period, it is hard to see them as much more violent than many of the other peoples they had dealings with, some of whose members were recording their activities. Rape, pillage, arson, murder, looting and theft were hardly the preserve of the pagan Vikings, Christian armies were more than capable of equalling Viking ferocity and brutality (Sawyer, 1997).

Historians have to try to understand the context within which the evidence they have was produced. While the employment of an empathetic approach to this critical analysis must be tempered by attention to the evidence, it nevertheless inevitably results in interpretations that are not always easily susceptible to proof and verification. The facts have to be interpreted by contemporary historians who will themselves be creatures of their own time and location. They in their turn will make decisions about what facts are significant and what are not. In doing this they cannot help but view the past with contemporary eyes and select facts with the benefit of hindsight which inform their decisions about what was or was not important (Rogers, 1987). In an important sense therefore, 'history is the projection of ideology into the past' (Keegan, 1989). Historians can and do argue fiercely not only over the accuracy of data but also over the interpretation that can be placed upon it.

Some examples of historical debates

Historians have argued over whether or not the last quarter of the nineteenth century saw Victorian Britain and other industrialized nations experiencing a great depression and what the effects of this were. For some the answer was yes while others contested the very concept of a depression and its impact on various sectors of society and the economy.

(Crouzet, 1982)

A study of the history of the causes of the Second World War offers further insight into the range of historical interpretation possible. While many historians agree that there is a link between the First and the Second World Wars, beyond this there exists an extensive range of differing interpretations on causes (Keegan, 1989). Some historians have sought to emphasize diplomatic and military rivalries between the great powers of the day, laying the blame at the door of Germany's ambition for world power or on the weakness and vacillation of the appeasing powers in the 1930s. Other historians have highlighted economic competition, including the struggle for colonies and overseas markets for

6

industrial goods. Some have even sought to apply ideas originating in Freudian psychoanalysis in an effort to explain events.

Historians therefore have to work with incomplete data that is open to interpretation. The fact that the activities of historians often result in a range of possible explanations requires those engaged in this work to retain a degree of flexibility and open-mindedness on the subject of how, why, what and when things happened in the past. The evidence they have to draw on may be open to a number of different interpretations. In the case of documentary evidence, the historian cannot assume that a chronicler was in a position that offered a complete overview of events and may need to seek verification by drawing on a wider range of sources.

So Can Historians Ever Know How Things Really Happened?

As all data is both incomplete and processed, all observers are partial and all historians are projecting their own ideas and beliefs onto events, it is hard at first to envisage how anything can be truly known about the past. It might at first appear as though every historical story or explanation is as valid as every other historical story or explanation.

Such a reaction, however, would be depressing, potentially dangerous and would not do justice to the understanding that historians have made possible through their efforts. It is possible to know about the past but the varied nature and, in some cases, the paucity of the historical evidence, combined with the inevitability of interpretation, mean that historical knowledge must be considered provisional, as historians and others seek to refine and improve their ideas about the past. Historians must continually question the facts, taking care over those they select and not ignoring important evidence that does not fit neatly into their theories or which calls them into question. They must weigh up competing interpretations and acknowledge and be open about their own involvement in the process of history, recognizing that this is likely to affect their judgement.

Certainly historians need to exercise caution in claiming truth and objectivity in their evidence but this does not mean that they should assume a relativist position, for historians can seek a degree of objectivity in their methods. While they may struggle to arrive at the *correct* answer they can try to ensure an intellectually rigorous approach to their enquiry, characterized by attention to the available evidence and an effort to ensure rational argument and debate based upon it. While objectivity as an abstract goal may be impossible, historians can and must strive to be objective in their practice. The evidence-based aspect of historical endeavour will impose a set of controls and limits simply in terms of what is available. Furthermore, as with other academic disciplines, historians are

Look at the image below. Do you see a goblet or do you see two faces in profile? The image does not change but it is possible to view it in different ways. Similarly, different historians may look at the same data and yet develop alternative ideas about its significance.

http://members.aol.com/Ryanbut/illusion4.html

Industrialization in late eighteenth- and nineteenth-century Britain

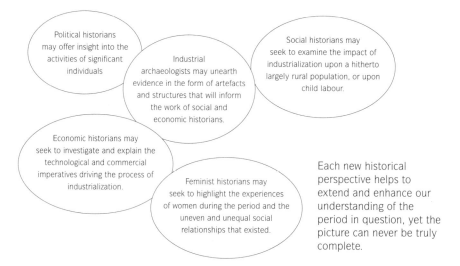

Political historians may offer insight into the activities of significant individuals

Industrial archaeologists may unearth evidence in the form of artefacts and structures that will inform the work of social and economic historians.

Social historians may seek to examine the impact of industrialization upon a hitherto largely rural population, or upon child labour.

Economic historians may seek to investigate and explain the technological and commercial imperatives driving the process of industrialization.

Feminist historians may seek to highlight the experiences of women during the period and the uneven and unequal social relationships that existed.

Each new historical perspective helps to extend and enhance our understanding of the period in question, yet the picture can never be truly complete.

part of a community and their ideas, theories and methods will be subjected to critical review within this community and this provides yet another mechanism with which they can seek to develop more reliable ideas about the past. The aim of the historian is not to produce the *right* history but to produce *better* history. Not perfect, not complete, but improved.

The study of history involves much more than mastering a prescribed set of universally agreed names, dates and events in the correct sequence. History is also an enquiry-based activity. It attempts to offer increasingly powerful ways of understanding and explaining the past, by developing increasingly plausible explanations of what happened and why things happened in the way that they did (cause and effect). In their efforts to develop this increasingly comprehensive body of knowledge, historians must utilize a range of investigative skills and techniques. History involves asking questions and different historians may highlight different features and develop a range of different interpretations depending upon the questions they ask. It would be wrong to see the procedural and content aspects of history as separate or sequential, whereby having inquired historians are then able to make a definitive statement about what happened, when and why. History involves a symbiotic relationship between the available evidence and its interpretation, an interplay between an enquiry carried out by a historian and the past events into which he/she inquires. The relationship between the two strands is iterative in nature and the outcomes are provisional. As we will see in Chapter 2, this is a pattern that is repeated in the teaching and learning of history in schools.

Why Study History?

How do you know who you are unless you know where you've come from? How can you tell what's going to happen, unless you know what's happened before? History isn't just about the past. It's about why we are who we are – and about what's next.

(Robinson, in QCA, 1999a, p. 103)

It is understandable to set great store by disciplines that can offer a degree of certainty or utility and as such are instantly recognizable as essential parts of any curriculum. The fundamental importance of English and mathematics in enabling children to function in the modern world and to get the most out of their education is indisputable. Similarly subjects such as science are essential if children are to comprehend the workings of the physical universe, while others such as Information and Communications Technology (ICT) are likely to play an increasingly important role in future employment. But what are the reasons for studying history? A failure to include history on the curriculum is unlikely to lead to children underachieving in other areas of the curriculum or result in pupils who lack key skills for employment in a modern industrial economy. Similarly studying humanity's past will shed little light on the laws of nature. Consequently, history could be seen by some as having little practical use and hence it could be regarded as interesting but, at best, peripheral to the real business of primary education. However, to draw the conclusion that disciplines which result in outcomes that are provisional, debatable or contentious should be regarded as less reliable and hence intrinsically less worthwhile and useful is in our view a mistake. Part of the worth and value of history is as a direct result of the fact that it involves enquiry and deals with uncertainty. It is our position that history can and does make an important contribution to children's education in general and a unique contribution to their social, cultural and intellectual development in particular. We therefore need to make a case for this, particularly in the light of changing national priorities and the resulting pressures on schools and nurseries. The final section of this chapter discusses four arguments in support of the teaching of history.

1. History offers children a means by which they can gain insights into the affairs of the modern world (HMI, 1988) by revealing examples of how the past has influenced the present and by offering lessons for the future.
2. History provides opportunities for the development of key learning skills of use across the whole curriculum and in adult life.
3. History involves subject matter that is intrinsically interesting and has the potential to motivate, stimulate and fire children's curiosity, while the process of historical enquiry fits well with social interactionist (Bruce, 1997) views of how children learn.
4. History plays a unique and pivotal role in personal and social development through the transmission of society's 'cultural heritages' (HMI, 1988) as children explore the choices, attitudes and values of people in the past.

1.   History is about 'what's next': avoiding past mistakes

An oft-made claim for the need to study the past is the lessons that can be learnt for the future. It is sometimes suggested that those who fail to appreciate the lessons of history will be doomed to repeat the mistakes of the past. It was said of the French, for example, that in their attempt to prevent a repetition of the slaughter of troops experienced during the First World War by developing the border defences of the Maginot Line, they had remembered everything and learnt nothing. According to this view, an understanding of history allows societies to avoid reliving and repeating past errors and to have a clearer picture of what action to take in the future.

However, there are problems with the view of history as provider of signposts for the future. First, it assumes that the concept of a *mistake* can be universally agreed upon and, as we have already seen, historians frequently disagree on exactly what the lessons to be learned might be. The policy of appeasement adopted by British governments towards Nazi Germany prior to 1939 is often cited as a mistake from which we must learn. The Iraqi invasion of Kuwait led to Saddam Hussein being likened to Adolf Hitler by Western politicians and some of the media. His regime was equated with the Nazi regime of the 1930s and 40s in Germany, his army's occupation of Kuwait likened to German territorial gains obtained by force. The *failure* of the inter-war policy of appeasement was held up as a lesson to all about the dangers of giving in to such people. Hussein and other similar individuals may well be ruthless and brutal but such simplistic analogies do not help our understanding of the situations in either Nazi Germany or the Middle East. The inter-war policy of appeasement may have failed to prevent the Second World War but it could be argued, given Britain's then lack of military preparedness for a major conflict, the politicians of the day had limited policy options prior to 1939–40.

Not only are the lessons to be drawn from past events often hotly contested, it is also too simplistic to think that because 'A' may have followed 'B' in the past the same will be true today. To take a handful of markers or characteristics and use these to claim comparability across all aspects of life in given situations risks masking real and important differences. There may be analogies and similarities between the past and the present but circumstances and characters will never be identical and this is bound to make prediction and prophecy difficult to say the least. This was graphically illustrated by the events in Kosovo in 1999. Western politicians cited a previous climb-down a few months earlier on the part of the Serbian leadership when threatened with air strikes as their reason for believing that threatening air strikes a second time would be successful in halting the actions of Yugoslav army and police units in Kosovo. Not only did the threat fail to deter the Serbian leader Slobodan Milosevic but the commencement of the bombing campaign signalled the intensification of ethnic cleansing by the Serbs and had only a limited impact on the Yugoslav army in the field. Milosevic did not cave in in a matter of days as Western public opinion had been led to expect. Instead the conflict dragged on for weeks.

Unfortunately the lessons learned through the study of history are rarely easily applied to complex contemporary realities. Different historians as we have seen may well draw different lessons from the same set of events. At the same time the historical evidence will be in no way complete and even if the historical record was complete and unanimity of interpretation prevailed amongst historians, it is frequently other groups that are involved in decision-making. Those seeking to draw exact historical parallels for the purposes of decision-making are taking a considerable risk by assuming that the similarities outweigh the differences and that the circumstances and variables are sufficiently analogous to ensure predictability. It is much more likely that contemporary decisions are made on the basis of contemporary analyses and priorities with history employed as justification. Where history has been used consciously and overtly to justify decisions and policies it has not always resulted in accurate assessments and its deployment is often driven by the desire to mobilize popular opinion in support of particular policies. Some of those who called loudly for Britain and other Western nations to save Balkan peoples from the *evil dictator* Milosevic during the 1990s appeared to be ignorant of the pivotal role of the Western powers, including Britain, in creating and exacerbating many of the regional tensions that caused much of the strife in the former Yugoslavia (Glenny, 1999). Furthermore where historical lessons are drawn and a *successful* outcome is the result, there is no way of proving that it was not in spite of the application of lessons from history, rather than because of them. We are a long way from Isaac Asimov's psycho-history (1953) and it seems unlikely that there are many historians who became historians simply in order to predict the future, even if from time to time they are asked to do so on national news bulletins. History cannot tell us what to do in the future. What it can do is assist people in having a better appreciation of their current state of affairs by illuminating, albeit partially, links, connections and continuities between the past and the present. As a result, what history offers is a more informed basis for decision-making, not a route map to success.

Finally, not only can the possibilities of learning from the past be overstated but to talk of society avoiding past mistakes seems to be a very grandiose claim to support the teaching of history in foundation and primary settings. Such a claim appears hard to reconcile with the task of the primary teacher. The likely outcome of teaching history to children is that there may be a reduction in the level of ignorance and misconception about the past (for example confusing D-Day with Dunkirk). Teaching history to children will not enable them to predict the future but it will offer them the chance to extend and improve their understanding of their current situation based on rational and critical analysis rather than prejudice and ignorance. This is a much more modest claim certainly but it is less likely to be proved spurious than to say that by teaching history to our children we will avoid the repetition of national and international catastrophes.

2. History's contribution to the wider curriculum and adult life

History can be a valuable instrument for learning in other disciplines (HMI, 1988). There is no doubt that history would offer an interesting vehicle for the development of literacy and numeracy as well as offering opportunities in many other areas of the curriculum such as art, geography or ICT (see Chapter 2). History can, therefore, be seen as a unifying subject offering numerous opportunities for work across the curriculum. Furthermore, in a society characterized by information overload, the study of history requires selection and discrimination in the location and handling of data. Coming to terms with a world that is transient, risk-laden, uncertain and unpredictable requires critical and creative thinking as well as reasoning and evaluation skills, also making history valuable educationally (QCA, 1999a). A case could even be made for history on the grounds of its potential contribution to children's future economic wellbeing. The Education Reform Act of 1988 (NCC, 1990) placed a statutory responsibility upon schools to provide a curriculum that would, amongst other things, prepare pupils for the oppor-tunities, responsibilities and experiences of adult life (ibid.). For most pupils these will include employment opportunities. Skills and knowledge acquired through the study of history may be highly transferable in an economy where a significant proportion of employment opportunities in the private sector are in service and leisure industries, such as tourism, heritage sites and information and communications technology.

History in foundation and primary settings can therefore be justified in terms of its usefulness to other subjects and areas of learning. It could also be justified in somewhat utilitarian terms on the grounds of preparing children for future employment opportunities. However, a number of subjects could claim to offer opportunities for supporting the development of literacy and numeracy. Equally a number of subjects or areas of learning could claim to offer a grounding potentially, at least, of use to pupils in the rest of their education as well as in their future adult life. Although important as reasons for including history on the curriculum, cross-curricular potential and a contribution to pupils' employment prospects are not reasons unique to history.

3. History is intrinsically fascinating and involves children in first-hand experience and 'finding out'

A case can be made in support of history teaching in terms of the contribution it can make to children's intellectual development. History is not always clear cut but this very fact, far from making it inappropriate as an area of study for children, makes it extremely valuable and relevant. The opportunities which history presents for encouraging children to think as well as remember are extremely important. History offers pupils the chance to begin to be critical about the world around them, encouraging the use of observation, evidence, logic and reasoning aimed at deciding what to believe or what to do. Effective provision in both foundation and primary settings offers children the chance to gain first-hand experience, ask questions, reflect and predict as well as experimenting and playing with ideas. Introducing young children to knowledge and understanding of the world and how it has changed or teaching history to Key Stage 1 and 2 pupils presents teachers with the chance to challenge pupil assumptions. Children have opportunities to find information for themselves, while their teachers provide experiences that allow them to explore important historical ideas such as cause and effect. Although the promotion of thinking is not unique to one subject, history is an interesting arena within which to encourage children to review their actions and thoughts, posing questions for pupils which foster speculation and elicit different points of view. With older children, history necessitates consideration of many different factors, including political, emotional, social, cultural and economic, in order to make sense of changes, developments and events. Teachers can model critical and creative thinking in history by practising thinking out loud in front of the children, demonstrating strategies and explaining the processes involved. Views of history as 'bookish', boring or dull are a direct consequence of misconceptions about history as a set of facts and ignore the requirement for enquiry and inter-pretation. History enables children to address issues such as uncertainty, inequality and conflict. It is hard to conceive of such opportunities as either boring or futile. History has something of interest for all.

4. Transmitting *cultural heritages*

One of the stated purposes for education as set out in the Education Reform Act of 1988 (NCC, 1990) was to promote the 'spiritual, moral, cultural, mental and physical development' of pupils and of society. In the same year, HMI sought to offer a rationale for the teaching of history which included the potential of history to contribute to the 'personal...development of children by encouraging attitudes such as tolerance, respect for diversity of opinion and background' (HMI, 1988). Beliefs about the past matter because they can have consequences in the present and where history is marginalized in the curriculum all manner of misconceptions and errors can find acceptance.

> The people of this country are forever in the debt of The Few who fought the Luftwaffe in the Battle of Britain. But that message has not reached most young people. They think the Battle of Britain was in 1066 and that the troops involved were the cavalry. They are not sure if we were fighting the Romans or the Normans and believe our great wartime leader was King Alfred or Richard rather than Winston Churchill.
>
> (Seymour and Cummins, 2000)

This finding from an ICM poll conducted for a national newspaper not only suggests a truly staggering level of ignorance on the part of 1000 18–24-year-olds concerning their own cultural heritage. It is also revealing of the cultural heritages that the authors and possibly the paper's readership deem appropriate.

History is an indispensable contributor to the attitudes, values and beliefs that permeate society. As such history can be twisted and distorted to lend plausibility to policies and practices such as racism or sexism. Alternatively history can play a vital part in challenging the non-historical myths, legends and folklore that result in discriminatory attitudes and beliefs and undermine a democratic society. History provides a wonderful opportunity to address wider educational aims associated with personal and social development. If a key aim of 3–11 education concerns the moral, spiritual and cultural development of children and society, including the development of a sense of justice, fairness, right and wrong, then what better subject could we choose than history for allowing children to encounter and deal with these ideas?

Ironic then that such a powerful argument for the teaching of history seems to be at odds with the principles of history itself. If teaching history is intended to result in the inculcation of certain values, attitudes and modes of behaviour is this history? Some past historians of the classical period would certainly have seen nothing wrong with the idea of history as a morality tale (Warren, 1999) but it doesn't sit comfortably with more recent views of the subject. Professional historians nowadays would probably aspire to be altogether more dispassionate and analytical. Can history that is seeking to promote a particular viewpoint, even a pluralist, liberal viewpoint be deemed sufficiently impartial and objective in terms of its methods?

Is it the job of the history teacher to promote and legitimize the present state of affairs or to examine, explain and challenge it? It is hard to argue for objectivity and balance when considering topics as emotive for children as the injustice of poverty and deprivation experienced by some of their peers in the past. Depending upon how one assesses right and wrong, is there a potential tension between being a *good* citizen and being a thoughtful, well-informed and critical citizen? If history is to be used to support a particular set of values in school, then perhaps that support should be qualified and careful, as teachers exercise their professional judgement.

Some Conclusions

When seeking to make a case for history we ask, how can history help our pupils to become better readers and writers? How can history help our pupils to become better citizens? How can history help our pupils to realize that our current institutions are legitimate and fair? How can history help children to gain insights into the workings of the modern world through examining the past? How can history help our pupils to be more employable? Each of these questions has one thing in common, namely that the justification for teaching history is couched in terms of its relevance, such as the direct links between teaching and employment or between teaching and perceived social good. Teaching history can contribute to an understanding of the now through an understanding of the past. Teaching history can also impart valuable skills of use in future employment. It is certainly a crucial part of the transmission of society's 'cultural heritages' (HMI, 1988). Our argument is not that these reasons in favour of teaching history are untrue or incorrect, only that they may be insufficient because they assume relevance is socially or economically determined. However, relevance could also be personally determined. Education is intended to meet the needs of society but as teachers we are also concerned with meeting the needs of individual children. While these interests will hopefully have many points of convergence they are not necessarily identical. What the teaching of history cannot ensure is that children will take up particular careers, be wholehearted supporters of parliamentary democracy as practised in Britain or be able to prophesy future international events. Education is concerned with motivating, enabling, enskilling and empowering children. History, as the study of the past, can make a unique contribution to this and can have great personal relevance for children, developing, for some at least, into a life-long hobby and interest. The absence of history from school would result in the impoverishment of children's educational experiences by denying them access to a body of knowledge and a set of practices not to be found in any other area of the curriculum. Perhaps the best way to appreciate the value of including history in the curriculum is to imagine the curriculum without it. What other subject would offer children the chance

- to become excited and interested in the past?
- to begin to understand the values of past societies and how attitudes and beliefs influenced people's actions?
- to extend their knowledge and understanding of past events and peoples?
- to understand that the past was different from the present?
- to recognize that there is continuity in human affairs?
- to develop a sense of chronology?
- to understand the nature of evidence (facts versus opinions)?
- to understand that events may have numerous causes and that one event may have influenced others?
- to understand that historical explanations are provisional, debatable and sometimes controversial?

(HMI, 1988)

In the next chapter we examine how ideas about the nature and worth of history have been translated into a curriculum for children in the Foundation Stage and those at Key Stages 1 and 2 of the National Curriculum.

REFERENCES

Arnold, J. H. (2000) *History: A Very Short Introduction*, Oxford: Oxford University Press.

Asimov, I. (1953) *Foundation*, London: Grafton/Harper Collins.

Bruce, T. (1997) *Early Childhood Education* (2nd edn), London: Hodder and Stoughton.

Crouzet, F. (1982) *The Victorian Economy*, London: Methuen and Co. Ltd.

Glenny, M. (1999) *The Balkans 1804–1999: Nationalism, War and the Great Powers*, London: Granta Books.

Her Majesty's Inspectors (HMI) (1988) *History from 5–16: Curriculum Matters 11*, London: Department for Education and Science.

Keegan, J. (1989) *The Second World War*, London: Pimlico/Random House.

National Curriculum Council (NCC) (1990) *Curriculum Guidance 3: The Whole Curriculum*, York: NCC.

National Curriculum Council (NCC) (1993) *History at Key Stage 2: An Introduction to the Non-European Study Units*, York: NCC.

O'Brien, M. and O'Brien, C. C. (1985) *Ireland: A Concise History* (3rd edn), London: Thames and Hudson.

Qualifications and Curriculum Authority (QCA) (1999a) *The National Curriculum: Handbook for Primary Teachers in England*, London: DfEE/QCA.

Rogers, P. J. (1987) *History: Why, What and How?*, London: The Historical Association.

Sawyer, P. (ed.) (1997) *Oxford Illustrated History of the Vikings*, Oxford: Oxford University Press.

Seymour, D. and Cummins, F. (15/9/2000) 'Baffled by the Battle of Britain', London: *Daily Mirror*.

Thompson, E. P. (1963) *The Making of the English Working Class,* Harmondsworth: Penguin.

Warren, J. (1999) *Access to History: History and the Historians*, London: Hodder and Stoughton.

www.britannia.com/history/docs/tacitus.html

2

History in Foundation and Primary Settings

This chapter examines the nature of history in the curriculum. For the youngest children, those in the Foundation Stage, history as a subject does not feature (QCA, 1999b). There is no organized body of knowledge about past periods that must be taught and no prescribed process of enquiry. Yet young children are not unaware of past events, nor are they incapable of asking questions or finding out. The chapter begins by offering suggestions on how aspects of the Early Learning Goals can be used to raise young children's awareness of concepts such as chronology, time, similarities, differences, patterns and change, based on their own experiences. To call such activities history could well be deemed a misnomer but the activities referred to could be seen as a starting point for history (proto-history), just as counting and sequencing activities in the nursery are part of early learning in mathematics. Perhaps, therefore, it is history but not as we know it.

The chapter continues by reviewing the current nature of the history curriculum at Key Stages 1 and 2. It begins with the process of history and discusses the knowledge, skills and understanding components of the National Curriculum Programmes of Study, providing examples that illustrate how some of the statements can appear in a real classroom. The chapter then outlines the content of the history curriculum, once again offering examples to illustrate the different ways that teachers have found to introduce children to past events and societies. Finally the chapter considers history in the context of the whole curriculum and especially in relation to the cross-curricular skills of literacy and numeracy.

History in the Foundation Stage

Children aged between 3 and 5 are working towards the Early Learning Goals rather than National Curriculum Programmes of Study. The Early Learning Goals are structured around broad areas of experience rather than the more narrow subject boundaries to be found in later phases of education. As a result no subject named history exists in the Foundation curriculum. Where history is seen as a clearly defined body of factual knowledge involving dates, famous people and world events it is hard to avoid the conclusion that such an area of study would be wholly inappropriate for young children. Such an approach to the subject would clash with the more holistic view of the world that younger children are thought to take. Similarly it does not seem to fit well with approaches to learning characterized by the use of play, first-hand experience and quality adult intervention and scaffolding, so important in young children's learning. It is difficult too to envisage how four-year-old children could realistically be expected to empathize with historical characters in the distant past when their own experiences of life upon which they would draw are so limited at this stage. Comprehending the timescales involved in the body of knowledge that is history would be equally problematic. If young children's comprehension is based at least in part on first-hand experience, then trying to appreciate the period of time between now and Tudor England could be seen as akin to being asked to gauge the distance between London and Brighton based on experiences with a 30cm ruler.

These difficulties would seem to support the notion that history cannot feature in the curriculum until children have matured sufficiently to be able to cope with the intellectual demands of the subject. However, although history as a coherent body of knowledge and systematic process of enquiry may not exist in the Foundation Stage, young children are still learning about the past and developing their ability to inquire and find out. While lessons on the Tudors would be inappropriate for such young children, learning to learn and finding out about changes and the passage of time are not. That young children will ask questions involving the dimension of time seems inevitable. That they will encounter stories from the past likewise.

There are opportunities across the Early Learning Goals for learning related to history whether in terms of building early ideas about time and chronology or in fostering early enquiry skills. Many of the routes into early ideas about history can be found in the 'Knowledge and Understanding of the World' aspect of the Early Learning Goals, although the integrated nature of the Foundation curriculum means that opportunities for developing early ideas about history are by no means restricted to this one aspect.

Knowledge and Understanding of the World

By the end of the Foundation Stage children should be able to:

- investigate objects using their senses;
- find out about and identify some features of objects;
- look closely at similarities, differences, patterns and change;
- find out about past and present events in their own lives and in those of their families and other people they know;
- find out about the place they live in;
- begin to know about their own cultures and those of other people.

(QCA, 1999b)

All of the above statements provide opportunities for early historical experiences enabling young children to begin to acquire some rudimentary historical knowledge and understanding and the development of historical enquiry skills based on familiar events, people and locations.

Similarities, Differences, Patterns and Change

Teachers need to start from the familiar when introducing ideas of chronology and change over time, namely the children themselves. Children who are still coming to terms with concepts such as *earlier than*, *later than*, *yesterday*, *today* and *tomorrow* are not necessarily incapable of understanding the concept of time. However, these ideas need to be introduced in ways that are appropriate and manageable for the children (Edwards and Knight, 1994; HMI, 1992). In nursery or reception classes, developing a sense of time or chronology in children might include activities such as naming the days of the week, work on the changing seasons, activities centred around annual festivals and events such as Bonfire Night, changes in appearance, friends, location/home, interests and families or encouraging children to remember and recount past events.

Questions to encourage younger pupils to remember:

What is the oldest . . . ?
What is your first memory . . . ?
What was your best ever . . . ?
Have you always . . . ?
Can you remember when . . . ?
Have you ever . . . ?
When did you . . . ?

Learning about chronology, change and the passage of time

Various ways in which children can demonstrate their understanding of chronology, change and the passage of time:

- recall and retell past experiences of their own;
- recall a sequence of connected events;
- classify, match and order objects, identifying similarities and differences and making comparisons such as old and new;
- demonstrate awareness of cause and effect;
- show sensitivity and empathy towards others;
- explore of the wider local environment;
- demonstrate an understanding of past, present and future;
- use stories as a familiar medium with which to introduce ideas about the past, such as cause and effect.

Children may confuse past events and make errors but such misconceptions or mistakes are not confined to learning about the past. Nursery and reception teachers encourage children to engage in finding out, problem-solving, decision-making and critical thinking as much as the acquisition of knowledge and history related activities fit well with all these areas.

Finding out

Activities that are aimed at improving young children's understanding of change, chronology and the passage of time provide scope for supporting children in finding out information for themselves through exploring, questioning or consulting. Teachers can ask challenging questions that push children towards speculation and exploration, at the same time encouraging and supporting children's speaking and listening. Critical thinking, essential for future learning in history, can be modelled for children. Thinking out loud with pupils is one way of illustrating the processes and strategies involved. Fostering talk and discussion with children about *how things used to be* contributes to language and literacy and personal and social development as children are encouraged to take turns and listen to others. It also represents the earliest stages in making children more receptive to and respectful of different points of view, encouraging debate and the exchange of ideas. Teachers of young children can use such activities to intervene, to sensitively challenge assumptions and bias. Teachers can also model a sense of wonder, fascination and curiosity in objects and activities from the past and first-hand experiences with artefacts from the past can be useful in helping children to acquire new vocabulary.

The skill of finding out can be fostered by encouraging children to

- ask and answer questions;
- hypothesize;
- forecast consequences and suggest possible solutions to problems, for example predicting outcomes in historical stories;
- participate in group discussions, listening to the views and ideas of others, commenting on others' ideas;
- use all their senses to gather information;
- initiate interactions with adults as information sources, seeking knowledge, clarification and reasons;
- use books and other sources of information;
- distinguish between fact and opinion, real and imaginary events.

The table below shows how Early Learning Goals for 'Knowledge and Understanding of the World' have been translated into a programme of work for a reception class in which enquiry skills and finding out are a key element.

Year group – Reception
Unit of work – 'Now and then'
Main areas of learning – Knowledge and Understanding of the World/Language and Literacy
Links to National Curriculum – History, English

Learning objectives	Activities	Organization	Resources
• Find out about past and present events in their own lives and in those of their families and other people they know.	Talk about past and present events in the children's own lives. What did they do yesterday? What did you do at the weekend/in the holidays/at Christmas/for your birthday?	Small group discussion.	
	Talk about the seasons or annual/regular events and how they affect the children's lives.		
	Discuss different generations in their family. Show sensitivity and be inclusive of different types of 'family'. Discuss other places where the children and their families may have lived previously. Make family timelines and albums.	Group 'tree'. Sequencing family 'portraits'/pictures.	Whiteboard and dry wipe marker.
• Investigate objects using their senses. • Find out about and identify some features of objects.	Compare and contrast past and present artefacts (for example, collecting toys that parents and grandparents may have kept from their own childhood and comparing them with toys today, or household items e.g. irons).	Class discussion. Small group observational drawings.	Museum loans/collected artefacts from home.
• Look closely at similarities, differences, patterns and change.	Use photographs of children to look at change and growth.		Museum loans.
• Find out about the place they live in.	Go on local walk to introduce children to appropriate historical language. What was the local area like in the past? How has it changed? Look at and discuss old photographs and pictures of the local area.	Whole class.	Old photographs of locality.
	'Interview' older relatives about how things used to be.	Brief interviewee and interviewers.	Tape recorder.

Much of what already goes on in nursery and reception settings can be utilized to promote learning about chronology, change and the passage of time and much of this learning will be of use to children in the later stages of their education as they encounter history as a subject.

History in the National Curriculum

History was not unknown to primary education prior to the introduction of the National Curriculum. History was a recognized part of the curriculum in both infant and junior schools prior to 1990–91. However, history was not always clearly defined as a subject in primary schools prior to the introduction of the National Curriculum. In terms of its delivery and its conception (Alexander *et al.*, 1992) it was frequently incorporated into cross-curricular approaches involving other areas of the curriculum.

Objectives for history in lower primary settings prior to 1991

- understand their own and their families' past;
- begin to understand concepts such as past, present and future;
- understand that evidence from the past can take a number of forms;
- sequence historical artefacts or events (e.g. before and after) offering reasons for doing so;
- acquire knowledge of certain key events in the past;
- distinguish between myths and legends and real events and people;
- make appropriate use of vocabulary related to time (e.g. now, long ago, after);
- use a mixture of imagination and evidence to describe life in the past.   (HMI, 1988)

Objectives for history in upper primary settings prior to 1991

- know of some of the major events in British and world history within a broad chronological order;
- demonstrate understanding of the development of societies (including British society) over long periods;
- demonstrate an appreciation of the breadth of history (e.g. technological, scientific and artistic achievements as well as economic, social and political developments)
- develop an understanding of the history of their locality and be able to relate this to wider themes;
- appreciate that past societies have held different beliefs, attitudes and values;
- understand that historical evidence is susceptible to a variety of interpretations;
- make appropriate use of chronological conventions (e.g. BC, AD, century, millennium)
- make use of primary and secondary sources to support interpretations of historical events;
- make imaginative reconstructions of the past based on and in accordance with the available evidence;
- make simple causal connections (e.g. between historical characters and their actions);
- recognize the similarities and differences between the past and the present day.

(HMI, 1988)

The development of history as a subject in the National Curriculum therefore resulted in fierce debates over what should be included (the conception of history) and teaching methods (the delivery of history) (Kettle, 1990). Some of those involved emphasized the importance of historical content and in some cases the content envisaged also had a distinctively English bias. At the same time others argued strongly for the importance of historical process and the acquisition of skills and concepts. For some of the proponents of this view, historical content was simply the vehicle through which the mastery of skills and the development of conceptual understanding could be attained. The History Working Party was faced with the unenviable task of attempting to steer a path between these competing ideas. The result was a history curriculum that acknowledged the need for both process and content and this has remained the situation throughout the reviews and alterations of both 1995 and 1999–2000.

> In order to know about, or understand, an historical event we need to acquire historical information. But the constituents of that information – the names, dates and places – provide only the starting points for understanding. Without understanding, history is reduced to parrot learning and assessment to a parlour memory game.

(History Working Party in Kettle, 1990)

The Programmes of Study for history are therefore characterized by two interrelated strands. First, children are expected to investigate and find out about the past by utilizing a mixture of knowledge, skills and understanding referred to as *key elements* in the 1995 version of the curriculum (DFE, 1995). Second, children are to be introduced to a selection of peoples and periods from the past through a series of historical study units. The curriculum therefore seeks to establish an iterative relationship between the historical content contained in the various study units and the processes by which historical knowledge and understanding are attained as set out in the key elements.

At present National Curriculum documentation leaves the choice of when and how to tackle the various study units to the discretion of schools. Consequently different schools are free to introduce different study units to pupils at different points during their primary education and could opt to deliver them as discrete history projects (blocked work) or, alternatively, as part of an integrated project involving one or two other National Curriculum subjects (linked work) (SCAA, 1995). However, schemes of work produced by the Qualifications and Curriculum Authority (QCA, 1998) have provided a suggested order which is becoming increasingly common. The following two sections outline the process and content of history as currently laid down in the National Curriculum.

Knowledge, Skills and Understanding

Chronological understanding

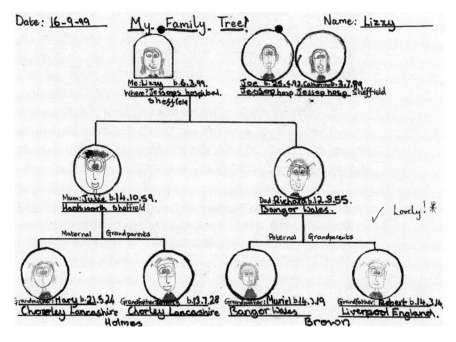

Date: 16-9-99   My. Family. Tree!   Name: Lizzy

Me:Lizzy   b.6.3.99.
Where? Jessops hospital.
Sheffield

Joe b. 25.4.93.Catherine b. 3.7.89
Jessop hosp. Jessop hosp. Sheffield

Mum: Julie b.14.10.59.
Handsworth Sheffield

Dad: Richard b.12.8.55.
Bangor Wales.

✓ Lovely! ✻

Maternal   Grandparents   Paternal   Grandparents

Grandmother: Mary b. 21.5.24   Grandfather: b.13.7.28   Grandmother: Muriel b.14.3.19   Grandfather: Robert b.14.3.14
Chorley Lancashire   Chorley Lancashire   Bangor Wales   Liverpool England.
Holmes   Brown

Monday
30th
September
1999

Catherine

Homes today	Tudor homes
Carpeted floors	Put mud and herbs on the floor
Built with Bricks and Cement	Built with wattle and daub or wood ✓
We have knives and forks	Tudors had knives and spoons. ✓
We have cups made of glass and plastic	Tudors had cups made of bulls horn ✓
Modern tiles and slates on the roof.	Roofs made of stone or thach or whatever was in the area. ✓
Electric lamps and lights	The Tudors had candles to see things with
Nowadays, people would like to have a tan.	In Tudor times

lovely, neat work.

Understanding the ways in which time is measured and knowing the chronology of major events and developments is central to the study of history. In primary settings this aspect of the history curriculum is often introduced through activities in which children are encouraged to recognize distinctions between the present and the past in their own and other (familiar) people's lives. As with pupils in the Foundation Stage, younger primary children can be asked to think about their own family's past. Activities to encourage this include creating photograph albums and constructing simple family trees or timelines showing siblings, parents/carers and other, older relations. Birthday charts and 'my life' timelines can also be used. The living memories of older 'generations' can help children to begin to understand periods prior to their birth and teachers can promote chronological understanding further by introducing the use of everyday terms about the passage of time such as *now*, *then*, *before* and *after*. Familiar artefacts that are close together chronologically can be used to support simple sequencing or comparison tasks such as *old* and *new*. As pupils become more knowledgeable and skilled sequencing and comparison activities involving the ordering of two, three and then more events and objects can be introduced. As children progress and mature they become better able to empathize with people in the past and can be asked to make comparisons with their own lives, for example comparing 'my life' to the life of a child from a different historical period such as a Victorian child working in a factory. Their comprehension may be limited, but it is unlikely to improve if we deny them opportunities to extend and enhance it. Increasing maturity is after all only one part of the equation for learning, experience and appropriate intervention also play a vital part. Furthermore, if we view history as an interplay between factual information and enquiry it is possible for primary children to engage in historical activities and make progress in their historical learning even though their chronological accuracy and ordering may be faulty, for example seeing Romans and Vikings as contemporaneous.

Chronological understanding

Key Stage 1

1 Pupils should be taught to:
a place events and objects in chronological order;
b use common words and phrases relating to the passing of time.

Key Stage 2

1 Pupils should be taught to:
a place events, people and changes into correct periods of time;
b use dates and vocabulary relating to the passing of time, including ancient, modern, BC, AD, century and decade.

(QCA, 1999a)

Knowledge and understanding of events, people and changes

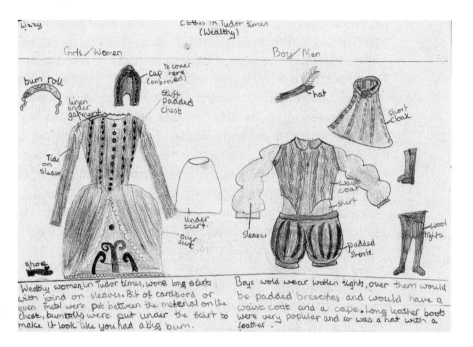

Diary
Clothes in Tudor times (Wealthy)

Girls / Women

bum roll
cap (embroidered) - to cover hair
linen under garment
stiff padded chest
Tied on Sleeve
Under scirt.
Over Scirt
shoe

Boys / Men

hat
short cloak
waist coat
shirt
Sleeves
padded shorts.
wool tights

Wealthy women, in Tudor times, wore long scirts with joind on sleeves. Bit of cardbord or even metal were put between the meterial on the chest, bumrolls were put under the scirt to make it look like you had a big bum.

Boys wold wear woolen tights, over them would be padded breeches and would have a waist coat and a cape. Long leather boots were very popular and so was a hat with a feather.

Me. and my clothes   Ryan.

Samuel Pepys. costumn

Opportunities need to be made for children to demonstrate factual knowledge and understanding of aspects of the past beyond living memory, including events and people that they have studied at school. Children need to be given opportunities to study the distinctive features of different periods and seek to find continuity, change and possible reasons for change. This may begin with well-known stories about significant events which children can be encouraged to discuss and recount, for example the 'Gunpowder plot'. There are opportunities here for children to develop still further their familiarity with the concept of change as they consider similarities and differences, for example finding out about the different forms of clothing worn by people in the past or changes in transport. Children also need to be helped to appreciate that people in the past did things for a reason and should be given activities that promote the formulation of hypotheses.

Knowledge and understanding of events, people and changes in the past

Key Stage 1

2 Pupils should be taught to:
a recognise why people did things, why events happened and what happened as a result;
b identify differences between ways of life at different times.

Key Stage 2

2 Pupils should be taught:
a about characteristic features of the periods and societies studied, including the ideas, beliefs, attitudes and experiences of men, women and children in the past;
b about the social, cultural, religious and ethnic diversity of the societies studied, in Britain and the wider world;
c to identify and describe reasons for and results of historical events, situations, and changes in the periods studied;
d to describe and make links between the main events, situations and changes within and across the different periods and societies studied.

(QCA, 1999a)

Historical interpretation

Historical interpretation provides pupils with the chance to examine the different ways in which the past is represented. Children begin by using their own experiences as a way of understanding the past and progress from there to an understanding of how events and actions can be interpreted differently. Historical interpretation draws heavily on children's ability to think rather than to remember and as such teachers need to encourage children to exercise these skills by providing historical activities that ask children to classify, evaluate, compare and contrast, hypothesize, empathize, use reason and logic and synthesize ideas. Children need to be made aware of different points of view and will need assistance in learning to appreciate and understand this diversity of opinion. Children are encouraged in history to use evidence critically, identifying bias and learning to distinguish fact from fiction and sources need to be handled in a way characterized by critical appraisal rather than acceptance. Children should be encouraged to question and challenge the accuracy and impartiality of historical testimony and evidence. Historical interpretation introduces children to the provisionality of historical knowledge and the need to differentiate between opinion and fact. Mistakes and errors are made in history and opinions vary, as do accounts, with some showing clear signs of bias. It is essential, therefore, that children be exposed to a wide range of images, evidence and objects from the past to facilitate the development of their interpretative skills.

Historical interpretation

Key Stage 1

3 Pupils should be taught to identify different ways in which the past is represented.

Key Stage 2

3 Pupils should be taught to recognise that the past is represented and interpreted in different ways, and to give reasons for this.

(QCA, 1999a)

Historical enquiry

Mrs B, a supply teacher, was working with a class of Key Stage 2 pupils for the day. The children's regular teacher had left work for the children to complete, including a history activity in the afternoon on rationing in Britain during the Second World War. As a war baby herself, Mrs B was in a unique position to talk from experience on the subject. The initial class discussion featured historical artefacts including ration books and coupons. Mrs B introduced the children to the idea of fairness that lay behind rationing. She helped the children to appreciate how small the amounts involved were, explained how some foods were completely unobtainable and told the children how she had never even seen fruit like bananas and oranges until after the war. Some of the children had not realized that some fruits cannot be grown in the British climate and therefore that they had to be imported. She also told the children about the black market, which many of the children regarded as unfair. Mrs B then explained that rationing even affected the availability of sweets, but that she was luckier than most children of the period and that in spite of the coupons, she always had plenty of sweets. She asked the children if they could work out why this might have been the case. The children asked questions and applied logic to the problem. Their responses included:

- 'Were you really rich Miss?'
- 'You went to the black market!'
- 'Your mum and dad had a sweet shop.'
- 'Did you know somebody who had a sweet shop?'
- 'Somebody you knew worked in a sweet factory.'

After the children had exhausted their ideas, Mrs B offered them a clue. She said that she did not have any brothers or sisters. The children were intrigued but were still unable to work out the answer. Then Mrs B explained that as an only child, only grandchild and only niece, not only did she not have to share her sweets, but she was also given the rations of all her adult relatives.

Most primary schoolchildren are naturally curious and history offers teachers chances to capitalize on this thirst for learning by providing opportunities for children to find things out for themselves. Through historical enquiry children gain experience of locating, examining and questioning historical evidence. They can be helped to find answers to questions about the past from a range of sources and ought to be supported in answering questions about the past based on study and observation. Historical enquiry draws heavily on children's investigative skills, skills that are not necessarily unique to history. Such skills include the ability to cooperate, sharing ideas and information, using all five of their senses, applying existing knowledge, asking questions and deploying their research skills. The process of enquiry may also require children to employ empathy and imagination, both of which have to be informed by knowledge of the context and content. Without attention to the evidence it would be impossible for children to develop a realistic sense of the possible and the probable. It is also important to remember the role of the teacher as a source of information in history. It is unlikely that primary schoolchildren will be able to discover history purely through skills and techniques so some degree of exposition on the part of the teacher will be necessary. This does not mean lecturing children on the historical facts. Exposition is one way of ensuring that they have access to essential and interesting information and is a means of helping to explain and justify why the information is accepted. Such exposition, when well articulated, may have the added advantage of motivating and stimulating children's interest in the subject.

Historical enquiry

Key Stage 1

4 Pupils should be taught
a how to find out about the past from a range of sources of information;
b to ask and answer questions about the past.

4 Pupils should be taught
   a how to find out about the events, people and changes studied from an appropriate range
     of sources of information, including ICT-based sources;
   b to ask and answer questions, and to select and record information relevant to the focus
     of the enquiry.

(QCA, 1999a)

30
_____

Organization and communication

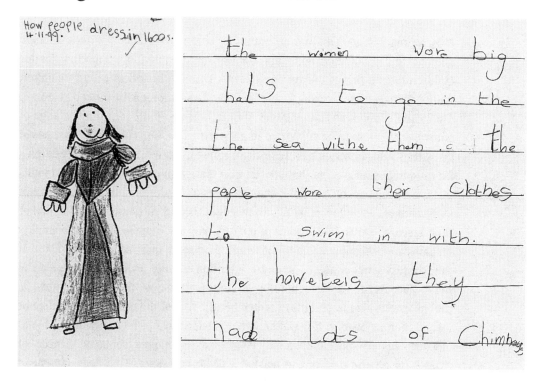

Children need to learn how to find and recall historical information, to select and
structure historical information and to communicate their historical understanding.
Children will also need opportunities for listening, describing, explaining, debating
and displaying their historical ideas and learning. As with historical enquiry
and historical interpretation many of the communication and organizational skills
required to do this effectively are not restricted to history alone. In history pupils will
find themselves recording their findings in a variety of written, numerical or artistic
ways. Many children will need assistance to cope with the demands of organizing and
communicating information. Writing frames (see below) can be used to direct pupils
towards certain lines of enquiry and ensure that written work is not just narrative or
descriptive in nature but can also be analytical and explanatory.

```
┌─────────────────────────────────────────────────────────┐
│  The Victorians                                           │
│  Looking at photographs                                   │
│  Man/woman _____                                │
│  Old/young _____ because _____│
│  _____│
│  Rich/poor _____ because _____│
│  _____│
│  Clothing _____│
│  _____│
│  Occupation _____│
│  _____│
│  Other information _____│
│  _____│
└─────────────────────────────────────────────────────────┘
```

When researching and organizing information, some children may be tempted to copy chunks of text from various sources and persuading children to use their own words can be difficult. While copying might offer insights into a pupil's handwriting skills it does not show that a child has learnt or understood anything about history. Question sheets that preclude copying and require children to demonstrate their learning are one way of overcoming this problem. Teachers may also need to spend time training children in how to take information from texts without copying whole sections. This can be done by jointly reading a text with pupils and asking them to identify any key words or ideas, making headings and sub-headings, substituting short phrases for long sentences and summarizing paragraphs.

Organization and communication

Key Stage 1

5 Pupils should be taught to select from their knowledge of history and communicate it in a variety of ways.

Key Stage 2

5 Pupils should be taught to:
a recall, select and organize historical information;
b use dates and historical vocabulary to describe the periods studied;
c communicate their knowledge and understanding of history in a variety of ways.

(QCA, 1999a)

Breadth of Study

History is selective, judgements have been made about what is relevant and meaningful and thus included and what is not. In the same way those involved in designing the history curriculum have also made decisions about the nature of the subject and those aspects of it that should be studied in primary schools and those that should not. It is clearly impractical and inappropriate to seek to place the totality of history as a discipline on the primary curriculum. Decisions have had to be made about what to include and what to leave out. It could be argued that the closer the proximity in time and space of the periods under study to Britain at the beginning of the new millennium, the smaller the number of differences, the easier it is for children to understand and hence the greater the relevance. Familiar frames of reference for children are most likely to be encountered in the recent past, while contrasts are most likely to be observed in the distant past (Rogers, 1987). At the same time those involved in the design of the history curriculum had to try to balance other aspects of historical endeavour. What should the relative weight given to British history be in comparison to world history? How much time should pupils spend engaged in social and economic history in comparison to political history? How far should children be introduced to narrative history in comparison to analytical history? Almost inevitably the result is a patchwork approach to the content of the history curriculum (Rogers, 1987). History in the National Curriculum is composed of *chunks* of the past, spanning recorded history from the civilization of Ancient Sumer to Britain since 1930, introducing children to significant individuals, social and economic trends and requiring both narrative and analytical competence.

During Key Stage 1 the knowledge, skills and understanding aspects of the history curriculum are delivered through four study units involving:

- changes in the children's own lives and those around them;
- the ways of life of people in more distant times;
- significant individuals from the history of Britain and the wider world;
- significant events from the history of Britain and the wider world (QCA, 1999a, p. 104).

The examples on the right show how these areas of study have been interpreted in three cases.

• changes in the children's own lives and those around them

A class of Year 1 children began the year with a topic on 'Our families and Ourselves'. As part of the topic the children experienced a number of activities in which they were encouraged to learn about changes in their own lives and the lives of other members of their families. Parents were asked to provide photographs so that the children could talk about how they had grown and changed since birth. The children were asked to find out about themselves when they were younger by asking parents and other relatives. The children were also encouraged to find out about the childhood of older relatives and this formed the basis of activities on how things had changed. As part of the topic the children produced simple timelines on growing up (see p. 32).

• the ways of life of people in more distant times

A class of Year 2 pupils were taken to a working water mill as part of a history and design technology project on 'Machines'. The mill was used to sharpen scythe blades. At the mill the curator started the water wheel and operated the grinding stones in the *grinding hull* through a system of belts and pulleys. Afterwards he took the children outside to look at the water wheel and explained the purpose of the *pentrough* and how different types of water wheel such as *overshot* and *backshot* operated. During the visit the curator explained how the machines worked and told the children about the lives of local people in the distant past who used to work as grinders. The children learned about how many of the workers had to come to the mill without shoes, and how they were employed in a building without windows in all weathers. The curator also told them about the terrible toll paid in terms of health and safety. Most of the workers did not live to become 30 years of age as they had either been killed in accidents such as grindstones exploding or had succumbed to lung disease as a result of the dusty working conditions.

• significant events and individuals from the history of Britain and the wider world

A class of Year 2 pupils were reading the Big Book *Historical Letters, Diaries and Journals* (Green, 1999) as part of the literacy hour. The section concerned a famous individual from the past, Mary Seacole, who had been a nurse during the Crimean War of 1854. Through reading and discussing the story the children learned that Mary had come to England from Jamaica and, on hearing about the suffering of the wounded in the war, she travelled to the Crimea to help. While there she tended the wounded on the frontline and was a skilful nurse who often found herself under fire. The children also learnt that she had written a book about her adventures.

34

In Key Stage 2 the knowledge, skills and understanding aspects of the history curriculum are delivered through seven areas of study. The areas include:

- a local history study;
- the development of British society prior to the Norman Conquest;
- Britain in Tudor times;
- Victorian Britain;
- Britain since 1930;
- a European history study;
- a world history study (QCA, 1999a, pp. 105–7).

The examples on the right illustrate some of the ways in which teachers have introduced the Key Stage 2 study units to their pupils.

• the development of British society prior to the Norman Conquest

A Year 3 class learning about the Vikings produced cardboard shields and helmets in their art lesson. Subsequently in history they went out into the playground and their teacher organized and ran a costumed role play lesson in which the children boarded their longboat, sailed to England and met Saxon villagers.

• Victorian Britain

Year 4 pupils studying the Victorians in history spent part of the term comparing and contrasting Victorian entertainment with entertainment now. Their teacher had obtained a pack of resources from a local museum and the children used the stencil and templates to make their own working zoetropes with which to create the illusion of movement.

• a world history study

Year 5 pupils engaged in a project on the Egyptians were given reference books and access to the computer in order to research the finding of Tutankhamen's tomb by Howard Carter in 1922. Their teacher discussed their findings with the different groups and assisted the children in organizing the information. Next the children looked at old and current newspapers and discussed layout and styles of writing before being asked to write a contemporary newspaper account of Carter's discovery.

Links to the Whole Curriculum Including Literacy and Numeracy

History makes a distinctive contribution to the curriculum in its own right but it also contributes to the wider aims of primary education (QCA, 1999a). Although sometimes thought about in terms of its constituent subjects, in reality the National Curriculum comprises much more than just these. The Education Reform Act of 1988 placed a statutory responsibility upon schools to promote the spiritual, moral, cultural, mental and physical development of pupils. The Act also made it clear that schools were expected to prepare children for the 'opportunities, responsibilities and experiences of adult life' (NCC, 1990). To support schools in meeting these requirements, the curriculum outlined in the 1988 Act also contained a set of cross-curricular elements including themes, skills and dimensions as well as the subjects. The inclusion of these elements was intended to offer schools opportunities to pull together the broad education of individuals and augment the basic curriculum as outlined in the core and foundation subjects (NCC, 1990).

> The **cross-curricular dimensions** include equality of opportunity for all including preparation for life in a multi-cultural society, and equality of access to the curriculum for children with special educational needs.
>
> (NCC, 1990)

The cross-curricular dimensions centre around the belief that all children have an entitlement to equality of opportunity in education. While the recent plethora of schemes of work originating from government agencies may give the impression that teachers are simply involved in the delivery of prescribed and prepackaged content, assessing and stratifying pupils by reference to standard norms, teaching is in fact a much more complex task. Schools and nurseries have a duty to work positively for equality of opportunity and history offers a wealth of opportunities with which to do this. Teaching and learning in history contributes to children's social and cultural development and can bring a European and global dimension to their understanding of the world as well as enriching and reinforcing the cross-curricular dimensions. These issues are addressed further in Chapters 7 and 8.

> The **cross-curricular themes** offer pupils contexts within which they can begin to think about and reflect upon values and beliefs as well as acquiring additional knowledge and understanding important for their future lives as adults. The themes cover economic and industrial understanding, careers education, health education, citizenship and environmental education.
>
> (NCC, 1990)

It is easy to see how teaching and learning in history make a contribution to children's understanding of some of these themes. Enquiry into Victorian working conditions and child labour would offer opportunities to draw comparisons with today's world of work and introduce themes such as health education and economic and industrial understanding. At the same time, work on the characteristic features of periods and societies including 'ideas, beliefs, attitudes and experiences' (QCA, 1999a) opens up possibilities for comparing and contrasting ideas about citizenship. Education for citizenship is seen as having three distinct but interconnected strands that will prepare young people for adult life: social and moral responsibility, community involvement and political literacy. History provides opportunities for children to acquire skills, understanding and attitudes that will contribute to their development as citizens including

- using an enquiry-based, participatory approach which involves critical thinking;
- developing ideas about fairness, equity and social justice;
- recognizing their own values and attitudes;
- sharing opinions, discussing and analysing relevant issues;
- recognizing other people's perspectives;
- working in groups;

- developing a sense of community;
- learning how decisions were made in the past;
- identifying how local, national and international events and issues are connected;
- identifying similarities and differences between people and places, locally, nationally or internationally, valuing diversity and developing positive attitudes;
- inviting members of the local community into school.

Cross-curricular skills are those skills that are relevant in varying degrees to teaching and learning in all subjects, but which are not the preserve of any one subject. These skills are sometimes referred to as key skills and include communication skills, numeracy skills, ICT capability, problem solving, interpersonal skills, thinking and study skills.

(NCC, 1990)

History provides opportunities for developing a range of skills. Some are subject specific, for example making appropriate use of chronological conventions. Others are common to several subjects such as enquiry skills, equally useful in science and geography as well as history. Other skills have near universal application in education. History offers numerous opportunities to foster children's research and study skills, for example evaluating the reliability and usefulness of different pieces of evidence. Chapter 1 includes comments on the potential of history for fostering children's thinking skills and Chapters 4 and 5 include examples in which interpersonal skills and problem-solving are being developed through history work. These chapters also include sections on the opportunities for including ICT as part of teaching and learning in history. Consequently the remainder of this chapter will focus upon literacy and numeracy skills.

History lessons should aim to develop children's historical knowledge, understanding and skills. However, history can also provide a powerful context for the development and practice of key skills in the areas of mathematics and language as well as applying learning from mathematics and language in a historical context. It is important though not to fall into the trap of assuming the existence of significant curriculum links when in reality they are at best incidental and frequently unfulfilled. The Literacy Hour can provide a context for exposition concerning historical content but it offers only limited potential for developing children's historical skills. Similarly historical material may provide a vehicle through which to develop children's understanding and capability in numeracy but such an approach would not secure children's systematic progress in history. Skills and knowledge of language and mathematics may be reinforced through history lessons but they are unlikely to be taught in them. In the same way, meeting the requirements of a broad and balanced curriculum which includes history cannot be achieved simply by inserting small amounts of historical content into the Literacy and Numeracy Hours.

Some history–language links

Speaking and listening	• Hot-seating activity in which a child is encouraged to demonstrate empathy with a child evacuee during the Second World War.
	• Asking questions and interviewing a visitor to the class about how life has changed within living memory.
	• Role-play activities on historical themes, for example the theme of Explorers and Encounters in which Cortez meets the Aztecs.
	• Preparing for, and participating in, class debates, for example on whether the decade of the 1970s was all 'trouble and strife'.
	• A class assembly presentation on Howard Carter's discovery of the tomb of Tutankhamen.
Reading	• Historical fiction, for example 'Carrie's War', 'Goodnight Mister Tom' and 'Tom's Midnight Garden'.
	• Newspaper articles about the locality in past times, for example during the Second World War or at Queen Victoria's death.
	• Accessing historical information using CD-Roms and the worldwide web.
	• Using reference books to find out about the life of a famous individual from the past.
Writing	• Diary extract/report about life on board Columbus's ship.
	• Writing a letter from an evacuated child to home about their new life in the countryside.
	• Writing poems about invasion by the Vikings.
	• Using persuasive writing, for example 'Why corporal punishment should not be brought back to schools'.
	• Using explanatory writing, for example 'How Lord Beveridge proposed to improve the lives of British people after the War'.
	• Using descriptive writing, for example 'Visiting the Crystal Palace Exhibition'.
	• Drafting questionnaires to take home, for example on 'Entertainment in the 1940s' or 'Fashion in the 1960s'.

Some history–mathematics links

Number	• Counting rhymes and songs involving number from the past. Exploring links to historical events or experiences, 'Sing a song of sixpence'.
	• Introducing historical artefacts associated with number, for example coins, adding machines, abacuses or Sumerian clay tablets.
	• Finding out about and comparing alternative counting methods such as Roman numerals.
	• Counting back from dates, for example 'If the date on the gravestone is 1856, how many years ago did the person die?'
	• Number in historical patterns and designs.

Shape, space and measurement	• Shape in the historical built environment such as in churches or bridges. • Measures of long time periods such as decade, century or millennium. • Past measurers of time such as sun dials, sand timers, water and candle clocks. • Calendars and diaries, for example using advent calendars to count down to Christmas. • Using/comparing Imperial and metric measures, for example using a Victorian recipe. • Geometric patterns and designs from the past.
Data handling	• Using and interpreting statistical data such as census data on lifestyles, life expectancy, employment or schooling. • Communicating numerical and statistical data in a variety of forms including graphs, charts and tables.

REFERENCES

Alexander, R., Rose, J. and Woodhead, C. (1992) 'Curriculum Organisation and Classroom Practice in Primary Schools: A Discussion Paper', London: DES.

Department for Education (DFE) (1995) *Key Stages 1 and 2 of the National Curriculum*, London: HMSO.

Edwards, A. and Knight, P. (1994) *Effective Early Years Education: Teaching Young Children*, Buckingham: Open University Press.

Green, J. (1999) *Historical Letters, Diaries and Journals*, Pelican Big Books.

Her Majesty's Inspectors (HMI) (1988) *History from 5–16: Curriculum Matters 11*, London: Department for Education and Science.

Her Majesty's Inspectors (HMI) (1992) *Aspects of Primary Education: The Education of Children Under Five*, London: Department for Education and Science.

Kettle, M. (4 April 1990) 'The Great battle of history' (DES Final Report of the History Working Group), *Guardian*.

National Curriculum Council (NCC) (1990) *Curriculum Guidance 3: The Whole Curriculum*, York: NCC.

Qualifications and Curriculum Authority (QCA) (1998) *A Scheme of Work for Key Stages 1 and 2: History, London: DfEE/QCA*.

Qualifications and Curriculum Authority (QCA) (1999a) *The National Curriculum: Handbook for Primary Teachers in England*, London: QCA.

Qualifications and Curriculum Authority (QCA) (1999b), *Early Learning Goals,* London: DfEE/QCA.

Rogers, P. J. (1987) *History: Why, What and How?*, London: The Historical Association.

School Curriculum and Assessment Authority (SCAA) (1995) *Planning the Curriculum at Key Stages 1 and 2 London*: SCAA.

38

3 Preparing to Teach History

Good teaching is characterized by, amongst other things, thorough preparation, clear planning, effective class management skills and a knowledge and understanding of the factors that promote learning in a particular area. This chapter considers the planning and class management skills necessary to underpin effective teaching in history. The chapter begins by considering the terms progression and continuity in the context of history teaching, before proceeding to outline and give examples of different approaches to the conception and delivery of history using blocked, continuing and linked strategies (SCAA, 1995). It then continues by illustrating the continuum of planning across schools from whole school, long-term planning through to the short-term session and lesson planning carried out by individual teachers. The second section of the chapter focuses upon class management and teaching skills that are a prerequisite for effective teaching and learning in any area of the curriculum. The chapter examines alternative approaches for grouping and organizing children as well as strategies for differentiation in history activities. The chapter then considers historical misconceptions that children may hold. Finally the chapter addresses the crucial teaching skill of reflection. Honest self-appraisal of strengths and weaknesses in the teaching of history, coupled with attention to research and inspection evidence, are vital if planning and teaching skills are to improve.

Planning

Good planning underpins effective teaching and purposeful learning and it takes place on three levels: long-term planning across the Foundation and Key Stages 1 and 2, medium-term planning of units of work and short-term planning of lessons or activities. History has a distinctive contribution to make to children's learning (see Chapters 1 and 2) and so should be planned for as rigorously as core subjects or literacy and numeracy. At each level it needs to be structured and systematic and not only fulfil the requirements of the National Curriculum Programmes of Study or Early Learning Goals (ELG) but also reflect a school's overall aims, objectives and policies. Different views exist as to how the history curriculum should be planned and where the emphasis should be placed and teachers need to make professional judgements about how to work within the current context to develop a worthwhile curriculum for their pupils. Before looking in more detail at long-, medium- and short-term planning for history, the chapter will outline some important areas for consideration that inform the planning process at all levels.

Planning for continuity and progression in history

Continuity and progression are often talked about in the same breath but they are different features of planning and the presence of one does not necessarily indicate the presence of the other. For instance, children may undertake work with historical artefacts on a regular basis but develop little in the way of historical enquiry skills unless these are specifically taught and practised.

When teachers refer to continuity they are describing those aspects of a child's history experiences that stay the same irrespective of their age. It should be evident in long-term planning through significant features of history education occurring on a regular basis. These might include historical content, ensuring that key concepts associated with chronology, time, change, similarities and differences feature throughout. Bruner's notion of a 'spiral curriculum' is useful here (Wood, 1998) as children revisit key elements of the curriculum throughout their school experience, each time at a higher level of understanding or refinement. Teachers also need to build continuity into the types of learning activity that children experience during their schooling to ensure the provision of both evidence-based and creative and imaginative approaches. Continuity also needs to exist in terms of the shared understandings amongst staff about the nature of history as active and enquiry-based, not simply a collection of facts about the past. A further area in which continuity can be sought is in the area of resourcing for history as schools try to ensure that throughout their education children have access to high-quality reference materials and historical literature as well as opportunities to work with artefacts, documentation, visual material and ICT.

Progression has been defined as 'the careful and deliberate sequencing of learning so that children can build their current learning on previous experience and also prepare for future learning' (Chambers and Donert, 1996). If continuity is shorthand for *what stays the same*, then progression is shorthand for *what changes*. Progression focuses on how children's learning advances in terms of the acquisition of knowledge and skills and the development of understanding, values and attitudes. Teachers plan for progression in two ways. First, the content and sequence of learning activities are structured through long- and medium-term planning. Second, teachers use individual children's records, assess their learning and match new tasks to their capabilities to enable them to make progress. The Early Learning Goals and National Curriculum Programmes of Study provide an important guide for identifying the next stage.

Progression in history involves

- an increasing breadth of historical knowledge (e.g. learning about new periods in the past);
- an increasing depth of historical understanding;
- an increasing time scale (e.g. starting from the recent and personal and progressing to the more distant);
- an increasing complexity in what is studied (e.g. from observing, naming and describing features to interpreting evidence and identifying patterns);
- the use of more abstract ideas (e.g. an increasing understanding of social, political and economic issues);
- the development and use of historical skills especially enquiry, whether in the classroom or in the field (e.g. from pupils answering questions to formulating their own questions).

Using Blocked, Continuing and Linked Approaches in Planning the History Curriculum

Students and newly qualified teachers may encounter a bewildering variety of formats for curriculum planning as schools and nurseries attempt to combine their own aims and priorities in history with effective coverage of the National Curriculum and Early Learning Goals. The School Curriculum and Assessment Authority (1995) outlined three possible approaches to curriculum planning (blocked, continuing and linked work), all of which can be utilized to support teaching and learning in history in the Foundation Stage and Key Stages 1 and 2. In some settings the majority of history lessons may focus on the subject with few or no links made between history and other areas of learning. At the other extreme, virtually all the history taught may be integrated with other subjects. Discrete history teaching and integrating history with other relevant areas of study both have their advantages and disadvantages as approaches to teaching and learning, consequently most schools find themselves utilizing a mixture of linked and blocked approaches when planning for history. The table overleaf shows how one school has mapped out some of its blocked and linked work across the year groups showing the subjects involved within each topic.

Topic Plan	Blocked work □		Linked work ⇔			
Year group	**Term 1**	**Term 2**	**Term 3**	**Term 4**	**Term 5**	**Term 6**
Reception	Ourselves	Festivals and celebrations	Shape	Books	Water	Weather
	⇔ His/Sci	⇔ RE/Art	□ Maths	⇔ Eng/ICT	⇔ Geo/Sci	⇔ Geo/D+T
Year 1	Stories	Light and colour	Clothing	Sound	Plants and animals	Houses and homes
	⇔ Eng/His	⇔ Sci/Art	□ D+T	⇔ Sci/Music	□ Sci	⇔ His/D+T
Year 2	Seasons	Moving toys	Old and new	Our world	Safety	Packaging
	⇔ Geo/Sci	⇔ D+T/Sci	□ His	⇔ Geo/ICT	⇔ Sci/D+T	⇔ D+T/Art
Year 3	Invaders and settlers	The body	Ancient Egypt	Habitats	Forces	Another country
	□ His	□ Sci	□ His	⇔ Geo/Sci	□ Sci	⇔ Geo/ICT
Year 4	The environment	Earth in space	Local study	Victorians	Electricity and magnetism	Writers
	⇔ Geo/Art	⇔ Sci/ICT	⇔ His/Geo	□ His	□ Sci	⇔ Eng/ICT
Year 5	Tudors	Materials	Food	The Aztecs	Pattern	Inventors
	□ His	⇔ Sci/D+T	□ D+T	⇔ His/Art	⇔Maths/ICT/D+T	⇔ D+T/Sci
Year 6	Entertainment	Ancient Greece	Machines	The Sea	Britain since 1930	Britain since 1930
	⇔ Music/Art	□ His	⇔ D+T/ICT	□ Geo	⇔His/Music	⇔ His/Art

Note: Shading indicates topics with history content.

Blocked planning for history

Blocked work is drawn from single subjects or areas of learning and is taught within a set period of time (not normally exceeding one term). Blocked work has a tight subject focus with a discrete and coherent body of knowledge, skills and understanding. Not only is blocked work an approach to planning in its own right but it also forms the basis for any attempts to link different areas of the curriculum (see page 47). These units will focus on distinct and cohesive bodies of knowledge and understanding related to particular periods and locations. However, although the historical themes covered by blocked planning

	Unit of work: **Old and new**	NC subject: **History**	Year group: **Year 1**

Continuing ☐   Blocked ☑   Linked ☐

PoS	Learning objectives	Activities	Organization/resources
1a	Placing events and objects in chronological order	Work with artefacts (toys). Sequencing old and new; new/old/oldest. Completing 'My toy' timelines showing old and new toys.	Organize toy collection (arrange labelling). Timeline worksheets.
2b	Identifying differences between ways of life at different times	Discussing holidays. Where have the children been on holiday? Finding out about holidays in the past. Where did parents/grandparents go on holiday? What did they do on holiday? Looking at old and new photographs, posters and brochures.	Homework task – talking to relatives. Collecting travel brochures, reproduction posters and postcards, pictures of holidays in the past.
4b	Asking and answering questions about the past	Visit to the living history centre. Children to experience the Victorian classroom. Talking to the children about modern schooling and schooling in the olden days, for example desks in rows, ink and pens, slates, abacus, boys and girls separate, getting to school, rules and punishment.	Book visit, letters home. Arrange preliminary visit to meet with curator. School log/punishment book for display. Old school reports.
6a	Learning about changes in their own lives and the way of life of their family and others around them	'Interviewing' older relative about how their lives differed as a child. What games did they play? Ask what things they could/could not do; what things they had/did not have.	Arrange visitor. Meet beforehand with visitor to discuss topics/answers. Children to prepare questions in advance with adult support. Group work and STA (specialist teacher assistant) support needed for recording lesson.
6c	Learning about lives of men, women and children from the history of Britain	Read *Victorian Adventure* (Hunt, 1990). Discuss similarities and differences in lifestyles between now and Victorian times. Children to complete comparison chart, 'In the past . . .', 'Nowadays . . .'.	Story book. Photocopy worksheet. Class discussion, individual task.

43

will change, core aspects of history ought to feature irrespective of whether the children are learning about the Victorians or the Romans. As children revisit these core elements at regular intervals irrespective of the topic heading, they will advance their learning towards higher levels of understanding. As a result children's experience of history will be continuous, insofar as they will study some aspect of the subject in each year, but the period involved is likely to alter in order to achieve coverage of the National Curriculum study units. However, this blocked approach to planning for history is likely to mean that children will have little contact with the subject at certain times during the year as is demonstrated in the table above. Thus it is also useful for teachers to plan for history to be taught in ways other than through discrete units of work. The planning sheet on p. 43 shows a piece of blocked planning for a Key Stage 1 class in which there is a clearly identifiable history focus.

Continuing planning for history

Continuing or ongoing work, like blocked work, is drawn from single subjects or areas of learning. Continuing work requires ongoing teaching and assessment to be planned across a Key Stage and is characterized by a progressive sequence of learning objectives in order to provide for progression in a pupil's learning (SCAA, 1995). Continuing work is particularly valuable where aspects of the curriculum – whether skills, knowledge or understanding – require time for their systematic and gradual acquisition, practice and consolidation (SCAA, 1995). Given the demands of literacy and numeracy in the primary curriculum it is unlikely that there will be much opportunity for continuing approaches in history planning at Key Stages 1 and 2. However, there may be opportunities for some occasional ongoing history work, for example locating news items with historical content in national and local papers or on television news programmes, or responding to local events and changes. Teachers can take advantage of these opportunities to plan questions that the children could be asked about the stories. Such activities might also present opportunities for children to practice their historical skills as well as extending their historical knowledge and understanding. However, opportunities for continuing work are more likely in the Foundation Stage where activities based on Knowledge and Understanding of the World will be a regular feature of children's experiences. Children in the Foundation Stage may regularly answer questions and discuss significant events in their own lives and the lives of their families, increasing their ability to make effective use of temporal vocabulary such as *then*, *now*, *before* and *after*. There may also be regular opportunities for the children to enhance their understanding that there was a past and that it was different from the present (Edwards and Knight, 1994). The table below shows planning for continuing work on Knowledge and Understanding of the World. Those aspects that include some opportunities for increasing children's sense of the passage of time and chronology have been shaded.

Continuing/ongoing work

Area of learning: **Knowledge and Understanding of the World**   Year group: **Nursery**

Learning objectives	Activities	Organization/area/resources
Finding out about changes in the natural world	Learning about seasonal changes Local walks, visiting park and collecting leaves Talking about clothing, keeping warm, dry, cool. Observational drawings of clothes, e.g. hats and gloves	Small group walks Parent helpers
Learning about patterns, similarities and differences	Looking at leaves, talking about lighter, darker, shape and size Mixing paints, leaf printing Leaf rubbings	Outdoor play area Powder paints, brushes, ready-mix paints Wax crayons
Finding out about living things	Identifying and naming animals Small-scale play (the farm, the zoo) Visiting 'Whirlow Farm' Listening to stories, e.g. 'The Hungry Caterpillar'	Tadpoles, tank and weed Feeding/looking after the goldfish Hatching eggs from the farm in the incubator
Finding out about materials	Paper Wood Plastics Metals	Tactile play area Careful supervision needed on bench
Asking questions about how things work	'Dark area' and torches Moving toys (e.g. wheeled) Building models that 'work' Talking about household appliances and the dangers of electricity/machinery	Torches Construction kits Mechanical/battery-powered toys
Looking closely at changes	Work with foodstuffs. Changes due to mixing or heating. Night and day, talking about time of day and people's actions	Cooker, sink unit, work surfaces, crockery, cutlery, bowls, utensils, etc. Adult support essential at all times Clocks and timers
Using technology	ICT number/literacy packages Pixie/roamer Talking about technology in the home (e.g. television programmes that children have seen)	Computer trolleys/area

continued

Learning objectives	Activities	Organization/area/resources
Finding out about past events in their lives/their families' lives	Discussions about their family (who is in their family, brothers/sisters/parents/grandparents. Talking about family events/experiences e.g. preparing meals, child-care activities, household routines. Collecting photographs, making family albums/books	Role play/home corner play
Finding out about the place they live in	Talking about where they live. House/flat names and numbers House books with doors and windows that open showing occupants. Road safety work. Shops and shopping	Role-play area shop
Learning about cultures and beliefs (their own and others)	Celebrations and festivals (New Year, Chinese New Year, 1st April, Easter, May Day, Bonfire Night, Divali, Christmas, Eid) Stories about different families Work with food	Displays of artefacts and images

Linked planning for history

Using a linked approach to history planning (for example planning a Year 5 project on the Aztecs, with history and art as the primary subject components) should not be confused with integrated lessons in which more than one subject is being taught simultaneously. Linked work is intended to increase the coherence of the curriculum by capitalizing on common or complementary knowledge, skills and understanding contained in different subject areas and by offering scope to stimulate learning in one area from work in another area (SCAA, 1995). The merits and limitations of linking work in different areas of the curriculum have been a source of debate for many years. Those in favour of integrated approaches would argue that a well-planned, carefully structured, linked approach reflects the holistic way in which children view the world and allows them to construct their own meanings, focusing on the process of learning rather than on the acquisition of facts that may become outdated. The whole curriculum also contains elements such as citizenship or research skills that are cross-curricular rather than fitting neatly into subject 'boxes' and linked approaches are a useful way of building these into teaching and learning. However, integrated topic work has also been criticized as undemanding and failing to provide for progression, with subjects losing their identity and characteristics within it. Subjects are 'some of the most powerful tools for making sense of the world which human beings have ever devised' (Alexander *et al.*, 1992, p. 17) and there are dangers that integrated or linked approaches to history teaching may result in history receiving only superficial or incidental treatment. In order to meet the statutory requirements of the National Curriculum, there has been a steady move towards more subject-focused teaching in primary schools and away from undifferentiated topic approaches. However, while the practice of trying to link ten different subjects in a topic approach can be criticized for failing to provide sufficient clarity and rigour in terms of teaching and learning, there are sound reasons for linking a limited number of different subjects or aspects of the curriculum. The benefits of linking subjects should be seen more in terms of providing relevance and curriculum coherence than saving time. The School Curriculum and Assessment Authority identified clear criteria for the integration of different subject areas in the National Curriculum. Units can be linked when

- they contain common or complementary knowledge, understanding or skills;
- the skills acquired in one subject or aspect of the curriculum can be applied or consolidated in the context of another;
- the work in one subject or aspect of the curriculum provides a useful stimulus for work in another.

(SCAA, 1995)

The planning sheets below show a linked project on the Tudors in which history and English are the primary subjects.

The most effective approach to delivering the history curriculum is likely to be one that is planned flexibly and combines teaching through separate subjects and teaching through linked work, exploiting the advantages of both approaches where appropriate. Children's learning can be kept focused by restricting the numbers of subjects or aspects of the curriculum that are linked and avoiding contrived or artificial connections. Whichever approach is adopted, the subject's basic concepts and skills must be clearly identified and incorporated into activities. Careful planning should also ensure that children are able to progress from one level of knowledge, understanding and skill to the next.

Unit of work: **Tudors**		NC subject: **History**	Year group: **Year 5**
Continuing ☐	Blocked ☐	Linked ☑	Linked subject – English

PoS	Learning objectives	Activities	Organization/resources
3	Learning how the past is represented in different ways	Using Tudor portraits Discussing how images are choreographed	Reproduced portraits, e.g. Henry VIII, Elizabeth I Reference books Lenses
2c	Learning to identify and describe reasons for and results of historical events	Henry VIII, the life of the King Pupil timeline of Henry's life	Reference books, 'Tudor Monarchs' ICT data base

PoS	Learning objectives	Activities	Organization/resources
Unit of work: **Tudors**	NC subject: **English**	Year group: **Year 5**	
Continuing ☐	Blocked ☐	Linked ✔	Linked subject – History

PoS	Learning objectives	Activities	Organization/resources
En3. 12	Using a range of forms of writing (biography)	Introduce Shakespeare as a historical figure to children, i.e. Tudor playwright Pupils to produce Shakespeare biographies	Reference materials Adapted play scripts
En1. 11a	Improvising and working in role	Trial of Mary Queen of Scots Pupils to research and role play	Reference material Role cards Classroom 'courtroom'
En3. 9b	Writing to inform and explain	Letter home from English sailor Children to emphasize conditions, dangers, weather, etc.	'Tudors' CD-Rom Exploration reference material

Long-term Planning

In addition to using blocked, continuing and linked approaches to the task of organizing a broad and balanced curriculum, planning in schools also assumes long-, medium- and short-term forms. The development of long-term planning is led by the relevant subject, year group or Key Stage coordinator, and requires contributions, review and ultimately the agreement of all staff. At Key Stages 1 and 2 long-term planning must meet the statutory requirements of the National Curriculum in terms of knowledge, skills and understanding within the Programme of Study for history as well as the breadth of study. A long-term plan, or *scheme of work* (see Chapter 9), outlines the historical content to be covered and how that will be organized. This will include details of

- when history is taught to each year group;
- how often;
- in what depth it is taught;
- whether it is taught separately or linked with other subjects, whether it is organized and taught as a distinct and cohesive unit of work ('blocked' units of work) or as 'continuing' work.

(SCAA, 1995)

The long-term plan will therefore contain units of work which are manageable and coherent, which have the focus and broad content of each unit clearly stated and which also clearly state any links with other subjects or aspects of the curriculum. Through long-term planning schools can ensure that children have worthwhile and recurring experiences of history throughout their schooling. Long-term planning provides a mechanism by which teachers can build in continuity as well as progression both within and between Key Stages in terms of knowledge, understanding and skills and breadth of historical study. In the Foundation Stage this level of planning should provide for a range of experiences that will enable children to work towards the Early Learning Goals. This can be achieved by completing a matrix, listing the ELG requirements and then indicating where these are covered within different units of work. The matrix should identify where the different aspects of early history are catered for. For example, are opportunities for pupils to improve their chronological understanding included? Are there repeated opportunities to look closely at similarities, differences, patterns and change? Will the children be given chances to learn about past and present events in their lives, their families' lives, other people's lives and the place in which they live? Will pupils be given opportunities to begin to find out about their own cultures and those of other people?

Long-term planning which will result in effective teaching and learning needs, however, to go beyond mere coverage of the history Programme of Study or Early Learning Goals. Any guidance for curriculum planning must be adapted to reflect a school's particular circumstances such as its location, the interests of the children, the expertise of the teaching staff and the resources available. Has the school built up a wealth of resources and contacts to support the teaching of history? Is the school located in such a way as to be able to take advantage of particular opportunities for teaching and learning in history in the local environment? Many schools make use of commercially produced schemes of work and/or use units of work from the QCA scheme (QCA, 1998) to assist in planning for history. These may be used either in their entirety or as a source of ideas. Whatever their source, published schemes should be scrutinized carefully and teachers need to examine them critically to ensure that they take the above points into consideration and that the materials used are relevant and appropriate. Whilst sometimes useful as a source of ideas, the suggestions contained in many schemes for history may require interpretation and adaptation in order to make them meaningful to children in a specific location. Furthermore, in the case of commercially produced materials, accompanying teaching resources such as worksheets will almost certainly be produced with reference to ideas about what ought to be appropriate for a typical child of a certain age. As many children will not be typical the teaching resources too may need modifying or even replacing. Unit 12, 'How did life change in our locality in Victorian times?' (QCA, 1998), for example, is likely to result in widely different outcomes depending upon the school involved, even though there may be considerable commonality in terms of the overall structure for the enquiry.

When developing long-term plans for history, the following points need consideration:

- How much time is available for teaching history or developing related 'Knowledge and Understanding of the World' and when does it occur?
- What opportunities are provided in the local environment for learning in history?
- What opportunities for learning about the past are offered by the school buildings and grounds?
- What links exist within the local community, regionally, nationally or even internationally to support teaching and learning in this area?
- What approaches to teaching and learning can resources (human as well as physical) support?
- What is the staff's level of subject knowledge, expertise and interest?
- To what extent can history contribute to other aspects of the curriculum, such as citizenship or the development of literacy and numeracy?
- How can planning reflect the school's aims, objectives and policies – for example on equal opportunities?
- What are the needs, abilities, interests and achievements of the children? What sorts of previous experiences do they have?
- How do children learn? How do they acquire knowledge and skills and develop understanding in history?

The planning sheet below shows a section of long-term planning for history at Key Stage 2 in which study units are allocated to different year groups and different aspects of historical 'Knowledge, skills and understanding' (QCA, 1999) are prioritized at different points across the Key Stage.

History – Year 6 – Year Planner

History – Year 5 – Year Planner

History – Year 4 – Year Planner

Historical knowledge skills, and understanding
- Characteristic features of Victorian period (ideas, beliefs, attitudes and experiences) (2a)
- Identifying and describing reasons for and results of industrial developments in Victorian period (2c)
- Investigating how an aspect of the local area has changed over a long period of time (7)
- Learning to use a range of sources for historical enquiry (4a)
- Selecting, recording and organising historical information (5a)
- Communicating historical knowledge and understanding in a variety of ways (5c)

Breadth of study
- The Victorians
- Local study

Medium-term Planning

Medium-term planning, usually for half a term, is produced by class teachers, supported by the relevant subject, year group or Key Stage coordinator. In Foundation Stage settings, particularly nurseries, all the teaching team will usually be involved at some point. Medium-term planning outlines the details of the programme to be taught to a particular class or year group and the unit of work set out for history should be interesting, motivating and relevant to the children's lives. Medium-term plans set out the learning objectives based on the Early Learning Goals or National Curriculum Programmes of Study. They set out a logical progression of activities through which these objectives can be met and include opportunities for pupil assessment. At this level of planning some

---

Unit of work: **Time**   Continuing ☐   Blocked ☐   Linked ☑

Main area of learning: **Knowledge and Understanding of the World**

Linked area of learning: **Mathematical development**

Year group: **Reception**   Half-term: **5**

Learning objectives	Activities	Organization/area/resources
Learning about patterns in time	Discussing school routines (assemblies, PE), daily, weekly events, holidays, special days (birthdays) Seasonal changes	Writing and drawing tables Seasonal photographs
Measuring time	Making sand timers, candle clocks, water clocks Drawing/disassembling mechanical/electrical clocks and watches Keeping diary (daily/weekly) Finding birthdays on calendars	Collection/display of clocks and timers (old and new)
Finding out about past and present events in their lives and the lives of others	Routines, 'a day in my life', 'a day in our class', 'a day in someone else's life' Birth, death and new life Growth – myself	Photographs of children showing change and growth Story books showing passage of time
Finding out about past and present events in their lives (Beginnings and endings)	Looking back Starting nursery/school ('How did I feel when I first came to school?') Moving house, making new friends, joining clubs The future, 'What am I looking forward to?'	Circle time
Look closely at similarities, differences and change	Clothing and costume; wigs, hats, dresses/skirts, sportswear, fashion, holiday wear	Collection/display of clothes from the past Photographs of past fashions Dolls' clothes

indication will also be given concerning resources to support teaching and learning in history, particularly where advance action such as booking museum loans or arranging speakers or out of school visits is required. Finally such plans will indicate teaching methods and classroom organization. Where the planning is part of linked work, indications of where the history activities will link with another subject or cross-curricular element need to be set out. Similarly, medium-term plans may also outline opportunities for teaching and learning in history to contribute to children's learning in literacy, numeracy or ICT. In the Foundation Stage medium-term plans will also provide information on the context within which the relevant Early Learning Goals will be addressed such as the role-play area, investigation table or outdoor play area. The medium-term plan on p. 51 shows a unit of linked work in the Foundation Stage involving Knowledge and Understanding of the World and Mathematical development.

Short-term Planning

Short-term planning is produced by individual class teachers or members of the nursery team. This level of planning, whether for a lesson or an activity, should be sufficiently detailed to indicate clearly what is being taught. It also needs to make clear how something is being taught, including ways in which teaching and learning may be differentiated to take into account the range of ability and how the children are expected to learn. Where lessons or sessions are going to be repeated with different groups the planning may need to be modified or adjusted in the light of previous teaching and assessments of children's learning. When planning lessons or activities, a teacher must make a number of decisions. A good lesson or session plan has the following features:

- A clear, specific, relatively small-scale learning objective, derived from the Programmes of Study or Early Learning Goals, which can be assessed, stating what the children will be able to do, know or understand at the end of the session. The learning objective will have been identified in medium-term planning.
- Clarity on the part of the teacher on whether the purpose of the lesson/session involves knowledge or a skill to be acquired, a concept to be grasped or whether it is concerned with the children's ability to engage in the enquiry process.
- Clarity over what will be assessed (linked to the learning objective) and how.
- Key teaching points and questions with pointers to desired responses.
- The incorporation of ICT where appropriate.
- Details of how the children will be organized.
- Stimulating tasks and resources matched to children's experience and ability and informed by previous assessments.
- Provision for differentiation.
- Precise details of resources.

- Opportunities for feedback to the pupils and time for plenary discussion in order to check on and reinforce pupil learning.
- Clear progression from the introduction to the conclusion.

Introducing the lesson or activity well plays an important part in determining the enthusiasm and involvement of the children. The children need to know what they are going to be learning. Children are more likely to learn effectively if they are told the purpose and plan for the lesson or activity. It also means that they are likely to be in a better position to reflect on their learning at the end of the session. The introduction is where key teaching points, key questions and new vocabulary can be introduced and it may be important to recap or recall previous experiences. The first few minutes of a lesson are crucial and it is well worth a student or newly qualified teacher spending time beforehand on thinking how she/he is going to gain the children's attention and interest them in what is to follow. In history this can be achieved by offering the children something interesting to look at or listen to, such as a photograph, a historical artefact, making reference to a display or telling a brief anecdote (true or fictitious) which introduces the lesson's content. Writing down key teaching points and any new vocabulary is essential, as it is easy on occasion for teachers to get sidetracked or interrupted. It is easy too, in the early stages of a teaching career, to try and pack too much into an introduction. It is important to remember that in history time needs to be built in for children to ask questions, clarify points and to ensure that they are clear about what they have to do.

Having given consideration to how the children's attention will be obtained and how the purposes and nature of the task will be shared, the lesson or session plan then needs to outline how the activity will develop. This section should include notes on the task(s) on which the children are engaged, how they are to be organized, what differentiation (other than by outcome) will be offered and the nature of any adult intervention. Teachers need to consider their role during this time and to explain this to the children in order to encourage them to work more independently. During any history lesson the teacher may adopt a number of different roles including working with a particular group, monitoring all the groups, deciding who needs more input, encouraging effort and extending learning by asking appropriate questions. This section of the lesson plan may also need to include provision for very able pupils or those who finish early in order to extend their learning. Such extension activities could include using different reference sources or applying a skill in a different context. Finally a lesson or session plan needs to incorporate sufficient time at the end of a lesson not only for resources to be put away but also for reviewing and consolidating the children's learning. Such consolidation and checking on pupil learning can be done through playing a game, children sharing and discussing their learning, connecting the work to future activities or by asking similar questions in a different context.

Lesson plan: **History 'Transport old and new'**   Class: **Year 2**   Date: **10/2/00**

Learning objectives: **Identifying differences between ways of life at different times (2b)**

Ask and answer questions about the past (4b)

Resources

- Photographs and pictures of old-fashioned bicycles, motor vehicles, aircraft, steam locomotives, horse-drawn vehicles, ships and boats

- Toy vehicles including old and new

- Reference books on transport through the ages

Introduction

- Explain lesson content and purpose

- Ask for pupil experiences of transport

Development

Teaching points/Questions

- Ask for pupil ideas/knowledge about transport in the past

- Introduce teaching resources

- Ask pupils to identify old and new and say why/what's different

- Put children into groups focusing on land transport/water transport/air transport

- Children to group as 'Old and new'

- Recording similarities and differences

Pupil activities

- Class discussion/question and answer

- Pupils work in small groups focusing on land, air or water transport. Researching similarities and differences. Resources available on tables in land/water/air sets

Differentiation
Blue group to use pictorial record, STA support with labelling

Plenary/conclusion

- Children to report back findings/learning to other groups

- Check on ability to identify similarities and differences

Assessment

Criteria: children demonstrate knowledge and understanding of aspects of the past beyond living memory
children can handle sources of information to answer questions about the past

Mode/method: observation/question and answer
pupil's written/pictorial work

Teaching and Class Management Skills

For the learning objectives contained in planning to be realized the documentation needs to be matched by effective teaching and good classroom management skills. The Early Learning Goals provide clear guidelines on how young children should be taught whereas the National Curriculum, except for the literacy and numeracy strategies, dictates much of the content of teaching but not the process. Children can learn in different ways and have different needs and, consequently, teachers need to use a range of teaching and learning strategies to ensure that history is accessible and of interest to all pupils. As a student or newly qualified teacher it can be tempting to focus on the content of lessons and getting through that content in the time available rather than on what the children are learning and how this is organized. Whilst the previous section focused on planning to enable children to learn, this section looks at different ways in which children can be organized in order for them to learn. It then considers how learning can be differentiated to enable all children to achieve success and make progress, before outlining some of the historical misconceptions that teachers may encounter amongst pupils. The chapter concludes with a discussion on how students and teachers can assess the effectiveness of their planning, organization and teaching in history through self-evaluation in order to improve and develop their capabilities in these areas.

Organizing the Children

The way in which teachers organize children for an activity is determined by practicalities such as the availability of resources, the nature of the task being undertaken and the type of learning that is anticipated. Children may work as a whole class, in groups, in pairs or on an individual basis and effective teachers choose the most appropriate form of organization for the task in hand.

Advantages of different forms of working:

- Individual work can be effective in developing children's ability to take more responsibility for their own learning by encouraging them to demonstrate a degree of autonomy and independence.
- Group work is a useful vehicle for promoting language and social skills as a means by which children can support, challenge and extend their learning together (Pollard and Tann, 1993).
- Whole-class teaching is an effective approach for direct teaching (exposition and questioning); for introducing new work, recalling and recapping on previous learning; for giving instructions and for summarizing, reviewing and consolidating learning.

Examples of particular forms of organization in history:

- group work – interpreting old photographs, socio-dramatic/role play, producing a report on an enquiry;
- paired work – working on the computer using a simulation game or searching the Internet;
- individual – observational drawing of historical artefact, using reference materials, writing an account of a day in the life of a Victorian child;
- whole class – a discussion of a recent site visit, listening to a history story, watching a history video.

In many history lessons a number of ways of organizing the children are likely to be employed sequentially as the following example of a Key Stage 2 history lesson on Britain since 1930 demonstrates.

A **whole-class** introduction in which teacher explains the purpose of the lesson. A visitor is coming to talk about their experiences as a child.

Pupils divide into **groups** to discuss and note down questions that will provide information on life in the past. The teacher circulates and offers help and assistance to groups and **individuals**.

The pupils come back together as a **class** when the visitor arrives. The teacher chairs a question-and-answer session, offering clarification and eliciting additional information.

The pupils work in **pairs** after the visitor has left to write a biography.

Most history lessons at Key Stage 1 or 2 will begin and end with the teacher engaging with the whole class and children working either individually or collaboratively in between. Effective teachers aim to achieve a balance between these different forms of organization in their teaching as each has its strengths and limitations. A focus on individual work for instance means that similar points will have to be repeated and children may make less progress, lacking the stimulus of other children and having limited contact with the teacher (Dean, 1993). At times children may have to work in groups on different tasks because of the availability of resources: this takes careful planning and again points may have to be repeated. Furthermore, true group work can be a slow process, as children have to manage the group dynamics as well as complete the task. Meanwhile whole-class teaching risks being directed at the middle ability range and there may be children who will be bored with the pace or who are unable to follow what is happening.

Whole-class teaching in history

Some degree of whole-class teaching is likely to take place in many history activities. This method of organizing the children relies on a high level of communication and presentation skills on the part of the teacher. Whole-class teaching in history will require good exposition skills, not least the ability to explain things in different ways in order to challenge the most able while ensuring the participation of those children who are struggling. It is important to *work* the whole room with both your attention and your presence. It is very easy to focus on a particular part of the class or certain children and this can lead to other pupils feeling excluded and risks causing disruption. Class activities require sufficient resources to be made available to the children with a minimum of fuss. In some cases it may be possible to set these out beforehand, in other instances, for example work involving historical artefacts, the resources may distract pupil attention and consequently a speedy method of introducing them part way through needs to be found. Class teaching needs pupil attention in order to be effective; this can be gained through appropriate pacing, interesting materials and enthusiasm on the part of the teacher. Pacing and timing are also crucial and *overdwelling* on a subject can result in fidgeting and disruption; the younger the children the less didactic teaching they will be able to cope with.

As with any other lesson, history lessons with whole classes will run more smoothly if classroom routines are clear to children. While many conventions in 3–11 settings concern behaviour in the interests of health and safety and social justice it is also possible to make use of routine in order to underpin effective learning in history. While such conventions are unlikely to be as overt as statements such as 'In our class we share things' or 'In our class we do not run', they can be made apparent to the children through praise, recognition and repeated experience. Routines and conventions in history could include expectations over how to handle artefacts and other historical evidence or what to do with finished work. Expectations on pupils to try and demonstrate an appropriate degree of independence and autonomy for example finding out, looking carefully or showing interest and curiosity are equally useful. Finally, in order to make routines work, teachers need to be clear, consistent, persistent and on occasion insistent.

Using group work in history

It can be extremely valuable for a teacher to work with small groups in history. There are numerous different ways in which teachers can group children, each with advantages and limitations (see table overleaf).

The benefits of children working as a group are well documented (Dean, 1993). Their discussion and collaborative enquiries on an aspect of history, for

Group work options	Benefits	Problems
Mixed ability	Mixed groups can be useful where different roles can be assigned to each child, for example in order to produce a report on an enquiry. They can also result in role models and support for less able pupils while encouraging more tolerance from more able pupils.	Dangers of more able pupils 'coasting'. Dangers too of more able children being used as substitute teachers, instructing others but learning little new themselves. There can also be problems with more able children becoming frustrated by the pace of their peers, resulting in a 'take-over' in which their peers are left behind.
Similar ability	Grouping by ability can be appropriate for specific differentiated tasks; for extending more able children; for giving closer attention to those requiring additional help or for teaching a group which has reached a particular stage.	This form of grouping can lead to children seeing themselves as good or bad at something if used permanently or inappropriately. Furthermore as groups are often determined on the basis of the children's ability in literacy and numeracy, it can also result in self-fulfilling prophecies with teachers under- or over-estimating pupil capability in history.
By age	Easy to organize.	Grouping by age in mixed year classes may not always be useful, as the groups will contain wildly different levels of ability, interests and needs.
By friendship	Popular with pupils and hence can be a motivating experience for the children.	This can be divisive, isolating children or reinforcing stereotypes, for example boys may only choose to work with other boys, while some children may find that no-one wishes to work with them.
By interest/ enthusiasm	A shared enthusiasm and expertise can produce high goals and high levels of commitment and perseverance.	Not practical as a long-term strategy as children's interests may converge and diverge according to the historical context.

example, may enable them to extend their understanding in a way which they would have been unable to do alone as they *scaffold* each other's understanding in the subject. It is sometimes claimed that children are engaged in group work whereas in fact they are working *in* a group *as* individuals rather than *in* a group *as* a group. Group work relies on children being able to behave considerately towards their peers, to observe class conventions and to resolve differences of opinion in a positive fashion. Cooperative group work of this sort, however, does not happen automatically and children need to be taught certain social skills from an early age to enable them to work effectively with others. To make the most of group work in history children need to be encouraged to develop their collaborative and cooperative skills. Children who have had only limited opportunities to experience sharing, taking turns, involvement in discussion and having to listen to the ideas of others may find group work difficult. Having a real role for children in a group can help them to get the most out of it. Children without a role, either self-chosen or conferred from above, are more likely to drift away from the task mentally and in some cases physically.

Differentiating in History: Responding to Individual Needs

Nurseries and schools have a responsibility to provide a broad and balanced curriculum for all pupils. The National Curriculum and Early Learning Goals provide a starting point for planning a relevant and interesting history curriculum. However, children learn in different ways, at different rates and have different levels of attainment, interest and confidence. Thus, the curriculum also needs to accommodate differences between children and match learning opportunities with individual learning needs. Differentiation involves providing all children with work at an appropriate level that enables them not only to participate but also to learn, to demonstrate what they know, understand or can do and to make progress. Differentiation is not just an issue in the core subjects. It is an essential element in effective teaching across the curriculum as it provides all children with access to the curriculum and with opportunities to fulfil their potential. It is also perhaps one of the hardest aspects of teaching to 'get right', particularly for student and newly qualified teachers who have less knowledge of the children in their class. It is far easier to identify differences between children than to work out what to do about them, particularly when teachers are trying to balance the need to use their time efficiently alongside meeting the individual needs of particular children.

Differentiation is not about creating 30 lesson plans for 30 individual children. This is not only impractical and unworkable but also undesirable as it may isolate children and they may not be able to reap the benefits from working in a group. Hart (1992) suggests that teachers should focus on the difficulties that arise from the curriculum rather than those related to pupils. There are a number of steps teachers can take at the medium-term planning stage to ensure that children are able to achieve and make progress. They can

- incorporate a variety of teaching and learning strategies (e.g. organize the children in a variety of ways and utilize alternative approaches to teaching and learning);
- plan to use a wide range of stimulating resources in history (e.g. videos may appeal more to some children than textbooks);
- identify different methods of assessment to enable all children to demonstrate their learning.

Strategies	Examples

By outcome

This is probably the most common form of differentiation. Children use the same resources and have a common task which is sufficiently open-ended for them all to achieve success at their own level. Activities and materials need to be equally accessible to all pupils and should not be dependent upon knowledge or skills that only some pupils have.

'Writing in the past'
All the children create timelines that sequence the various examples and artefacts (fonts/scripts, alphabets/hieroglyphs/runes, writing accessories, envelopes, stamps, seals, writing tools, pens, quills, chalk, slates, tablets).

By task

When differentiating by task, not all children will have the same experience. This can be achieved in a number of ways. Children may be engaged on different tasks with the same objective; alternatively, a task can be made open-ended for some and more structured and clearly sequenced for less confident children.

'Writing in the past'
All the children create timelines that sequence a range of examples and artefacts, however different groups are given different types and quantities to sequence with the most able being asked to produce the most demanding timelines.

One way to alter the task involves using different recording techniques. There are many different ways in which children can record their learning and experiences in history. A second approach involves classroom organization in which children with similar abilities or needs work together on a particular task.

Famous person's timeline. Children with reading and writing difficulties use a 'cut/paste/name' technique on a preproduced timeline. The majority of children draw their own lines and are required to give more information than just the name.

Differentiation by task can also be achieved through the introduction of stepped tasks in which the pace and depth of learning will vary. Here, children are given a series of increasingly demanding tasks with some children completing all tasks and others completing only some. Teachers need to ensure that children do not see this as a form of competition or that more able, but lazy, or less motivated children do not linger unduly on the less demanding tasks. Stepped tasks can also cause difficulties in that children may not have a common starting point for a subsequent history lesson. One possible strategy for overcoming this problem is to have a common core task that guarantees a common starting point but to employ different extension activities to cater for pupils who are capable of taking their learning further in the time available.

Historical enquiry activity into fashion in the 1960s. More able pupils finishing more quickly are given the opportunity to use bookmarked websites on the Internet as a research tool.

Finally teachers can differentiate their history teaching by task by providing different children with different resources and materials. Resources can be provided which are more or less demanding, materials can be varied to allow for a wider range of skills.

Differentiated worksheets. Cloze procedure with words included. Cloze procedure, with words to be located in the literature.

Through teacher/adult support

One variation on the theme of altering the pupils' experiences in history is to adapt and adjust the level and quantity of adult support. In some instances this may be achieved by planning to work with particular children during a lesson or part of a lesson in response to a specific need. Alternatively the teacher intervention during a lesson may be responsive to pupil progress as teachers make prompt and accurate judgements about the apparent level of understanding or ability amongst the children, responding appropriately at the point of need to enable them to progress. Varying support in this way can include the types of questions directed at different children, the emphasis placed on reinforcing and recapping certain learning during plenary sessions and the focus of discussions to feedback and target set for future learning.

While moving around her class to assist children in writing about the development of the Health Service after the Second World War a teacher noticed that Daniel was writing about the 'National Hospitality Service'. She stopped, sat down with Daniel and asked him if he could see what was wrong with his title. She clarified the vocabulary with him and then moved on to monitor children's progress at the next table.

Experienced teachers often differentiate their lessons without consciously acknowledging that they are doing so. Meeting the needs of all pupils can therefore be further facilitated by ensuring that the following features of daily good practice are present in the teaching and learning of history

- give clear instructions and explanations;
- have clearly stated expectations;
- identify clear learning objectives that you share with children;
- sequence your questions towards the learning objective;
- recap on previous knowledge;
- ensure that learning is consolidated. Make time at the end of sessions to reinforce the main points;
- provide resources that are appropriate and easily accessible for the children concerned;
- use appropriate language that ensures every child comprehends the task;
- balance teacher exposition with times when children are working independently or collaboratively;
- produce interesting and exciting displays that encourage learning and reflect your high expectations;
- value the children's responses (and not just the correct answers);
- give positive, high-quality feedback to the children on their progress in history. This can be written or verbal but it should be given promptly and with points for improvement;
- promote a supportive classroom atmosphere, which focuses on positive discipline and praise.

Planning for differentiation makes it more likely that all the children will be able to participate in history lessons. Within these lessons, there are a number of ways in which children's needs can be catered for, both in classroom-based work and work beyond the school. The table on page 60 shows three major strategies for differentiation and provides examples of how history lessons can appear when these strategies are employed.

Pupil Misconceptions in History

Children may hold a number of misconceptions in history. In some instances confusion can exist over the sequencing of events and periods in the past. In others vocabulary, and the concepts described by it, may be unfamiliar and difficult to comprehend. Catherine Parr brought Henry VIII's children to live at *court* but what would that mean to many children? Similarly, as language evolves with new words being introduced and older ones becoming progressively more redundant some vocabulary could be very strange indeed to children. Children can also draw on their previous experiences in ways that may actually be misleading. Observing that items tend to display wear and tear after a certain amount of use could lead a child to assume that anything shiny must be relatively new. Similarly, experience of old films or photographs could result in pupils assuming that black and white equates with old, while colour implies recency. Even starting from the familiar can result in misconceptions (Kimber *et al.*, 1995, p. 163) as children can approach the subject from a highly personalized perspective. The ways in which these misconceptions in history are tackled needs to be based on observation and assessment of a pupil's knowledge and understanding. Without accurate appraisal of where children are experiencing difficulties, the teacher's efforts to assist them to higher levels of understanding are likely to be hampered. Chapter 6 offers a number of methods for conducting assessments of pupils in history. Once a teacher has established that a pupil has made an error or holds a misconception of some kind, then they can employ one of the strategies below in order to help the pupil progress.

- Offer additional experiences through evidence-based approaches to the subject that challenge preconceived ideas or misconceptions.
- Remember that there is a social dimension to learning. Interactions with peers and teachers through which ideas and explanations can be shared and discussed can be an effective way of overcoming misconceptions about the past.
- Talk and exposition are central to the task of helping children to overcome misconceptions. Teachers have an important part to play in offering children analogies or clarification. On the one hand this talk can draw on children's previous experience, trying to make a link with things they already know to aid comprehension. Alternatively the talk can be more ambitious and seek to open up new ideas to children. Kimber *et al.* (1995) pointed out that it is possible to underestimate children's abilities to cope with new and sometimes abstract ideas in history.

Improving History Teaching: Using Self-evaluation, Inspection Evidence and Research

Using self-evaluation

Trainee and newly qualified teachers who think critically about their own practice in teaching history are more likely to increase their repertoire of effective teaching methods in the subject than those that do not. Self-evaluation and becoming a reflective practitioner by monitoring, evaluating and revising practice are important aspects of teaching. Teachers should continually reflect upon and refine their own practice. Such evaluation is not simply a summative activity to be conducted at the conclusion of a history lesson or at the end of a particular unit of work. Evaluation also has a formative and continuous dimension. Much of it may be informal and based on classroom observations, for example the teacher who sees that a particular word or phrase in a book is archaic and no longer widely used and that her pupils do not appear to understand it, will immediately rephrase the word or provide a definition in order to enhance the children's comprehension.

When evaluating teaching and learning during history lessons it is more motivating to start with the positive. What went well? Then think about any aspect that did not appear to go as well as it should or as you would have liked. Reflect upon your learning objectives and the extent to which you think they were achieved. How appropriate were the teaching methods, structure and content of the history lesson for the range of ability in the group/class? How effective was the organization and timing of the session? Were these aspects suitable given the age and experience of the children? What would you do differently next time to improve the lesson? What do the children need to do next? At every stage of this process there ought to be careful consideration of the question 'How do you know?' and appropriate criteria need to be employed. The fact that children appear to have enjoyed a lesson is a positive point but it is not evidence of learning.

Read the description of the history *lesson below and try to evaluate its strengths and weaknesses. A commentary is provided at the end for you to compare with your own ideas.*

Criteria that could be used include

- the appropriateness of selected teaching and learning strategies for individuals and groups;
- the effectiveness of groupings;
- the quality of learning resources;
- the timing of learning activities;
- motivation by content and teaching and learning strategies.

During break time Mrs S set out the resources her Y4 pupils would use that afternoon. On Wednesday afternoons the class had PE or games before break, followed by history or geography.

The children entered the room following PE and whilst they settled at the tables Mrs S rolled down the blackboard on which she had written the words 'The Egyptian Gods'. Shaida asked Mrs S 'What are we doing today, Miss?', who replied 'We're not doing anything until everybody's sitting quietly!' When she had the children's attention Mrs S then informed them that the afternoon's lesson was about the Egyptian gods. She told the children that they would be finding out the names of some of the Egyptian gods and what they were gods of, using their history scheme plus other reference books that were available on their tables.
'I want you to work in your English groups. You're going to draw one of the gods from the books and colour it in. Under the picture I want you to write the name of the god and what they were the god of.'
'Can we use any colours, Miss?'
'No, I want you to look carefully at the pictures and use the same colours. If your work is neat I'll use it in the display I'm putting up for parents' evening this week.'
Mrs S then proceeded to tell each group which god she wanted them to copy and told the most able group that they could do more than one god.

'All the resources you will need are on your tables. There are books, paper, pencils and colouring pens. Off you go.'

The children quickly organized themselves into their groups and got on with the task. One group started squabbling over access to the books and pencils but after a quick word from Mrs S they settled down to draw. All of the children appeared to be on task and Mrs S moved around the tables overseeing the activity and responding to pupil questions. She made supportive comments to those children whose drawings were good representations and spent time with a statemented pupil, helping him to complete the activity. One child asked if he could paint his picture but Mrs S responded that there was insufficient time and that he should use the resources provided. At this point Mrs S checked her watch and realized that it was 3.15. She called out to the class that there were only 10 minutes remaining and that she wanted the drawings finished for the display. She continued to encourage the children to try to complete the activity and at 3.25 she told them to stop what they were doing, put their names on their drawings, put them on her desk and tidy up. The children responded efficiently and the bell went at 3.30. Mrs S complimented the children on their work and selected a couple of examples to show the whole class. She then asked to see which tables were ready to go home and let the children out of the classroom table by table. On the way out Paul said to Mrs S, 'That was *brill*, Miss.'

Mrs S stayed on in the classroom, mounted some of the drawings and put them on the display board. A passing colleague admired the quality of the drawings.

Commentary on evaluating history teaching

Strengths	Weaknesses
• The resources required for the task were organized before the start of the lesson and were accessible to the children.	• Copying and colouring in on its own is an insufficiently challenging task for most Y4 pupils.
	• The purpose of the task appeared to have more to do with parents' evening and displays rather than learning about history.
• The children were largely on task.	• Opportunities for historical enquiry, including asking and answering questions about the past were largely absent.
• Mrs S made sure that she retained a degree of mobility and spent time with the statemented pupil in order to facilitate completion.	• Children were grouped according to their performance in English rather than historical knowledge, skills or understanding.
	• Asking more able pupils to draw more gods does not constitute differentiation.

Using inspection evidence and research

While being a reflective practitioner is one way of improving your ability to teach history, it is equally important to make use of the experiences and learning of others. Much educational theory has been criticized in the past and in relation to other disciplines has sometimes had low or lesser status. Yet all teaching is underpinned by theories of how children learn and what therefore constitute the most effective teaching methods. Foundation and primary practice has been influenced by a range of researchers. Some of these influences have become accepted as unquestionable characteristics of primary practice (Clegg and Billington, 1994) rather than being features open to scrutiny and question. Teachers should not cling on to the notion of *good practice* as immutable, an uncontestable and indisputable set of rules for teaching and learning. Good practice should always be the subject of debate and argument. Alexander *et al.* (1992) pointed out that if *practice is introduced from a sense of obligation rather than conviction* it is likely to have adverse effects on children's learning.

The sources of information available to students and teachers wishing to update and develop their teaching and learning in this area include professional journals, documentation from government departments and agencies and commercially produced curriculum materials. In addition, many sources of information and ideas on history can now be located through the Internet. It is important to use such sources critically, particularly the Internet, as the lack of editorial control means that the quality and suitability of material can vary widely. A further source of information can be derived from Ofsted inspection reports that can also be accessed through the Internet. Such reports can be instructive in setting out what is considered to be good practice in teaching and learning in history.

Sources of information to support high-quality teaching and learning and the development of teacher expertise in history

Journals and other publications

Teaching History
History Today
The Curriculum Journal
Education 3–13
Infant Projects
Junior Education
Child Education/Early Education
TES Primary

Other sources

History Channel: www.historychannel.com
BBC History Hour Online: www.bbc.co.uk/education/hours/history/

Government agencies and departments

Office for Standards in Education (Ofsted): www.ofsted.gov.uk
Department for Education and Employment (DfEE): www.dfee.gov.uk
Qualifications and Curriculum Authority (QCA): www.qca.org.uk
The Standards website: www.standards.dfee.gov.uk/schemes/history/
National Grid for Learning (NGFL): www.ngfl.gov.uk

Reflective Questions

Planning

- Does your planning contain clear learning purposes based on National Curriculum Programmes of Study or Early Learning Goals?
- Is your planning for history part of a whole-school approach set out in long-term plans?
- Do you use a variety of planning approaches, including continuing, blocked and linked history work?
- What would you expect to see in terms of continuity in history in the Key Stage with which you are currently working?
- What would you expect progression would look like from the Foundation Stage to the end of Key Stage 2 in terms of children's knowledge and understanding of events, people and changes in the past (QCA, 1999a)? Think about how the children will work as well as what they will learn and do.

Teaching and class management

- How would you avoid a queue of children asking the following questions during a history lesson
  - What do I do?
  - What do I do next?
  - Where is . . .?
  - How do you spell . . .?
  - Can I . . .?
  - Is this right?
- Do you make appropriate use of alternative ways of organizing and grouping the children?
- What skills would your children need to be successful in working as a group? Do you train/assist children to acquire the skills and techniques necessary for working cooperatively and effectively with others?
- How effective are your presentation skills when introducing new history work?
- How effective is your pacing and timing of large group or whole-class lessons?
- Do your history lessons contain opportunities for children to engage in debate, discussion, questioning and hypothesizing?
- What sorts of history activities would be appropriate for children working as a group?
- How do you differentiate your history teaching for the range of ability in your class?
- How effective are you at questioning the children as a way of eliciting information about their understanding?
- Do you chair discussions about history in such a way as to encourage contributions from all?

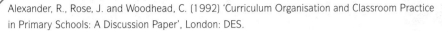

REFERENCES

Alexander, R., Rose, J. and Woodhead, C. (1992) 'Curriculum Organisation and Classroom Practice in Primary Schools: A Discussion Paper', London: DES.

Chambers, B. and Donert, K. (1996) *Teaching Geography at Key Stage 2*, Cambridge: Chris Kington.

Clegg, D. and Billington, S. (1994) *The Effective Primary Classroom: The Management and Organization of Teaching and Learning*, London: David Fulton.

Dean, J. (1993) *Organising Learning in the Primary School*, 3rd edition, London: Croom Helm.

Edwards, A. and Knight, P. (1994) *Effective Early Years Education: Teaching Young Children*, Buckingham: Open University Press.

Hart, S. (1992) 'Differentiation: part of the problem or part of the solution?', *Curriculum Journal* **3**(2): 131–42.

Hunt, R. (1990) *Victorian Adventure*, Oxford Reading Tree, Stage 8, Magpies. Oxford: OUP.

Kimber, D., Clough, N., Forrest, M., Harnett, P., Menter, I. and Newman, E. (1995) *Humanities in Primary Education*, London: David Fulton Publishers.

Pollard, A. and Tann, S. (1993) *Reflective Teaching in the Primary School: A Handbook for the Classroom*, 2nd edition, London: Cassell.

Qualifications and Curriculum Authority (QCA) (1998) *A Scheme of Work for Key Stages 1 and 2: History*, London: DfEE/QCA.

Qualifications and Curriculum Authority (QCA) (1999a) *The National Curriculum: Handbook for Primary Teachers in England*, London: DfEE/QCA.

Qualifications and Curriculum Authority (QCA)(1999b), *Early Learning Goals*, London: DfEE/QCA.

School Curriculum and Assessment Authority (SCAA) (1995) *Planning the Curriculum at Key Stages 1 and 2*, London: SCAA.

Wood, D. (1998) *How Children Think and Learn* (2nd edition), Oxford: Blackwell.

67

Effective Teaching and Learning Strategies in History

This chapter examines some of the different types of activity that can be used in the teaching of history and illustrates these throughout with examples from the Foundation Stage and Key Stages 1 and 2. Any planned teaching method ought to be informed by an understanding of how children learn if it is to have a better chance of being effective. Children are perceived as active learners who benefit from, and are thus provided with, relevant first-hand experience. Schools and nurseries assist pupils in making sense of the world by exploring objects, materials and feelings in meaningful situations. The children's natural curiosity is harnessed as they are encouraged to ask why and how things are as they are. Nurseries and schools also recognize that children gain a great deal personally, socially and cognitively from interacting with others, as well as with their environment, through play and talk.

These comments should be viewed as a summary only. There is not the space within a book such as this to cover the various theories in detail, nor is there time to do justice to the interplay between children's cognitive development and their development in other areas, for example social and emotional development. The purpose is to make the case for why various teaching methods are justified in history. The chapter addresses two broad approaches to teaching and learning in history, namely evidence-based and imaginative-creative approaches. It is worthwhile stating at this point that the boundaries between these two approaches may not always be clear cut and certainly there is much to be said for teachers utilizing a mixture of approaches and capitalizing upon the interplay possible where one approach can inform another. The chapter begins with a look at a range of evidence-based approaches that teachers can use in their history teaching. The list includes the use of historical artefacts, setting up a class museum, outside visits to historical sites, audio and visual materials, using teacher exposition and oral work, using written evidence, using timelines, and using new technologies. The second part of the chapter considers the use of imaginative and creative approaches to teaching and learning in history. It outlines and defines different categories of imagination in history and then reviews some of the options for learning through play, and fictional accounts set in actual events.

Evidence-based Approaches

The use of historical evidence in all its forms is a vital part of the history curriculum. Evidence-based approaches to the teaching of history involve the introduction of images, information and objects from the past to the children as a way of extending their historical knowledge and skills. Good practice in helping the youngest children to formulate some early ideas about the past and to develop skills and attitudes useful in finding out about the past is informed by the same principles of good practice that inform all learning in nursery and reception settings. Children benefit from time to explore and manipulate their environment and high levels of high-quality interaction between children and adults make a major contribution to learning. While there is no subject called history in the Early Learning Goals there are many opportunities for early years practitioners to introduce children to ideas about the passage of time through the use of evidence. Early years practitioners work from the familiar in using evidence-based approaches by focusing upon the home, the family and the locality. They help children by modelling observation and examination techniques and by introducing and reinforcing descriptive language.

The history curriculum at Key Stages 1 and 2 encourages the understanding of artefacts, systems and environments from different times and cultures. Not only is the introduction of such materials into the classroom highly motivating for children, it also fits well with theories of how children's learning can be enhanced through first-hand experiences particularly, though by no means exclusively, with younger pupils. The table on page 70 outlines some of the ways in which evidence-based approaches can support pupils' learning in history.

Using Artefacts

Introducing objects into history teaching offers pupils first-hand experience and opportunities for questioning and enquiry. A significant development in the understanding of how children learn came with the advent of Piaget's work. Piaget did not regard children as passive learners (Donaldson, 1978), for him children actively construct meaning and ideas about how the world works. He used the concepts of assimilation, disequilibrium and accommodation to explain the process of learning. Children assimilate knowledge about the world around them through first-hand experience. Subsequent experiences force children to re-evaluate their original ideas in the light of new information in order to accommodate to the new reality. The lack of equilibrium or disequilibrium caused by encountering new data which does not conform to or extends their old model (schema) of the world is resolved as they incorporate the new knowledge and

Aspect	Learning	Example of evidence-based approach
Chronological understanding	Developing an understanding of concepts such as change over time and continuity through the introduction of historical evidence in its many forms.	A class of Year 6 pupils watched the BBC Landmarks video on 'Britain Since 1930' (BBC Publications, 1999) and discussed significant features such as poverty in the 1930s, gradual economic improvements in the 1950s and increasing affluence and freedom in the 1960s and 1970s.
Past events and people	Children's knowledge and under-standing of events and people in the past is also informed by evidence. These approaches enable children to make concrete links with other times and cultures and expose them first hand to examples of diversity, similarity and progress, for example by considering design, function, aesthetics, fashion, style, taste or communication.	A class of Year 3 children visited a Tudor building (Bishop's House) in Sheffield. During the visit the children were encouraged to look for similarities and differences between Bishop's House and their own homes in terms of construction, fixtures, fittings and furniture. After the visit the children were given an opportunity to record their experiences and learning through the construction of a model using lengths of soft wood, found materials and textile remnants.
Historical interpretation	Learning to formulate and test hypotheses; discussing, predicting and identifying; moving on from guessing.	A Year 1 class were shown some coins as part of a project on 'Old and new' and asked to identify them and tell their teacher what they could buy with them. The teacher then introduced some old pre-decimalization coins covering the 1890s–1970s. She asked the children if they knew what they were, seeking theories, ideas and explanations, before looking in detail at the images, writing and dates on the artefacts.
Historical enquiry	Developing generic skills such as handling, storing, observing and examining. Learning to look; slowing down, taking time to study, not simple cursory glances. Learning to ask questions; moving beyond the 'What is it?' stage. Learning to classify; using colour, texture, shape, smell, sound, weight, size, materials, design, structure and purpose.	A Year 2 class were finding out about holidays in the past based on the ideas contained in the QCA planning sheets (QCA, 1998). Their teacher collected old postcards, posters and photographs and the children were encouraged to find out about the holidays their parents and grandparents could remember.
Communication	Learning to describe requires and develops a broader vocabulary extending children's historical language. Learning to record includes organizing historical information and using a range of techniques including drawing, annotation, notation, writing for different audiences and using small tape recorders.	A class of Year 3 pupils compiled Invaders and Settlers timelines at the end of a unit of work on pre-Norman Britain. They used a range of reference materials including the CD-Rom to help them in the task.

experience into their existing mental models, thus improving and enhancing them (Donaldson, 1978; Bruce, 1997).

For Piaget, progression in intellectual development was the result of the loss, and subsequent restoration at a new higher level, of equilibrium. In Piaget's model, the older and more mature the children, the more adept they are at taking into account increasing quantities of information and exploring increasingly complex strategies to help them solve problems and operate effectively in their environment. First-hand, concrete experience therefore had a positive impact on children's learning.

Most children are curious and are often enthralled by the arrival in the classroom of artefacts from earlier times. Teachers may wish to start from what the children are familiar with such as household items or toys so that children will be able to make connections and draw upon their previous experience. The inclusion of modern parallels can help children to develop a sense of chronology, change and development by comparing and contrasting the old and the new and creating three-dimensional timelines. Equally, bringing strange and unusual objects into the classroom can introduce an element of mystery and excitement. Artefacts can be highly effective as a means of generating discussion about the past and introducing new vocabulary. It is important to remember that children will benefit from being able to use senses other than vision alone. Smell and touch can also be important. Given what is known of the ways in which young children learn it is important to include a range of objects none of which are hazardous and many of which can be handled by the pupils.

Communication artefacts

A vertically grouped class of Year 2 and 3 pupils were involved in a half-term topic on 'Communication'. The primary subject focus was English and ICT, however through a personal contact the teacher discovered that the education officer at one of the local museums was a collector of old technology, including telephones. The teacher visited the education officer at the museum to discuss a visit to the school to allow the children to look at how the technology had changed since its inception. During his visit to the class the education officer was able to provide the children with hands-on experience with a wide range of historical artefacts, some dating back nearly a century, which graphically illustrated the changes over time in terms of factors such as design and materials. As an *expert* (in both the history of the artefacts and education) the visitor was also able to talk knowledgeably and at an appropriate level when answering the children's questions. Following the visit the children did a variety of work including recording their experiences on the computer and mounting a timeline display using observational drawings made on the day.

While first-hand experience plays an important part in pupils' learning so too does quality intervention on the part of adults. One of the consequences of Piaget's ideas on children's stages of development was the notion of readiness. If a child found an experience too difficult to comprehend then this constituted evidence that the child was not yet ready to learn. Bruner's research (Wood, 1998) built on that of Piaget but he suggested that children were capable of intellectual achievements at an earlier point than that predicted by Piaget as a result of instruction and carefully structured environments. This idea challenged the idea of readiness. For Bruner, passively waiting for children to become ready to learn might necessitate a very long wait indeed. As a result, the concept of readiness could actually lead to a lowering of educational standards and teacher expectations. While teachers do need to be sensitive to a child's needs, abilities and development, they also need to be prepared to intervene, through questioning, guiding and instructing in an effort to extend and challenge thinking. In Bruner's model, facilitating pupils' progress through the use of appropriate support materials and intervention would provide children with *scaffolding* upon which they could construct increasingly advanced ways of thinking and understanding the world. In handling artefacts children may have their own ideas about features that are significant. A black and white photograph might be thought to be older than a colour one not because of its subject matter but simply because it is black and white. Similarly children may make assumptions concerning the chronology of artefacts based on the wear and tear in evidence. By utilizing a series of focused questions teachers can help children to think about, examine and interrogate artefacts. Such questions can be used to focus pupils' attention on a number of areas. With younger pupils the focus is likely to be on description rather than hypothesis and identification. With older children questions can target physical features, methods of construction or manufacture, the function and design of objects, the value that objects might have had and notions of how value can be relative and is subject to change over time. Structured questioning of this sort helps to reduce the incidence of wild guessing. It may be useful to include observational aids such as magnifiers, particularly where small details such as the insides of a clock or watch are the focus of the observation.

Suggestions on how you could direct children's attention when examining artefacts

Observation questions

1. What does it feel like?
2. What does it look like?
3. Is it heavy or light?
4. What materials is it made from?
5. What colour is it?
6. Does it smell of anything?
7. Is there any decoration or a pattern on the object?
8. Is there any writing on the object? Do you know what language it is? Does it tell you anything about the object?

Interpretation questions

1. What do you think it was used for?
2. How old do you think it is?
3. Do you think it was handmade or made by a machine?
4. Do you think it was made for personal use or to be sold or exchanged?
5. Where do you think it comes from?
6. Why were these materials used?
7. Who might have used/owned it?
8. Do we have similar objects today? How are they different/similar?

Setting up a Museum

Photographs on loan from local school library service.	**Class 10's Museum of the Second World War**	Imperial War Museum posters.

Collected artefacts loaned from home including ration books, uniforms, gas mask, shrapnel, newspaper cuttings, coins, medals, photographs, paintings and sketches.	Reference books on Second World War. Imperial War Museum and Eden Camp teaching resources.

School or class collections of artefacts are a useful resource for history teaching and can be augmented through the use of museum loans, loans from parents and the local community or through purchase. While many class collections may have a clearly defined lifespan related to the duration of a specific history topic, others may be much more long lived and form part of a wider school museum in which the exhibits are rotated over the academic year. Setting up a class museum can be a valuable way of involving children in the communication and organization of historical information. Keeping a record of the exhibits is important where a large number of artefacts have been gathered from pupils and their families. Items that are on loan will need to be returned to the rightful owner at the end of the project so it is important to keep a record. Parents need to be cautioned about loaning valuable items given the fact that children will be handling them. The exhibits therefore ought to be labelled and children can play a role in researching the history of individual artefacts, arranging and producing information to accompany the displays, designing and constructing the display area, as well as managing and caring for the collection and the display. Older pupils can take responsibility for this themselves.

Setting up a class museum creates opportunities for children to

- act as curators;
- produce tickets;
- schedule visits by pupils from other year groups;
- act as *experts*;
- set up a loan system to other classes;
- catalogue displayed artefacts;
- write labels, dating and ordering objects;
- seek the advice and involvement of local museum staff.

Storing the objects also needs to be thought through, particularly where there may need to be some rotation of the exhibits to reflect a particular focus for a week.

For example, a class museum linked to a topic on 'Britain since the 1930s' might focus on houses and homes during the first few weeks and exhibit crockery, cutlery and other household items. During the latter part of the topic the focus might shift to the impact of the Second World War and the display would change to include ration books, posters, a gas mask and an ARP (Air Raid Precaution) helmet. Some instruction on handling the artefacts may well be needed in order to minimize the risk of accidental damage. Highly fragile items may need a sealed display case, other items may stain or mark and gloves may be needed. Detailed guidelines on setting up class and school museums can be found in the Historical Association's *Occasional Paper 7* (1994).

Outside Visits to Historical Sites •

Taking children out of the classroom on visits to museums, galleries, exploratories and historical sites can extend the opportunities for evidence-based teaching in history. There will be occasions when, for practical reasons, it is not possible to bring historical artefacts to the children. In other circumstances, encountering artefacts *in situ* can help the children to make greater sense of them. Using sites and outside collections can make a significant contribution to the development of pupils' historical knowledge and understanding, for example developing pupils' sense of chronology and change over time, as well as offering a new context within which to practise their historical skills. Outside visits also offer opportunities for community interactions and for linking nursery and school experiences with the wider world, enabling children to become more aware of the diversity of people, places and objects. As with any other aspect of history teaching, planning and preparation are essential in order to get the maximum educational benefit from a visit, as well as safeguarding the health and safety of the children.

Teachers need to weigh up the appropriateness of the visit for their children. Younger children may benefit more from sites closer to the nursery/school, while older pupils may be better able to cope with a long journey and make more sense of the history associated with a more distant location. A preliminary visit without the children is advisable in order to familiarize yourself with what the site has to offer. Checking on the readability of labels, the height of displays, the ease of access and lines of sight, will be useful in assessing whether or not it will be appropriate for the children. Such a preliminary visit will also feed into the process of risk assessment. Teachers will need to think about the logistics, health and safety and housekeeping issues associated with outside visits, for example conducting a risk assessment and making the arrangements for travel, toileting, feeding and sheltering the children. A preliminary visit may also provide valuable information for drafting letters to parents dealing with issues such as pocket

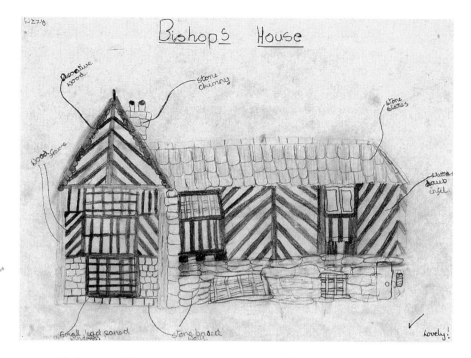

money, clothing and footwear. Finally, conducting a preliminary visit to a site will enable teachers to talk from experience when matching pupils to adults and issuing reminders about standards of behaviour and risk avoidance. For further information on historical visits see Chapter 5.

It is important to establish clear educational purposes for a visit. In some instances, such as visits to museums, it is neither possible nor desirable to try to do or see everything. This is not to say that some free time to look more widely at the site and exhibits is a bad thing, merely that this should not distract children from the main reason for the visit. First-hand experience alone is no guarantee of learning. Putting a pupil on a site will necessitate preparatory work if intended learning is to predominate.

Planning to get the most from a site visit

- What do children need to know or have experienced prior to the visit in order to get the most out of it?
- What preparatory work will you need to do with other adults accompanying the children? Are the group leaders briefed on the purpose, skills, concepts and attitudes associated with the visit?
- What will happen during the visit? Do you need classroom space; input from education officers/guides; opportunities for handling artefacts?
- Will the children be using worksheets? Some sites produce their own. They can be useful in helping to focus attention and structure the collection of information and can result in a visual as well as a written record. However, children also need opportunities for reflection, therefore teachers need to ensure that questioning takes place to encourage empathy and

higher levels of intellectual activity. Children also benefit from opportunities to exercise choice and set their own agenda. Overreliance on worksheets can reduce such opportunities and can sometimes result in children racing to be the first to finish rather than really looking and learning.

• What will happen after the visit? What follow-up work will the children engage in? Remember that with young children the chance to talk about their observations and experiences fairly soon after the visit is likely to aid retention and learning.

Below is an example of a briefing sheet and notes for parent helpers.

Site: Botanical Gardens

Year group: Year 3
Information for parents

Purposes of visit

• To study how an aspect of the local area has changed over a long time.
• To learn about some of the attitudes and experiences of people in the past.

The Botanical Gardens were opened in 1836 on 19 acres, bought for £3600 raised by subscription. A competition was organized to find the best design and it was won by Robert Marnock. He won first prize of £10 and was paid £100 per year as the Gardens' first curator. Robert Marnock had travelled all over the country gathering ideas for his design including talking to Joseph Paxton, the head gardener at Chatsworth and later the designer of the Crystal Palace in 1851. There was a belief at the time that there was a need for green and open spaces in industrialized towns as an antidote to crime, grime, drink and poor housing. Some of the Victorians talked about the 'lungs of the city' and saw parks and gardens as sources of clean air. Others thought that by encouraging social contact between the classes the workers could be 'civilized'. On their first four days of opening there were 12,000 visitors who all paid 2 shillings to get in, but not many workers could have afforded 2 shillings. Furthermore, after their opening the Gardens were normally only open to the subscribers except on special occasions. What is more, visitors to the Gardens had to meet a strict dress code, and anyone caught swearing or drinking alcohol in the Gardens would be thrown out.

By the end of the nineteenth century the Gardens were in financial trouble. In 1897 they had debts of £22! Many of the gardeners were sacked and some people tried to sell the land for housing to make a lot of money. There was a scandal and the local council took over and opened the Gardens to the public for the first time. However, there were still commissionaires on the gates to stop *undesirable* people coming into the Gardens.

Suggested questions for the children

Observation questions

1. What are the site and its surroundings like?
2. Who is the statue in the Rose Garden of? (Peter Pan)
3. How are the glass houses different from glass houses today?
4. What does the large statue at the bottom of the main drive commemorate? (Crimean War)
5. What can they find in the top left corner of the Gardens? (bear pit)

Interpretation questions

1. What do the children think conditions were like for the workers?
2. What do they think about keeping bears in a pit? Why do they think the pit is not used now?
3. Why do they think the Gardens were built?
4. What do they think about having to pay to get into the Gardens?

Carder, J. (1986) *The Sheffield Botanical Gardens*, Sheffield Town Trust

Using Audio and Visual Materials

Audio and visual material can tell children a great deal about past times by offering a highly accessible and exciting source of evidence, one moreover which provides an interesting dimension to children's deliberations on how it is possible to conclude that something is old. Younger children can begin with what is most familiar to them, namely themselves and their family. Common activities include collecting and sequencing photographs of themselves in chronological order or creating photographic timelines of significant events in their own lives such as birthdays, bonfire night, religious festivals, weddings or christenings. Children can also be asked to compare old photographs and pictures with recent ones, for example examining still photographs of a local town centre to gain an insight into how much things have changed locally with the passage of time. In some cases evidence on the back of photographs and paintings, for example names, dates, addresses and messages may supplement the evidence on the front. Alternatively children might be given the chance to listen to popular music from past periods and to compare styles and instruments with those of modern popular music.

Audio material

- Records
- CDs
- Taped accounts, broadcasts

Visual material

- Photographs e.g. museum loans
- Postcards (often reproduced)
- Paintings
- Cartoons
- Posters
- Film/video
- ICT simulations

An important part of using audio and visual historical material concerns critical appraisal. Visual material in particular can provide a rich and vivid insight into the past as long as we encourage children to use this sort of material to practise historical interpretation and questioning the evidence (Morris, 1989). Children need to be encouraged to listen and to look critically. With younger children this may arise from purely descriptive discussion to begin to make judgements about what people might be thinking or feeling. With older children it is possible to alert them to the fact that audio and visual material does not necessarily constitute an unbiased representation of the past. Visual reading and listening skills need to be fostered by teachers, as not everything the children hear will be accurate or uncontested and not everything they see can be taken at face value. Furthermore, some material could be deemed inappropriate in our contemporary society, for example lyrics or radio broadcast material in which racist or sexist language is used. Teachers will wish to look carefully at some resources to eliminate offensive material.

OUR COUNTRYSIDE

A SERIES OF 48 — No. 22

HENLEY ROYAL REGATTA

To anyone who has had the good fortune to enjoy a fine day at Henley Regatta, this picture will bring back happy memories. The crews straining every nerve at the finish are, of course, the chief attraction, but in between the races nigger minstrels and purveyors of luscious fruit, both plying their trade in punts, compete with one another for the attention of the ladies, whose gaily coloured dresses find a challenge in the blazers of their escorts.

SENIOR SERVICE
CIGARETTES

HENLEY ROYAL REGATTA

This cigarette card was part of a collection of views of Britain from 1936 and donated to a Y3 teacher for use with his pupils. Not only is the language used on the back totally unacceptable, displaying or using other cards in the set might necessitate some discussion about health education.

In her book on using portraits in history Susan Morris (1989) offers excellent insights into the messages contained in visual material. Although mainly concerned with paintings and photographs that have been consciously posed for, many of her ideas can be applied to other visual material. When using images that have been consciously posed for, children ought to be encouraged to think about who was portrayed in this way; certainly not everyone in the past could afford the services of a portrait painter or had the time to sit for them. The choreography involved in portraits constituted a conscious attempt on the part of the sitter and the artist to say or show more than just a good likeness. A plethora of items that would have had significance for contemporary viewers are clearly visible in visual material of this sort. The costumes and clothing on display were intended to say something to the viewer about the status of the subject, as do medals, badges of rank and other symbols of office. Similarly the portrait may seek to convey positive ideas about the character of the subject through the pose and expression adopted.

In the centuries before photography, portraits were sometimes used to aid marriage negotiations between wealthy or aristocratic families. The couple might not meet until the ceremony itself, especially where members of royal households in one country were marrying members of another royal family in another country. This presented portrait painters with an interesting dilemma. The recipient of such a portrait probably wanted accuracy, yet the sender was probably more interested in flattery. Artists could conceal or play down deformities, alternatively they could accentuate fashionable physical attributes. Philip of Spain is reputed to have cursed Mary Tudor's portrait painter. One wonders what she thought of his!

An examination of portraits, for example as part of work on the Tudors with Key Stage 2 pupils, will reveal how attitudes have changed towards fashion and perceptions of attractiveness. Children can be encouraged to look for the *handsome* male with his 'finely turned legs' or the *beautiful* woman with her translucent white skin and her veins showing, blond curly hair, smooth hair line and a narrow waist. Mary Tudor's half-sister, Elizabeth I, was keenly interested in the way in which she was portrayed (Kimber *et al.*, 1995).

The Roman Emperor Augustus was unlikely to be seen in person by most citizens of the Roman Empire. As a result he sent 'youthful, attractive' images of himself, including statues, paintings and reliefs, all over the Empire. Roman legions even took statues of him with them on campaign and set them up in conquered territories. He also made sure that the image that people were most likely to encounter, namely the one on his coins, portrayed him as 'young, imperial and benevolent' (Grabsky, 1997) throughout his reign, even though he remained Emperor until his death aged 76.

Portraits and pictures therefore could be used as much for propaganda purposes as for their contribution to a family album. An examination of portraits of individuals such as Henry VIII or Queen Victoria says a great deal about the sort of images that the sitters and/or the artists were seeking to portray. Looked at in this way, portraits begin to take on the status of propaganda as much as accurate representations of the real person.

Examining visual material

Although family portraits may be less professionally choreographed they can be just as revealing about the past.

Observation questions

1. What is the clothing like?
2. What does the subject look like (happy, stern, wise, beautiful)?
3. What is in the background?
4. What are they carrying?
5. Who is with them?

Interpretation questions

1. When do you think it was painted/photographed?
2. What does the background tell you about the subject and the time in which they lived?
3. What do the following things tell you about the subject(s)?:

- clothing (for example textiles or armour);
- expression;
- pose;
- accessories;
- pets or other animals.

Using Teacher Exposition and Oral Work

Visitors and experts

The use of factual accounts and personal histories through the introduction of people who can talk about their experiences of how things used to be can be very stimulating for children. To get the maximum educational benefit from using human sources of evidence in this way, visitors to the class need to be briefed and the children too need to be prepared. They should already know something about the topic and should have prepared questions to ask. Meanwhile the visitor should be notified beforehand about the areas of questions that the children are going to raise, so that he/she can give his/her answers some forethought and perhaps gather some concrete evidence such as artefacts or photographs with which to support his/her account.

Oral history

Miss J's Year 5 pupils were studying Britain since 1930. During an after school conversation with the caretaker she learnt that he had been born in an air raid shelter during a bombing raid. Miss J persuaded the caretaker to come and talk to the children about this and his early experiences as a child growing up during and after the Second World War. Prior to the visit she met with the caretaker after school to talk about what the children had been learning about and what things might be useful and interesting to bring into the discussion. The children were informed that the visit was going to take place and, working in small groups, they drafted a series of questions to ask in order to find out about the past. The questions included:

What did you wear?
What was school like?
What did you do after school?
What sort of things did you eat?

During the interview Miss J chaired the question-and-answer session making sure that all the groups were able to ask questions and that answers were as full as possible. At the end she made sure that the children thanked the caretaker for agreeing to talk to them and once the visit was over the children went back into their groups.

   The final task was to organize and communicate their historical learning and the methods chosen were differentiated by task. The majority of the children wrote a biography of the caretaker's early life using dictionaries and thesauruses where necessary. Some children who experienced difficulties with reading and writing were given support in the form of a writing frame as well as teacher support with spelling and a key words list.

Teachers as sources of information

John knows his mother and grandmother are friendly. He asks how they first met. The resultant adult hilarity and subsequent explanation lead him to a better understanding of his past.

One source of oral information for children engaged in evidence-based history activities is the teacher. It is essential to be able to present information and ideas on history to children in ways that gain their attention and focus upon the significant features of the past. The ability to explain and paint a verbal picture of the past plays an important part in motivating and enthusing pupils as well as providing them with basic historical information. Such direct teaching is also a feature of the conclusions to lessons in which it is important to gain a sense of what the children have learned. A precursor to and co-requisite of discussion is the need to think things through in your own mind and as such the discussion of historical evidence can be an important approach to learning. Pupil–teacher discussions involving some teacher exposition can be a useful way of introducing or reinforcing children's knowledge of historical language in areas such as time (century, decade), artefacts (galleon, chariot, baldric) and people (peasant, centurion). Factors to consider when introducing and concluding history lessons include the use of appropriate language, clarification of unfamiliar historical vocabulary and the sensitive use of questioning and discussion.

Handling discussions and asking questions in history

- Be clear about what you want the children to learn and plan for the questions and prompts that you will use to start the discussion:
  - recall questions, some of which may be 'closed' requiring one word answers and playing to the strengths of those with good memories.
  - reasoning questions are likely to be 'open-ended' in nature, offering children the chance to demonstrate understanding and thinking skills as well as creating opportunities for children to express a point of view or opinion and make use of historical evidence in doing this (Blyth, 1986).
  - speculative questions require the children to move beyond the evidence and start to employ their structural imagination (Dean, 1993; Little, 1989).
  - personal response questions draw on pupils' feelings and introduce the notion of empathy in history (Dean, 1993).
- Think of definitions, explanations, clarifications and exemplar material that you might need.
- Receive pupil contributions in a positive manner and be sensitive to the feedback from the children (including non-verbal feedback). Use this to gauge any possible mismatch between content and capabilities as well as the pace and timing of the discussion to avoid over-dwelling.
- Try to be inclusive of all children not just those sitting at the front and centre of your position.

Using Written Evidence

While first-hand oral accounts are useful in helping children to find out about the past they are limited in so far as they can only reach as far as living memory will permit. Documentary evidence therefore can be a useful starting point for historical interpretation and enquiry for times in the more distant past. While all stories may throw up issues that can have a personal relevance for some children, factual documentation and personal accounts may put this into particularly sharp relief and may need careful handling. Such accounts may raise subjects such as death, family breakdown, illness and disability, as well as different cultural values and attitudes. Any written account of an event will inevitably be a summary, the writer could not record everything, they may have forgotten or overlooked certain details, alternatively they may have made conscious decisions about what to include and what to leave out which can tell the reader something about the observer. A further problem with documentary evidence can lie in the text. The language may be archaic, the script difficult to decipher. Children grappling with the intricacies of writing as part of the National Curriculum may struggle therefore to make sense of Victorian copperplate handwriting or Elizabethan scripts in which letters are used differently. As a result it may be necessary for teachers to precis, translate or transcribe documentary evidence in order to make it accessible to children.

Sources of documentary evidence

- Personal records – letters, telegrams, diaries, wills, inventories, accounts, certificates, bank books, greetings cards, newspaper cuttings, medical reports.
- Non-fiction texts – teach children to skim and scan texts as well as using contents pages, indexes and glossaries (Blyth, 1986).
- Local records – parish registers, school logs, street names, place names, local maps and plans, census returns in local libraries.
- Literature – novels, biographies, plays, poems.
- Newspapers – local, national, international. Compare stories about the same event in different newspapers to examine similarities and differences in the accounts. Compare front pages on different newspapers; how would history differ depending upon which document you were working with? Use a story about an historical event to initiate a discussion/enquiry with children (Cockcroft, 1986).
- Transcripts of speeches and proclamations. A number of Internet websites contain modern transcripts of historical documents, for example the Peace of Wedmore, which established the Danelaw around 878 or the transcript of Chamberlain's 'Peace for our time' speech which followed his return from Munich in 1938.
- National records – parliamentary papers, Acts of Parliament, Royal Commission reports, maps, census data.

Using Timelines

Children's chronological sense may be imperfect but this does not necessarily mean that they cannot be introduced to simple ideas about sequencing (Blyth, 1986). While children's understanding of chronology will be affected by their stage of development, equally the way that activities are organized and presented, and the level at which they are pitched, can make it possible for even young children to begin to handle the abstract concept of time.

Variation in timelines

• Simple timelines involving vocabulary such as before, now, then and after.

• Sequence lines (often personal/family driven). These may require parental input and help and can be useful in introducing children to the idea of ordering.

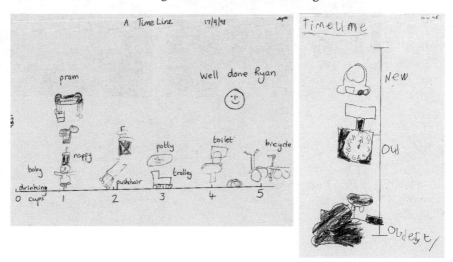

• Photograph timelines.

Great-great-great-grandma   Great-great-grandma   Great-grandma

Grandma   Mum

• Themed timelines, for example dress/fashion, transport, toys.

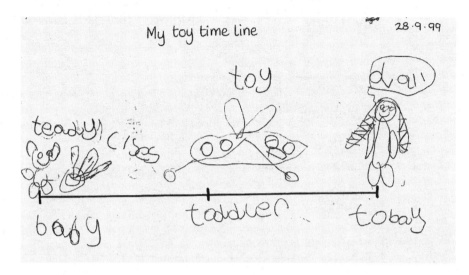

• Short timelines with lower juniors such as Henry VIII and his wives.

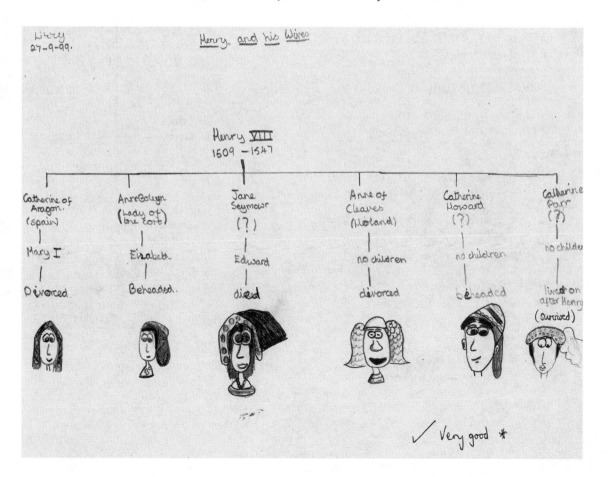

EFFECTIVE TEACHING AND LEARNING STRATEGIES

• Clocks and diaries, 'a day in the life of . . .'.

My Diary.   Name Sally Jackson

Monday 22.11.99	I went in the hall to watch a christmas play.
Tuesday 23.11.99	I did a Poem about a Clown
Wednesday 24.11.99	we went in the hall to do large apparatus. and I wrote in my
Thursday 25.11.99	We went In the diary hall to Pratis the Songs for the christmas Play
Friday 26.11.99	I am Finishing Off my model.

- Extended timelines, for example invaders and settlers from the Romans to the Normans.

3000 BC	2900 BC	2800 BC	2700 BC	2600 BC	2500 BC	2400 BC	2300 BC	2200 BC	2100 BC
Dynastic Period				Old Kingdom				1st Intermediate Period	

c.3000 BC
Egyptians invented hieroglyphic writing after seeing Mesopotamian writing.

c.2500 BC
Egypt did not fight wars with any big countries.

c.2600 BC
Egyptian kings organized the country well so there was lots to eat.

c.2200 BC
Climate change. Water levels in the Nile were low for many years. Many people starved and there was civil war.

2000 BC	1900 BC	1800 BC	1700 BC	1600 BC	1500 BC	1400 BC	1300 BC	1200 BC	1100 BC
Middle Kingdom			2nd Intermediate Period		New Kingdom				

c.1800 BC
The idea for the shaduf came from Mesopotamia. The shaduf lifted water from rivers to canals and from canals to fields.

c.1600 BC
The Hyksos kings from Palestine invaded lower Egypt and controlled it for just over a century.

c.1400 BC
Egypt fought other countries and often won. Gold, silver and slaves were brought back to Egypt.

c.1200 BC
Moses left Egypt with his relatives. They were descended from Joseph, who had been sold as a slave to Egypt years before.

c.1400 BC
The Pharaoh Ankhanaten decided that there was only one god, the Sun. He built a new city and new temples.

c.1100 BC
Egypt used up most of the gold from its gold mines.

c.1500 BC
The Egyptian Queen Hatshepsut sent boats to Ethiopia to explore. They brought back strange trees and animals.

c.1500 BC
Egypt conquered Nubia, south of it on the Nile. There were gold mines in Nubia.

c.1500 BC
Kings dug huge tombs in the Valley of the Kings. When they died they were buried there with many precious things.

c.1500 BC
Horses were brought into Egypt from Syria and Mesopotamia.

1000 BC	900 BC	800 BC	700 BC	600 BC	500 BC	400 BC	300 BC	200 BC	100 BC
3rd Intermediate Period			Late Period				Greek Period		

c.700 BC
The Assyrians from northern Mesopotamia conquered Egypt. They took much gold back to Assyria with them.

c.300 BC
The saqiyia was invented to lift water from rivers to canals and canals to fields.

c.300 BC
Alexander the Great, a Greek king, conquered Egypt. One of his generals became Pharaoh and started a new dynasty.

c.The birth of Christ
Rome conquered Cleopatra, the last of the pharaohs from the Greek dynasties. She killed herself.

Using New Technologies

Children are increasingly enthusiastic and proficient users of information technology (HMI, 1989) and increasing numbers of them have access to some form of ICT in the home. The use of ICT in the nursery/classroom offers considerable potential for enriching and enhancing the history curriculum as well as providing opportunities for interactive learning, the promotion of fine motor control, personal and social development and the development of reasoning skills. Using information and communications technology in a variety of ways and contexts will also aid children in becoming increasingly familiar, confident and positive about their skills as users. ICT can provide valuable tools for reinforcing first-hand and practical historical experiences, for example through the use of writing packages. Children's abilities at recalling, selecting and organizing historical information (QCA, 1999) as well as communicating their knowledge and understanding in a variety of ways (QCA, 1999) can all be enhanced and enriched through the inclusion of ICT. Similarly ICT can play a part in widening pupils' historical knowledge and understanding as well as offering yet another context within which to engage in historical enquiry.

Using ICT in history teaching

- Themed software

Some of these packages set out to provide information in support of specific periods within the history curriculum such as a Vikings CD-Rom. Others may introduce children to notions of temporal sequencing and ordering or encourage children to develop vocabulary related to time. Speaking and listening can be enhanced through the use of audio-equipped historical CD-Roms. Software also exists which enables young children to develop their appreciation and awareness of a wide range of different types of music and art from the past (HMI, 1991). The Parents' Information Network (PIN) reviews ICT packages and comments on their quality. Although designed to support parents who wish in turn to support their child's learning at home, the information provided can be equally valuable for teachers (www.learnfree.co.uk/pin/about.asp).

- Open-ended software

This software is not specifically related to any particular history topic but can be used to extend and enhance children's efforts to communicate and organize historical information. Examples would include the use of data collection and handling packages and the use of word-processing packages. Editing and redrafting benefit in particular (HMI, 1991) from the use of open-ended software. Using drawing or painting packages, for example, offers advantages for pupils in terms of the quality of the finish and the opportunity to adjust their art work in a way that does not require excessive use of materials or messy outcomes (HMI, 1991).

- The Internet

Numerous websites exist with historical content. Many are not suitable for direct use by children, although some schools have started to produce their own websites in which historical topics feature (www.wickham.newbury.sch.uk/topics/tudors/tudors.html). Those sites that are not appropriate for children as a result of the subject matter or the level at which the text is written can still offer teachers a considerable source of information with which to inform their teaching. Examples of websites are included in Chapter 5 on resources for history teaching.

Imaginative and Creative Approaches to History

Ultimately it could be said that all approaches to teaching and learning in history are evidence based. It is hard to envisage how children could engage effectively in creative and imaginative approaches to history without access to some evidence with which to inform their work. However, it is perhaps a mistake to see the relationship between evidence-based and imaginative approaches as hierarchical with nonpermeable boundaries between the two. The idea of introducing creative and imaginative approaches into the teaching of history fits well with our current understanding of how children learn. Bruner argued convincingly that there is a social dimension to cognitive development (Wood, 1998). A child's learning is influenced and affected by those experiences involving interaction with others, both children and adults, and this combined with current understandings of the importance of first-hand experience, offers support for collaborative play as a way of learning. At the same time, his arguments in favour of the importance of language and communication lend weight to the use of story in history. The impossibility of time travel means that understanding the past requires acts of imaginative reconstruction, albeit based on evidence, in order to make sense of the world. The use of creativity and imagination in history can take a number of forms and requires children to make use of their cognitive, emotional and communication abilities.

When trying to establish what imagination and creativity in history might involve it is useful to draw on the work of Little (1989), who outlines three aspects to the use of imagination in history. Structural imagination draws on children's cognitive abilities and involves 'filling in the gaps', creating generalizations in order to highlight the significance of events, to see things as a whole and thus to make greater sense of the past. Examples of historical generalizations could include terms such as the Industrial Revolution, the Reformation, the Great Depression or the Iron Age. Little offers as one example of filling in the gaps the fact that documents testify to the presence of Julius Caesar first in Italy and then subsequently in Spain. While there is no corresponding documentation relating to his journey from one location to the other, clearly the journey must have been made. Structural imagination however must be tempered by caution, particularly over the application of contemporary ideas onto the past. Our current parliamentary democracy, for example, is regarded as having its origins in ancient Greece, however the parallels between Britain in the twenty-first century and the Athenian democracy of Pericles with its limited franchise and use of slavery can easily be overstated. Ornamental imagination (Little, 1989) draws on children's communication skills as they seek to set the scene, flesh out historical characters, organize a narrative or create an image. The third aspect of imagination, empathy (Little, 1989), introduces the idea that feelings as well as thought can impel behaviour. Teachers need to remember that empathy is not the same as sympathy. The former involves understanding, while the latter is about agreement. Historians try to understand why someone in the past did something without necessarily agreeing with them or applauding them for doing it. The notion of empathy is open to criticism from those who regard the purpose of history to tell the true story of the past. It is certainly the case that caution needs to be exercised when putting oneself into someone else's shoes. It is never possible to truly understand in this way and the further back in time one journeys, the more difficult the task will be. That said there is no shortage of evidence of the power of emotions to motivate behaviour and learning (Hyson, 1994). Memory and learning can be enhanced in creative and imaginative approaches to history that heighten children's interest and enjoyment and can offer them opportunities to experiment with and try out feelings and behaviours in an attempt to make sense of them. Through story and play children can begin to reinforce their understanding of the actions and behaviour of past people. Although the ability of children to imagine and move beyond the evidence will inevitably be limited, as they do not possess the previous life experiences of adults with which to interpret the actions of past individuals, nevertheless there are still possibilities for imaginative and creative approaches in history.

Learning about the Past through Play

Tina Bruce (1997) sees play as central to young children's learning. It enables the integration of children's learning, making it deeper, broader and more relevant than might otherwise be the case. In history first-hand experience through play offers the chance to manipulate, explore, discover, practise and apply knowledge and ideas. Exploratory play of this sort can help children to gain a deeper understanding of history through first-hand experience of artefacts. Imaginative and creative interaction with artefacts can help them to improve their understanding of the purpose of an artefact and to begin to empathize with the original user(s). Other forms of play also offer children opportunities to increase their understanding and their ability to express thoughts and feelings. Although most children will play spontaneously, in an educational setting teachers will need to structure some play opportunities to make the most of the potential for historical learning. In some cases it will be necessary to provide a time for play and to establish a physical environment to promote play, including the provision of props such as historical artefacts and clothing. Teachers may also need to act as mediators, intervening sensitively to advance children's play by modelling, explaining and promoting cooperation and consideration. Teachers may also find it useful to engage in more active participation as a co-player, offering suggestions and information that will help to sustain the play. Finally, the teacher is charged with making an assessment of children's learning in history and therefore will have to act as assessor and communicator, using observations and data to make judgements about pupil development and learning and recording that information.

Although play is not as prominent in many primary settings as it is in the Foundation Stage, it is important to remember that older pupils too can gain an understanding of the past by

- acting out and taking on the persona of individuals from the past;
- trying to adopt a viewpoint from the past to understand why people took a particular course of action.

Types of role play in primary history	Examples
Hot-seating	A child researches (sometimes with assistance) a historical character and takes on the role of this individual. Other children can then ask questions, for example Florence Nightingale being asked about conditions at Scutari.
Reconstructing the past	Examples might include making and writing with quill pens, cooking and eating using old recipes or putting on a Punch and Judy show. (Some discussion about violence towards women would probably be appropriate for the last example!)
Non-costumed role play	Children act out historical scenes and events, for example, charging the walls at Conisborough Castle, imagining how hard it would be running down the moat and up the mound wearing heavy protective clothing, carrying shields and swords and being bombarded from above.
Role-cards	Children are given cards produced by the teacher which give information on a historical character, including details on name, age, status and circumstances. Children take on the role in a debate or role-play situation.
Costumed role play	Visiting the living history Victorian classroom and being taught in the Victorian style and having a Victorian school dinner of gruel. One school in Sheffield has a classroom fitted out in the Victorian manner. Schools can book to take classes there and experience first hand what it was like to be in a Victorian lesson. The children wear Victorian clothes and experience Victorian teaching methods.
Analogous role play	Creating an analogous situation in the class, then debriefing children on the parallels with history. For example different education for boys and girls. The debriefing is extremely important both as a way of reinforcing learning and as a way of dealing with feelings and emotions that may have been raised by the activity. Emotions can run very high particularly where a perceived injustice has been perpetrated.
ICT simulation	Some software packages offer children a simulated experience requiring them to engage with a past world on screen. These can be useful where direct experience may not be possible. Alternatively they can be used to supplement or reinforce such experience. Simulations of this sort can also provide starting points for further study and the use of evidence-based approaches. To the extent that simulations are a form of role play, their use may be instrumental in fostering empathy in the children for people and situations in the past. For example, trying to make a living grinding flour in a water mill only to have your livelihood swept away by flooding.
Predicting what happened next	The teacher tells part of a historical story and pupils produce what they consider to be the likely ending, either orally or in writing. The teacher then completes the story and initiates a discussion about the similarities and differences between the actual outcome and the children's predictions.

Planning drama and role-play scenarios with historical themes offers older children opportunities to extend their ability to empathize with people in the past and they can be used both in school and on site visits. These imaginative and creative approaches in history have to be based on evidence and not on uncontrolled flights of fancy. Provided this is done, such activities can underpin historical enquiry and interpretation as children are offered an exciting and stimulating context within which to draw upon and apply their previous learning based on the evidence of literature, visits, artefacts, ICT and interactions with the teacher. They can also be used to promote empathizing with past characters and as a way of communicating historical understanding to others. Preparation matters and teachers ought to have a clear focus for role play activities in history. In addition, it is important to give some thought to where the children will locate the information (evidence) with which to inform their role play. Watching historical reconstructions can offer children useful pointers by helping them to picture the past and build mental images that will aid their understanding and help retention of learning. Finally, role play works best with those pupils who are used to working in this way. Consequently if such an approach represents a departure from normal practice it is best not to make unrealistic demands of the children.

- What skills, previous experiences or games would help them to work in this way?
- What resources, such as costumes or props, will the children need to make the most of the opportunity for play?

Fictional Accounts Set in Actual Events

One approach to fictional accounts and actual events involves imaginative writing, which has the potential to enable children to make personal sense of the past and may reinforce retention and learning. It can, however, be a highly demanding task for children to put themselves into a previous time in a meaningful way, particularly where those children are at the early stages of mastering written English. Success in this approach is heavily dependent upon access to sufficient information if the process is not to stall or degenerate into sheer fantasy and stereotyping.

The use of story offers an alternative to creative writing and is a common occurrence in 3–11 settings. Stories can be extremely powerful vehicles for examining different periods and cultures and are a useful tool in developing pupils' under-standing of the past. They constitute a powerful way of making history accessible to children, as they provide a means of helping pupils to

- identify similarities and differences between now and then;
- acquire some early 'time markers';
- examine historical evidence;

- communicate historical understanding (e.g. re-enacting historical stories as part of a socio-dramatic play) (Edwards and Knight, 1994);
- understand concepts such as continuity and change;
- draw parallels with their own experiences (e.g. stories about children in the past).

Even the youngest children can find their understanding and awareness of the past, their vocabulary related to time and their historical skills (such as enquiry skills or identifying similarities and differences) being enhanced through the use of story. They offer a familiar medium through which to encounter unfamiliar worlds by introducing children to situations and events beyond their own experiences and transmitting basic information about the past. Historical fiction of this sort can provide children with information on a wide variety of topics including dress, transport, food, the built environment, the natural environment and society. It can also introduce higher order concepts, such as change and continuity over time and the simultaneous nature of events (Little, 1989), as well as offering opportunities to discuss the distinction between fact and fiction. Stories can provide teachers with opportunities to help children challenge stereotypical attitudes and assumptions and to respect and under-stand the similarities and differences that exist between people. Teachers, therefore, need to give careful consideration to the stories that they employ to ensure that they support a positive approach to diversity rather than undermining it. When using story as a starting point for historical activity or as a way of developing and extending a particular theme teachers need to try and provide a balance of material including fiction set within historical contexts (e.g. *Goodnight Mister Tom*, *The Silver Sword*), myths and legends (e.g. Greek, Egyptian), stories that the children have created themselves, factual stories and personal accounts (see evidence-based approaches above).

Reflective Questions

- Do you ensure that first-hand experience and evidence-based approaches play a significant role in your history teaching?
- How do you ensure that pupils and adults are properly prepared prior to a site visit?
- Are there audio-visual images in your resources for history that perpetuate stereotypical and offensive attitudes and beliefs?
- How could you use photographs e.g. those on pages 81 and 86 to teach children about the past?
- How do you make written evidence accessible to your pupils?
- To what extent is the use of ICT integrated into teaching and learning in history in your class?
- Do you make use of appropriate imaginative teaching methods in history including play and story?

REFERENCES

BBC School Programmes (1999) *Landmarks: Britain Since 1930*, London: BBC Worldwide (Educational Publishing).

Blyth, J. (1986) *Place and Time with Children Five to Nine*, London: Croom Helm.

Bruce, T. (1997) *Early Childhood Education*, 2nd edition, London: Hodder and Stoughton.

Carder, J. (1986) *The Sheffield Botanical Gardens*, Sheffield: Sheffield Council.

Cockcroft, J. (1986) *In my Time*, London: Collins Educational.

David, T. (Ed.) (1999) *Young Children Learning*, London: Paul Chapman Publishing Ltd.

Dean, J. (1993) *Organising Learning in the Primary School*, 3rd edition, London: Croom Helm.

Department for Education and Employment (DfEE) (1997) 'Starting with Quality'. The 1990 Report of the Committee of Enquiry into the Quality of the Educational Experience offered to 3- to 4-year-olds, chaired by Mrs Angela Rumbold CBE MP', London: HMSO.

Donaldson, M. (1978) *Children's Minds*, London: Fontana Press.

Edwards, A. and Knight, P. (1994) *Effective Early Years Education: Teaching Young Children*, Buckingham: Open University Press.

Grabsky, P. (1997) *I, Caesar: Ruling the Roman Empire*, London: BBC Books.

Her Majesty's Inspectors (HMI) (1989) *Information Technology from 5–16: Curriculum Matters 15*, London: DES/HMSO.

Her Majesty's Inspectors (HMI) (1991) *Aspects of Primary Education: The Teaching and Learning of Information Technology*, London: DES/HMSO.

Historical Association (1994) *Occasional Paper 7: School Museums and Primary History*, London: Historical Association.

Hyson, M. C. (1994) *The Emotional Development of Young Children: Building an Emotion Centered Curriculum*, New York: Teachers College Press.

Kimber, D., Clough, N., Forrest, M., Harnett, P., Menter, I. and Newman, E. (1995) *Humanities in Primary Education*, London: David Fulton Publishers.

Little, V., 'Imagination and history' in J. Campbell and V. Little (1989) *Humanities in the Primary School*, London: The Falmer Press.

Magorian, M. (1981) *Goodnight Mister Tom*, London: Puffin Books.

Morris, S. (1989) *Using Portraits in History*, London: English Heritage.

Qualifications and Curriculum Authority (QCA) (1998) *A Scheme of Work for Key Stages 1 and 2*, London: QCA.

Qualifications and Curriculum Authority (QCA) (1999) *The National Curriculum: Handbook for Primary Teachers in England*, London: DfEE/QCA.

Serrallier, I. (1956) *The Silver Sword*, London: Puffin Books.

Wood, D. (1998) *How Children Think and Learn*, 2nd edition, Oxford: Blackwell.

The Learning Environment and Resources for History

The learning environment can have a significant impact upon teaching and learning in history. An environment that stimulates the children, is accessible to them and contains high-quality resources is likely to support and encourage learning. For the purposes of this chapter the term 'learning environment' will include the physical surroundings both inside and outside the nursery or school. Some information on resources for teaching history has already been given in the previous chapter, the further consideration of the resources available here will also include attention to the most important resource of all, the human resource.

This chapter will consider ways of creating a learning environment that will support pupils' learning in history and make the best possible use of the human resources available. It will begin with the physical environment and the need to ensure that children's health and safety is addressed in line with the Health and Safety at Work Act 1974 as well as teachers' common law duty of care to act *in loco parentis*. The chapter goes on to examine how the learning environment can be used to foster pupil interest in history through a variety of means. This section considers the provision of varied resources and the need to stimulate and interest children in the past and the passage of time through exciting and attractive use of display. The section also addresses the use of ICT, worksheets and adults in supporting pupils' learning in the subject. Finally the chapter examines the use of environments and resources beyond the classroom to foster children's historical learning, including organized visits and parental involvement in teaching children about the past.

Organizing a Safe Learning Environment

There is a duty on teachers to establish a safe learning environment in which children can feel secure and confident and in which they can operate safely. A key consideration in history is the presence of artefacts in the classroom. Teachers are expected to be familiar with the likely actions of their pupils in a given situation and are expected to be able to exercise a degree of foresight. Failure to prevent injury or harm to a child in the classroom when the dangers could be reasonably foreseen constitutes negligence. A major problem for teachers trying to exercise this foresight is that no environment, and certainly no 3–11 setting, can be made entirely risk free. It is inevitable that children will fall over, trap their fingers or mishandle objects from time to time. Risk avoidance, risk awareness and, ultimately, risk management are important skills for children to acquire given that they cannot be supervised 24 hours a day. However, children's abilities in these areas develop over a long period and teachers therefore need to make every effort to ensure their children's safety and not behave in a thoughtless fashion, exposing pupils to unnecessary hazards. Foresight therefore requires an understanding of the children themselves. Teachers need to make judgements about the extent to which their pupils

- are mature enough and dexterous enough to handle certain historical artefacts;
- can be expected to take responsibility for themselves and their actions;
- can understand and observe nursery/school rules and conventions (e.g. no running).

These assessments form an important part of the decision-making process when establishing a safe learning environment. Once these issues have been thought through a teacher can then employ his or her common sense to reduce risks to acceptable levels when deciding on what artefacts to introduce into the nursery or classroom and by thinking carefully about the organization of space and resources. Storage areas containing history resources ought to be properly labelled using words and pictures and children should be encouraged to refer to the labels and take some responsibility for organizing their own learning when selecting and handling some of these resources. When resources are stored effectively pupils can be encouraged to make choices, to select appropriate equipment and materials, to take responsibility for keeping the classroom tidy and to develop their own resource management skills.

Some history activities, for example those requiring children to examine artefacts, seek out information or re-enact historical events, may be quite noisy and dynamic, while others, such as recreation activities, are potentially messy. As a result, it may be necessary to plan and establish a mixture of clearly defined areas and general purpose spaces in the nursery or classroom, with sufficient and varied space for a range of activities. Furniture is often used to mark out and define areas, such as quiet areas and ICT areas, in which children may seek out historical information or complete history tasks, and it is important to make sure that these arrangements do not hinder your ability to observe and monitor children's learning.

In addition to a teacher's common law duty to care for his/her pupils, he/she is also bound by the provisions of the Health and Safety at Work Act 1974. Under the provisions of this Act all employees, including teachers, must not meddle or interfere with anything provided for the purpose of ensuring people's health and safety. They must also have a care for their own safety at work and the safety of others that might be affected either by their actions or their failure to act. Teachers are required to cooperate with other members of staff who have duties under the Act such as the school's/nursery's health and safety representative or the first aid specialist. Schools and nurseries have health and safety policies (often based on LEA policies) and staff are expected to be familiar with the contents of these policies. Children need to be helped to understand the importance of safety and where necessary the usage of some resources should be restricted to adults only.

Ensuring the health and safety of pupils in history

- The learning environment in the classroom must be properly cleaned in the interests of health and hygiene where children have been working with foodstuffs (e.g. making and tasting food from the past).
- Activities involving potentially hazardous tools need very careful supervision and in some cases will necessitate adult intervention (e.g. designing and making Victorian picture frames or cutting the nibs on quill pens using a craft knife).
- Preliminary visits are valuable as a way of trying to anticipate potential hazards when working outside the classroom (e.g. visiting a historical site).

Organizing an Interesting Environment

Resources

Artefacts and reference materials

Some history resources will be assigned to individual classes or teachers, some will be available to teams of staff (for example the nursery team, the Year 2 classes or Key Stage 2), others may be held centrally for use by the whole school. In the case of shared resources and loans, advance action may well be needed in order to ensure access to them at the right moment, for example booking library and museum loans, liaison with colleagues and contacting parents. Within classrooms, many teachers operate a mixed economy with their resources, some of which will be teacher controlled while others are on open-access, as they seek to include a wide range of interesting objects, materials and equipment to create a stimulating environment. Determining the issue of access ought to be shaped by your commitment to children's health and safety and an awareness of the constraints of the classroom. Consequently, arranging and organizing classroom resources for history used on a daily basis means thinking carefully about ease of access and rules.

- Select and use a range of up-to-date, appropriate resources that support active, investigative learning.
- Check that resources are clearly labelled and easily accessible so that the children know where to find them and where to return them. Organize resources for history in such a way that children are encouraged to take responsibility for obtaining them, using them appropriately and looking after them.
- Identify resources that may need to be booked or borrowed in medium-term planning
- Ensure that there are sufficient resources for the task in hand.
- Check that resources are well maintained – dog-eared photographs, crackly videos and tatty reference books are not motivating.
- Ensure that children know how the school/class library system works.

Examples of useful resources for history

- For Key Stage 1, the 'Watch/Magic Grandad' materials produced by the BBC include video and photographic resources on a range of topics to support history teaching with infants, such as holidays, famous individuals from the past and life within living memory. The BBC also produce the 'Zig Zag' and 'Landmarks' materials for lower and upper junior pupils, covering the National Curriculum Key Stage 2 study units. Many of the materials are televised and CD-Rom resources, including useful databases, can also be obtained to provide historical evidence for inquiries.
- Non-fiction publications form an important resource and can be obtained in many bookshops or through specialist educational publishers. Examples include the Longman 'A Sense of History' series, or Scholastic's 'Horrible Histories' series written by T. Deary.
- Fiction can offer a useful insight into chronology or past times (see Chapter 4). Examples of use with younger pupils could include Ahlberg, J. and Ahlberg, A., *Starting School* or *Peepo* by the same authors or Amery, H. and Cartwright, S., *The Old Steam Train*. At Key Stage 2 examples could include Magorian, M., *Goodnight Mister Tom*, or Serrallier, I., *The Silver Sword*.
- Museums – Virtual Teachers' Centre – www.timeplan.com/vtc/muse.htm
- Sources of primary documents – http://library.byu.edu/-rdh/eurodocs/uk.html
- Other useful websites
  The Romans – www.bbc.co.uk/education/romans/index.html
  The Tudors – http://home.hiwaay.net/~crispen/tudor/index.html
  Victorian industrialists and social reformers – www.spartacus.schoolnet.co.uk
  Britain since 1930 and the National Health Service –
      www.nhs50.nhs.uk/nhsstory-before.htm
  British history – www.britannia.com/history/
  A walk through time – www.bbc.co.uk/education/history/walk
  Horus Web Links to History Resources – www.ucr.edu/h-gig/horuslinks.html
  History's Happening – www.saber.net/~paloeser/
  BBC history site – www.bbc.co.uk/history

  Key Stage 1 and 2 schemes of work – www.stndards.dfee.gov.uk/schemes
                      www.qca.org.uk
                      www.nc.uk.net

Worksheets

A well-designed worksheet can be a useful resource to support teaching and learning in history. However, poorly thought-out sheets and over-reliance on commercial worksheets, often as a means of keeping children occupied and where little thought is given to what might be learnt through their completion is unlikely to lead to high standards of attainment amongst children in history. Worksheets are no substitute for quality interactions between pupil and teacher. A worksheet cannot rephrase or explain things further to children, nor can it offer praise and recognition for effort and outcome. Where the majority of history lessons involve the children in completing worksheets, no matter how well designed and produced, there is a very high likelihood of frustration and boredom setting in for some children. Worksheets can also suffer from the problem of readability, picture clues can only go so far towards overcoming this problem and the need to match tasks to ability can result in multiple versions of a basic sheet.

Worksheets produced by class teachers can be a useful tool for teaching and learning as well as for assessment purposes, however for teachers to get the most out of them, they need to do two things. First, teachers need to make sure that the layout and presentation are of a sufficiently high quality to encourage similar pride in the children's work. Using ICT to produce worksheets means that they can be of high quality, include scanned photographs or documents if appropriate and, thus, be attractive and motivating for children to use. Second, teachers need to make them part of their teaching strategy and not a replacement for it. Worksheets can be used to start and promote talk and discussion amongst pupils. They can also be employed to help foster children's enquiry skills, such as study skills. They can even be used to support practical activities, requiring pupils to follow instructions or acting as an *aide-mémoire* for children. When children are involved in a site visit, for example, it is important that they are encouraged to observe closely, use their senses and talk about what they can see. However, there are times when worksheets are useful both as a way of stimulating enquiry and providing a structure for recording. The principles underlying devising effective worksheets are similar whether they are to be used in or out of the classroom. They should

- be well laid out and clear;
- be motivating to use, perhaps with some graphics included;
- be easy to understand, with straightforward vocabulary;
- not be overloaded with text;
- have a clear purpose;
- be open ended or graded to provide for differentiation;
- provide for independent and collaborative working;
- ask questions such as *how?, why?* and *which?* that promote higher order thinking as well as questions which require a factual response.

In addition, worksheets for use during site visits should:

• include questions which involve thinking rather than simply doing;
• require different types of response, such as drawing, deciding or estimating;
• not contain too many directions;
• encourage children to use their different senses where appropriate and safe.

The worksheet example below was used to evaluate pupil progress and encourage Key Stage 2 children to engage in self-assessment.

TOPIC EVALUATION   Name: Lizzy Brown

What did you know about Tudors before you started?

I knew that Henry VIII had six wives.

Give 10 facts that you know now.

Elizabeth was the last Tudor monarch.

The Tudors began when Henry VII won the war of the Roses. Mary I, Elizabeth I and Edward VI were children of Henry VIII. Henry VII was the 1st Tudor monarch.

Henry VIII liked hunting and writing poetry.

The Spanish Armada occured in Elizabeth I rule.

Mary I, called Bloody Mary. Elizabeth caught small pox.

Mary I killed lots of people.

Edward VI was only on the throne for 6 years.

What (or who) was your favourite part of the Tudor Topic?

My favourite Tudor King or Queen was Elizabeth I and the Spanish Armada work.

Are you pleased with your work? Why/Why not?

I am pleased with my work because I enjoyed it, I think if you enjoy your work you do it better

Signed Lizzy

Teachers Comment:

Definitly - some super work Lizzy.

J. Exell

THE LEARNING ENVIRONMENT

ICT

Information and communications technology (computers, calculators, video, tape recorders, etc.) has had a profound effect upon all our lives and its growth in recent years has been exponential. The presence of computers in nurseries and schools has increased considerably since the 1980s. Many bases and classrooms have more than one machine and some primary schools even have dedicated ICT suites. Consequently the access for teachers and children to the technology has also improved. The Education Reform Act 1988 requires that by law all pupils are entitled to access to these important and influential tools (NCC, 1990a). There is no shortage of ICT history software available to teachers particularly at Key Stages 1 and 2. Teachers ought to make effective use of ICT in history through the introduction both of history-specific software (e.g. CD-Rom Vikings database, historical simulations) and of open-ended packages that will allow pupils to communicate and handle historical information, including the use of ICT in the aesthetic areas of drawing, designing and composing (see Chapter 4). In recent years, the burgeoning of the Internet has provided teachers with a considerable source of information to support their history teaching, even though the majority of the sites are likely to be inappropriate for use by the children themselves.

Using ICT can enrich and extend learning in the history curriculum while simultaneously helping children to acquire confidence and pleasure using the technology. ICT can also be a particularly valuable resource when teaching history to pupils with special educational needs (see Chapter 8). ICT offers children a means of communicating historical information and ideas, as well as capturing, storing, gaining access to, changing and interpreting historical information. Older children should be encouraged to engage critically with the technology, judging both the content and the presentation of historical information. ICT resources, particularly the Internet, can carry an authority that is not always deserved and older pupils need to be encouraged not to accept things as being beyond debate just because they appear on screen.

Having a resource is one thing, using it effectively is another matter. Whatever use is being made of ICT, teachers should make time to play with and explore the technology prior to using it with children. When seeking to make effective use of ICT resources in history, it is necessary to consider the need for planning, effective management of the equipment and developing the necessary teaching skills. The steady improvement in the availability of ICT resources in 3–11 settings since the 1980s has meant that all teachers and children now have the opportunity to use computers at regular intervals. This, in turn, means that the children's experiences of history through ICT can be properly planned for; crucial, if continuity and progression are to be assured. The medium-term planning sheets below are an example of how planning for ICT has formed part of the planning process generally.

Unit of work: **'Toys and games'**   NC subject: **ICT**   Year group: **Year 2**

Continuing ☐   Blocked ☐   Linked ☑   Linked subjects – Design technology and History

2d	Trying things out and exploring what happens in imaginary situations	Exploring ICT simulations and adventure games.	Albert's house Granny's garden
3a	Using ICT to present information in a variety of forms	Using the computer to sketch designs for toys. Recording toy experiences using the word processor.	Splosh Writer
5c	Talking about the uses of ICT outside the school	Discussing ICT games and simulations that they have played at home and elsewhere.	

Unit of work: **'Toys and games'**   NC subject: **Design technology**   Year group: **Year 2**

Continuing ☐   Blocked ☐   Linked ☑   Linked subjects – ICT and History

PoS	Learning objectives	Activities	Organization/resources
1a	Generating ideas, drawing on their own and other people's experiences	Designing and making a soft toy for a younger child.	Collection of early learning toys, dolls and teddy bears
2d	Assembling, joining and combining materials and components		Fabric/textile resources Less resistant materials e.g. paper, card
5a	Investigating and evaluating familiar products	Comparing old and new toys. Discussing quality of finish, materials used, design, and construction.	Collection of toys from parents/relatives

Unit of work: **'Toys and games'**   NC subject: **History**   Year group: **Year 2**

Continuing ☐   Blocked ☐   Linked ☑   Linked subjects – ICT and Design technology

PoS	Learning objectives	Activities	Organization/resources
1b	Placing objects in chronological order	Sequencing series of toys (e.g. old and new; new, old, oldest). Simple timelines.	Collection of toys from parents/relatives Contemporary toys
2b	Identify differences between ways of life at different times	Comparing old and new toys. Discussing similarities and differences. Old and new grids (i.e. 'Toys in the past . . .' 'Toys today . . .'	
6a	Changes in their own lives and the way of life of others around them	Interviewing older relation about toys and games in the past. Learning and playing old playground games. Recording rules and instructions.	Tape recorder Balls, ropes Writer, tape recorder

In addition to planning for ICT to be a feature of teaching and learning in history, it is also important to ensure that history software, accompanying documentation and equipment are kept in an efficient and organized manner. In most foundation and primary settings at present, children encounter ICT within their normal classrooms rather than in specialized ICT areas and the comments that follow are therefore aimed at managing ICT resources in these contexts.

- Establishing a permanent place in the classroom for the computer helps to reduce disruption.

- When using history software as part of teaching and learning, prepare a list of any additional information that children might need in order to use the software effectively. This might include preparing 'cheat sheets' (see below). Give some thought too to any skills or previous knowledge that the children might require in order to use the software. Have support equipment or materials ready, for example note-taking materials, and make sure they are easily accessible to the children.

An example of a cheat sheet for scanning pictures of Henry VIII's six wives

1. Put the picture into the scanner facing downwards.
2. Open **Adobe photodeluxe**.
3. Go to **File** – open **special** – **scan photo**.
4. When the scan window opens click **Preview**.
5. When the picture has been previewed pick the place that you want to scan by moving the selection frame around.
6. Click to scan on whatever kind of picture it is, e.g. photo, text or print matter.
7. Save in **My Photos** and give it a name that you will remember.
8. Make sure **My Photos** window is open. If not go to **File** – **Photos** – **Show my photos**. Click on **Acquire**.
9. Find the picture you have just scanned and double click on it.
10. To take it to Clarisworks click it to select it. Go to **Edit** – **Copy**. Go to **Finder**, open the Clarisworks file, make sure tools are selected, choose arrow tool and then paste.

- Give some thought to how you are going to introduce the software to the children. One option is for teachers to teach the pupil(s) at a point of need. Although of high relevance for the child and offering instant feedback, this can be problematic when there are 30 other children and non-teaching support is unavailable. Introducing the software to the whole group and allowing pupils to rotate around the activity during the day/week(s) is a second option. However, it can be hard for 30 children to observe such an introduction clearly where only one machine is available. Furthermore, unless the children are able to use the technology fairly quickly they are unlikely to remember much of the introduction and such an approach almost certainly would not work well with younger pupils. Finally, teachers have the option to use pupils as experts who can cascade the skills and knowledge to the rest of their peers. This is certainly attractive as an efficient approach, however it does require careful monitoring of the group dynamics to ensure that the children being 'taught' by their peers are actually gaining access to the technology and learning.

- Use a range of open-ended and thematic software to promote the development of a wide range of ICT skills and allow time for children to master these skills. Commercially produced thematic software can be useful in introducing children to the keyboard and the mouse in a structured and systematic fashion. At the same time, keyboard skills will also develop as a consequence of using the computer in a variety of purposeful contexts, for example word-processing historical stories. Providing regular and frequent turns at working on the computer will be much more effective at increasing computer skills and confidence than infrequent but longer turns.

- Make use of concept keyboards to replace or supplement the computer keyboard when working with younger pupils or pupils with special educational needs. Some software allows teachers to develop their own overlays on historical themes. Below is a teacher-designed history overlay using Touch Explorer Plus. The first overlay has pictures of the different queens. Levels 1 and 2 show what information the children get on the screen when they press a picture and move between levels.

Overlay sheet for the concept keyboard

Catherine of Aragon	Anne Boleyn	Jane Seymour
Anne of Cleves	Catherine Howard	Catherine Parr

Catherine of Aragon was the widow of Henry VIII's brother. She was Henry's first wife.

Anne Boleyn was a former maid of honour of Catherine of Aragon. She was Henry's second wife.

Jane Seymour was one of Anne Boleyn's ladies in waiting. She was Henry's third wife.

Anne of Cleves had never met Henry. The marriage was arranged. She was Henry's fourth wife.

Catherine Howard was a relative of one of Henry's dukes and was nearly 30 years younger than Henry. She was Henry's fifth wife.

Catherine Parr was a widow and Henry saw her as an ideal stepmother for his children. She was Henry's sixth wife.

Text level 2

Catherine of Aragon was popular and loyal to Henry, but her only surviving child was Mary, and Henry wanted a son. After eighteen years of marriage Henry divorced Catherine.

Anne Boleyn also gave birth to a daughter, Elizabeth, but Anne too did not give Henry a son. He accused Anne of being unfaithful to him and after a trial she was beheaded.

Jane Seymour married Henry eleven days after Anne Boleyn was executed. She gave birth to a son, who was also called Henry but she died soon after.

Anne of Cleves and Henry had not met before they were married and when they did meet Henry did not like her. He said she looked like a horse. Henry divorced Anne after only six months.

Catherine Howard was accused of being unfaithful to Henry. She was tried for treason and beheaded.

Catherine Parr enjoyed family life and brought the three royal children to live together at court. Luckily for Catherine Henry died before she did.

108

Planning to include ICT and managing the resources effectively are only part of the answer to making the best use of this resource in history. The teacher also has to monitor and control the process to foster positive ICT experiences for all the children in the nursery or classroom. It is easy to be seduced on occasion by the quality of the resource and the obvious enthusiasm of some pupils but the need to monitor and ensure quality in teaching and learning, not least in terms of equality of opportunity, is very important. Grouping the children is an important first step, as too many children round a computer will lead to redundancy and possible exclusion. Making sure that all the children involved have a clear role or task to perform, whether it is operating the keyboard or mouse, reading the screen or recording information, helps to promote inclusion. There may be occasions where putting girls in single sex groups is an effective way of helping them to gain computer experience and reduces the likelihood of their being excluded or marginalized. Similarly, children of similar ability or children with similar personalities and dispositions tend to generate lively and rewarding discussion in which the pace tends to be agreed and exclusion is less likely. Mixed-ability groups can be useful particularly where there is a lot of reading to be done, however there may be a tendency for the better reader(s) to take over. In the same way, a child with more previous ICT experience can be a great asset to a group but once again there is the danger that this child could come to monopolize the activity. The group dynamics therefore need to be considered and teachers must be ready to step in and intervene if necessary. Careful thought in grouping and offering access does not guarantee equal participation. As a result, be prepared to alter your groupings in the light of experience and step in to encourage children who appear reluctant or intimidated by the resource. Some children appear to let others tell them what to do, while some always opt to read the screen or record information even when the group has been told to share the tasks. By observing children soon after they have started, there is still time to intervene at an early stage if you become aware of unrest in the group or to stop unacceptable behaviour leading to the exclusion of certain children. Watch out for children who

- dominate the activity by making unilateral decisions;
- monopolize the keyboard/mouse;
- operate the keyboard/mouse too quickly for others to keep up;
- tell other children what to do in a bossy manner leading to squabbles and bickering;
- are being excluded by other children who ignore their ideas and contributions irrespective of whether they prove to be right or wrong;
- do not appear to understand the nature of the task.

Display

Display in history might involve history resources, children's history work or a mixture of the two. The use of display helps to create an attractive learning environment and as such can play a valuable role in motivating children, setting standards and communicating information to parents and other visitors about the children's experiences and work. A good display of historical artefacts is one example of an evidence-based approach to learning and can start children talking, thinking, asking questions and working. A well-presented display of pupils' work in history offers a means of praising, recognizing and encouraging children by demonstrating the value that you place on their efforts in this area, while simultaneously offering opportunities for children to engage in the communication and organization of historical information. At the same time using displays in teaching and learning can offer a further source of historical information for the children. Children's involvement in some of the decision-making about what and how to display history resources and the results of their history work can help to ensure that a display is used and referred to.

When displaying children's work in history it is useful to think about whose work is displayed, how and why. Displays should be professionally presented; sloppy displays make good work look poor and fail to do justice to the efforts of the children. However, there is a difference between high standards of presentation and forgery.

A display on the Aztecs

Aztec masks

Drape with Aztec pattern/motif

The Aztecs

Three-dimensional Aztec objects including cardboard model of Aztec temple, feathers, beads, coffee beans and jewellery

Pupils' work on different aspects of Aztec life including religion, trade, rituals, traditions, housing, food and warfare.

If one of the aims of display is to motivate pupils, then it ought to be the children's work, not the teacher's, that is displayed. The inclusion of *effort* alongside *outcome* as criteria for judging which pieces of work are put on show is essential. If effort is not used as a criterion for selection, then some children may be consistently overlooked while others may receive disproportionate recognition. History displays should also reflect the variety and breadth of the history curriculum, showing practical activities as well as written work, and showing the development of skills as well as the acquisition of knowledge. Utilizing a range of techniques that include 2-D as well as 3-D and hands-on interactive displays as well as static ones can provide new and exciting stimulus for children. Finally, history displays ought to be changed over on a regular basis if they are to fufil their potential for inspiring and motivating pupils. There can be few things less likely to persuade children of the excitement and interest to be found in history, than the sight of a tired, old, dog-eared display on the Tudors as a reminder of lessons long since gone. There is no doubt that assembling and maintaining attractive and worthwhile displays takes a considerable amount of time and effort. Some teachers seem to possess a natural flair for it, whereas it takes others some time to develop the requisite skills. Many schools have guidelines about display, for example about mounting and colours for backing paper. The Reflective Questions at the end of the chapter include a section on some of the other considerations that may need to be taken into account when displaying pupils' history activities and experiences.

Adults as a teaching resource

Teachers and other responsible adults are the most valuable resource available for teaching and learning in any area of the curriculum. High adult:child ratios help to make the most effective use of materials and equipment. Most teachers are involved in working with other adults in the classroom. These may include special needs teachers, language support teachers, students and ancillaries as well as parent helpers and other volunteers. Indeed, it would be unusual to find a school that did not encourage the involvement of parents and other adult helpers in the classroom. They help to foster a sense of security and are important in reinforcing pupils' learning. Adults are also very important as role models for children and one of the behaviours they can model in history is interest and enthusiasm. Apart from providing more support for children, other adults may have particular skills and knowledge of use in history teaching. Organizing and managing possibly older and more experienced adults can be a daunting task for beginning teachers. This is particularly true for those working in the Foundation Stage where the tradition of team work in a teaching situation is much more well developed than in many primary settings. Nursery nurses often have very similar roles and responsibilities to those of qualified teachers yet do not attract the same level of pay or status. It is important that the role of each staff member is made clear in order to establish good working relationships. In the case of voluntary helpers, most schools have policies to follow which will cover issues such as volunteers' suitability for work with children and the need to maintain confidentiality.

There are a number of steps teachers can take in order to make the most of adult support in the nursery/classroom

- make the classroom a welcoming place;
- find out about the role of support staff and procedures for briefing them;
- discover the interests and abilities of potential helpers;
- find out if they can help on a regular basis – this will provide more continuity for the children and perhaps more satisfaction for the helper;
- avoid assigning helpers on a stereotypical basis (women help with cooking samosas while men assist children in using the computer or work on the woodwork bench);
- involve non-teaching colleagues in planning activities – they need to be clear about what you want the children to learn and how you want them to go about this;
- make sure that roles and responsibilities (e.g. discipline) are clear – to the children as well as to the adults involved.

Using the Wider Environment in History

An important resource and additional learning environment is the space outside the nursery/classroom. Many teachers make extensive use of outdoor areas and the local environment when the weather permits as trips and visits can be a wonderful stimulus for teaching and learning in history. Educationally, outside visits offer real opportunities to link nursery and school experiences with the wider world, enabling children to become more aware of change, similarities and differences and the diversity of people, places and objects. The world outside the nursery/school provides a rich source of evidence through which to introduce children to the idea of chronology and change over time. Starting points for using the local environment to support teaching and learning in history and developing an awareness of change over time could include

- looking at changes in the built environment such as new housing;
- looking at buildings that have altered their usage, for example churches into businesses, banks into restaurants;
- examining old structures such as bridges, canals, monuments, statues, clocks;
- comparing and contrasting old and new street furniture, such as signs, post boxes, phone boxes and lighting;
- visiting religious sites such as churches and graveyards to find out about some of the people who used to live in the area;
- looking at street names that suggest changes have taken place in the local environment such as Coal Pit Lane, Dog Kennels Hill, Infirmary Road, Packhorse Lane, Leadmill Street;
- looking at street names that celebrate past people(s) such as Tudor Way, Churchill Road,

Disraeli Grove, Drake Terrace, Elizabeth Avenue, Kier Hardie Way, Queen Victoria Road, Wilberforce Road;
• looking at street names that commemorate past events such as Mafeking Place, Trafalgar Road.

Using the local environment as a teaching resource

A class of Y2 pupils was taken on a walk around the locality of the school as part of a topic on houses and homes. The curriculum focus of the topic was history and technology. The area contained a wide variety of housing ranging from Victorian/Edwardian terraces to modern flats and semi-detached properties.

Staff were keen to use the visit as a way of encouraging the children to look for similarities and differences and to consider how the properties in the area had been changed and altered over time. Prior to the visit the children's teacher initiated a class discussion on changing houses by introducing samples of wallpaper and DIY catalogues and explained to the pupils that she was having some renovations done to her own house. She asked the children to talk about their own experiences of decoration or changes in their own homes. She then discussed with the children the sorts of things they could look for. She also discussed the visit with the two parent helpers and the Classroom Assistant who would be accompanying the children and gave them all a checklist of points to make and questions to ask during the walk.

During the walk the children were told about how many of the older terraced houses did not have indoor bathrooms or separate kitchens when they were originally constructed. Many of the properties observed had 'offshot' kitchens built onto the backs years after their original construction. The old outdoor toilets at the bottom of the yards had also become surplus to requirements and were used as sheds or left unused. Other changes were more recent and included a loft conversion to create additional sleeping space. Many of the newer properties had new porches constructed over the front door and one householder had built a small conservatory on the side of the house to extend the living area. Other features which were pointed out to the children included new doors, the introduction of double-glazed windows, alterations to chimneys and the addition of satellite dishes.

Whenever pupils are taken beyond the confines of the nursery/school staff have to consider the health and safety implications. Once outside the school gates, the children are beyond their normal *closed* environment and consequently they are not so easily observed, not as easily held accountable and are subjected to wider influences. In this looser context it is not as easy for teachers to exercise control and a lack of control carries with it potential risks to the health and safety of the children. A well-organized and executed visit can inspire and enthuse children about the past and the momentum can last for a long time. A poorly organized and riotous visit endangers the children and is unlikely to result in much planned learning. Preparation can greatly increase the chances of a successful and safe visit. Local walks can give young children useful training in crossing roads, public behaviour and staying with designated adults as well as opportunities to talk

Visit planner/Risk assessment

Year group   Number of children

Details of adult helpers

Destination   Transport

Date   Timing

Preliminary visit made: YES/NO   Adult helpers briefed: YES/NO

Learning objectives

Activities

Resources

Hazards	Level of risk (high/medium/low)	Action taken

Pupils with special needs likely to affect safety

Action required

Mobile phone number   School telephone number

Mobile and medication held by

Signed	Date	Emergency procedures
		• Secure safety of group
		• Contact emergency services if necessary
		• Contact teacher responsible

about chronology and change in the locality and beyond. Such walks provide teachers with good opportunities for making it clear to the children that in the outside world the standards of behaviour expected are even more rigorous than those in school or nursery. Ensuring good behaviour is not just a matter of the teacher's peace of mind, it is a prerequisite for safety and learning. Teachers should always conduct a risk assessment prior to visiting a site, copies of which should be given to adult helpers with a further copy remaining on file in the school. It is important to bear in mind when assessing risk there is a need to give consideration to *likelihood* as well as *severity* and to take steps to minimize the risks to the children.

Parents and Family as Resources for Learning about the Past

Excerpt from nursery newsletter

Please send a photo of your child when he or she was a baby for us to use on a display. Please put your child's name on the back. Through our topic we will be talking about how we change as we grow.

A successful partnership with parents is often cited as a vital prerequisite for successful education of children. Teachers are continuing a learning process that has been begun by parents, consequently parents should be valued as active partners in their child's continuing learning. Both parents and teachers want children to be happy and successful at nursery/school. The potential generic benefits of an effective partnership with parents are numerous. Parents can support schools and nurseries by exhibiting positive attitudes towards education. They can also become much more knowledgeable about children's learning and the curriculum, for example being persuaded of the value of play in learning, or undertaking activities with their children that will help to support their learning. The gains for the children and their teachers can include increased motivation, better behaviour and positive relationships. These outcomes may help to avoid conflict between the home and the nursery/school and minimize confusion for the children in the process.

Effective partnership and liaison between teachers and parents can also have much more specific benefits for children's learning in history. Where teachers communicate with parents about the nature of history (see Chapters 1 and 2) parents will be in a better position to support their child's achievements in this area of the curriculum. Parents' own ideas about history may be based on their own secondary school experiences. Their own historical knowledge may be limited and as a result they may feel that they are unable to support children's learning in this area. It may therefore be important for schools and teachers to stress the importance of observation, enquiry and analysis and to offer parents strategies and ideas for how they can support their child's learning in history.

Ways in which parents can help with the concepts of time and change

- Using vocabulary and expressions such as *now*, *then*, *before*, *after*, *old* and *new*, *olden days*.
- Verbally ordering events chronologically including family events, such as birthdays and other celebrations.
- Talking about the passage of time and introducing the terms with which we measure it, such as *minutes*, *hours*, *days*, *weeks*, *months*, *years*.
- Reading stories about the past and discussing the context. Parents are increasingly being encouraged to engage in reading activities with children and this could include historical material that introduces children to sequences of events and the passage of time.
- With older children fiction related to particular historical periods and non-fiction material can be introduced.
- Providing access to ICT in the home including software with historical content.
- Taking children on visits to historical sites and discussing the experience.
- Looking at family 'heirlooms' with children and discussing their significance and function.
- Comparing old and new artefacts in the home.
- Talking about changes in the local environment.
- Looking at old photographs of people and places.
- Using 'discoveries' to talk about change, for example decorating and changes in the home can throw up opportunities to consider change such as lifting an old carpet to discover the original floor covering or old newspapers.

Keeping parents informed about history is vital if teachers are to be able to draw on this resource for supporting children's learning in history. By displaying planning in the classroom parents can see what history will be taking place. Displaying children's history work and timelines around the classroom also helps to keep parents informed about the history curriculum. Parents and other older relatives can be invited into the classroom to talk about the way things used to be, for example using toys, games, transport or holidays as their theme. Parental involvement can also be sought in providing resources to support the teaching of history, such as providing artefacts from clothing to crockery and documentation to photographs. Parents may offer artefacts that are too precious or fragile and so it may be best to minimize the risk of damage by returning them after a short interval and by restricting their use to teaching only and not including these items in displays or general resources. Parents and carers may also have a part to play in supporting homework tasks. Homework can be useful as a way of actively involving parents in their child's learning, extending attainment in school through the provision of additional learning opportunities. Liaison is important and teachers need to be considerate of parental concerns as well as the age and maturity of the children involved. In any request for parental support show consideration and awareness of the constraints on many parents in terms of both time and money, not every parent, for example, can afford to fund trips and visits. One great advantage that parents have over teachers is that they are not con-strained by the curriculum. Consequently, not only can parents support children's learning against the National Curriculum Programmes of Study for History and the Early Learning Goals, they can also go beyond this and open children's minds to a much wider historical field.

History/Time/Chronology homework examples

Foundation Stage

Week 1 – 'Please show your child photos of themselves when they were babies. Tell them what they were like, what they liked to do.'
Week 2 – 'Please show your child photos of yourself when you were a baby/small child. Talk to your child about the things you did and liked when you were a child.'
Week 3 – 'Ask grandma and grandad to show your child photographs of themselves when they were a child and to talk about the things they did/liked when they were young.'

Key Stage 1

Ask the children to find out about the toys that their parents/grandparents played with when they were children.
Ask the children to find out about the games that their parents/grandparents played when they were children. Ask the children to learn the game and teach it to the class.

Key Stage 2

At the beginning of a unit of work Year 5 pupils were asked to research major events in Britain or involving Britain since 1930. Pupils were asked to use encyclopedias at home, to ask family members, to use ICT or to visit the local library. Children fed back on a decade by decade basis as a class and this was used to set the scene for the coming project.

Reflective Questions

Space and resources

- How do you make effective use of the available space when teaching history?
- How does the layout of the classroom foster independence and responsibility in the children?
- Are your resources for history organized in a way that makes them accessible?
- Do you plan ahead for history resources to ensure that they are available at the right time?

THE LEARNING ENVIRONMENT

Display

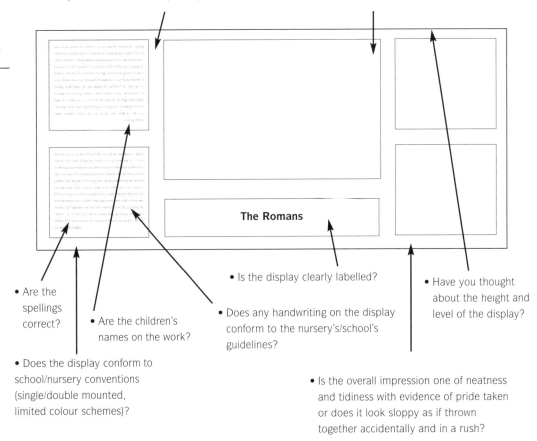

• Does the display look too crowded? Remember that the spaces between work are as important as those occupied by the work.

• Are the mounts cut straight and even with square corners? Are the margins equal? If they are unequal, is this deliberate or carelessness?

The Romans

• Are the spellings correct?

• Are the children's names on the work?

• Is the display clearly labelled?

• Does any handwriting on the display conform to the nursery's/school's guidelines?

• Have you thought about the height and level of the display?

• Does the display conform to school/nursery conventions (single/double mounted, limited colour schemes)?

• Is the overall impression one of neatness and tidiness with evidence of pride taken or does it look sloppy as if thrown together accidentally and in a rush?

Using ICT in history

• How do you group the children? Do you opt for homogeneity, putting children with similar ability, personalities or dispositions together? Do you opt for diversity, creating mixed-ability groupings where some children have more previous ICT experience or are better readers?
• How many children are able to work with the computer at any one time?
• Do you use a computer timetable to show each group's turn, either by time of day or order of groups?
• Does your timetable give equal time to both boys and girls? How long do children have on the computer? Do you measure this in time or by task?
• How do you ensure that all the children have a real role to play when using the computer? Do they know what this role is?
• Do the children change over their roles? When and how often?

- How do you make sure that you can mediate the group dynamics from time to time in the interests of equality of opportunity and personal and social development?
- Do you alter groupings that do not appear to work?
- How do the children learn to use the software? If children are going to demonstrate the use of software to their peers, do girls as well as boys have the chance to demonstrate their expertise?
- Do you encourage all the children to talk about and share their successes on the computer?

119

Using the wider environment in history

Planning a history visit

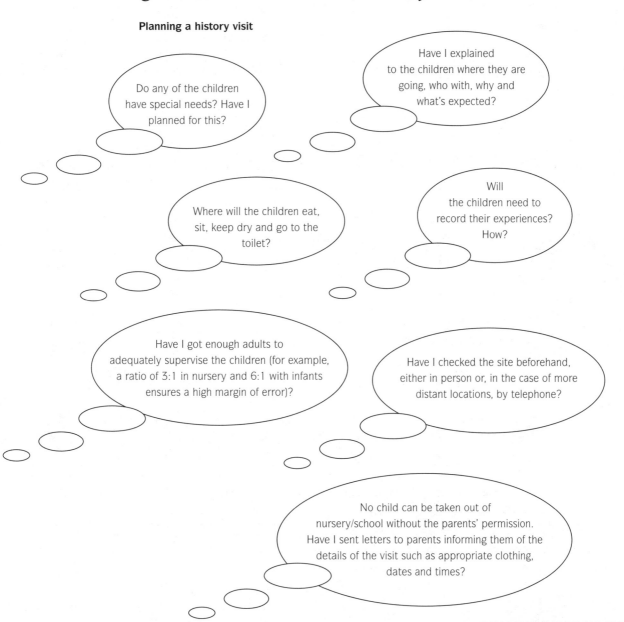

Do any of the children have special needs? Have I planned for this?

Have I explained to the children where they are going, who with, why and what's expected?

Where will the children eat, sit, keep dry and go to the toilet?

Will the children need to record their experiences? How?

Have I got enough adults to adequately supervise the children (for example, a ratio of 3:1 in nursery and 6:1 with infants ensures a high margin of error)?

Have I checked the site beforehand, either in person or, in the case of more distant locations, by telephone?

No child can be taken out of nursery/school without the parents' permission. Have I sent letters to parents informing them of the details of the visit such as appropriate clothing, dates and times?

Planning a history visit (continued)

Have I checked the route? What are the safest crossing points and are there any toilets en route just in case? Do I know the bus times, stopping places and alternative routes in the event of a non-arrival? Have I told the bus company that we are making the visit?

Have I briefed accompanying parents/adults about the visit and their role? Which children are they to accompany? What should they wear? Have I explained why the children are going, and what the learning purposes of the visit are?

What are the procedures in the event of an emergency or accident, for example a fire alarm? Do I have an emergency kit (sick bags, 'wet wipes', spare clothing)?

Are there any particular hazards to avoid?

REFERENCES

Ahlberg, J. and Ahlberg, A. (1981) *Peepo*, London: Puffin Books.

Ahlberg, J. and Ahlberg, A. (1988) *Starting School*, London: Puffin Books.

Amery, H. and Cartwright, S. (1993) *The Old Steam Train*, London: Usborne.

BBC 'Landmarks' series, London: BBC Educational Publishing.

BBC 'Watch' series, London: BBC Educational Publishing.

BBC 'ZigZag' series, London: BBC Educational Publishing.

Department of Education and Science (1989) *Curriculum Matters 13: Environmental Education from 5 to 16*, London: HMSO.

Health and Safety at Work Act 1974 (1974) London: HMSO.

Magorian, M. (1981) *Goodnight Mister Tom*, London: Puffin Books.

National Curriculum Council (NCC) (1990a) *Curriculum Guidance 3: The Whole Curriculum*, York: NCC.

National Curriculum Council (NCC) (1990b) *Environmental Education*, York: NCC.

National Museum of Scotland (2000) *Looking for Vikings*, CD-ROM, Chepstow.

O'Hara, M. (2000) *Teaching 3–8: Meeting the Standards for Initial Teacher Training and Induction*, London and New York: Continuum.

Serrallier, I. (1956) *The Silver Sword*, London: Puffin Books.

Assessing, Recording and Reporting on Pupils' Learning

Assessing children's learning in history offers a way to ensure progression and greater continuity for pupils as the results of assessment provide reliable information upon which to plan the next step of a teaching programme. Teachers assess pupils in order to inform future learning experiences by celebrating and building on successes, helping children to set targets for future learning and by diagnosing and responding to difficulties (O'Hara, 2000). Teachers need to make sound assessments of pupils' progress and use these to gauge the amount of scaffolding required to support learning. The results of assessment also provide teachers with a more valid base for evaluating their own practice and the history curriculum provided by the school, helping them to monitor and raise standards. At the same time, accurate and constructive feedback from the teacher, based on assessment, can be helpful in enhancing pupils' motivation and confidence. Assessment also serves to inform parents and future teachers about children's achievements to date. Information on pupil attainment to date can be used to make the transition within and between schools more streamlined.

This chapter considers assessment in history. It begins by summarizing those aspects of the subject that should be assessed and then continues by outlining alternative forms of assessment. Brief descriptions of formal, informal, diagnostic, formative, summative, evaluative, baseline, criterion and norm-referenced assessment are provided with examples to illustrate how these forms can appear in the context of history. The chapter then proceeds to outline alternative methods of assessment including classroom observations and monitoring pupil work. Recording provides an important evidence base for teachers which they can use to support their judgements and the chapter contains a section on different types of record, again with examples for history. The final section covers accountability and reporting. This section includes suggestions on how to give feedback to children, reporting on pupil progress and reporting on the nature of the history curriculum.

What to Assess

When assessing children's attainment in history teachers need to look not just for pupils' abilities to demonstrate factual knowledge and understanding of past events, as set out in the various study units, but also for evidence of attainment in relation to the process of historical enquiry. This is particularly important with younger children for whom demonstrating detailed knowledge of the Romans or Britain since 1930 is an inappropriate goal. Clearly a great deal more would be expected of older pupils than younger ones, however the list below outlines the areas that teachers can consider across the 3–11 age range. When assessing children's historical capabilities and knowledge, teachers can focus on the following areas:

- **Skills in history**. For example, using a wide range of evidence; thinking as well as remembering; observation; study and research; classifying; evaluating; comparing and contrasting; hypothesizing; applying existing knowledge; synthesizing ideas; application of reason and logic; asking questions; organizing and presenting information; identifying bias and distinguishing fact from fiction or opinion.
- **Concepts in history**. For example, historical measures such as century, decade, chronology or cause and effect.
- **Knowledge of history**. For example, familiarity with continuity and historical similarities; distinctions/differences between the past and the present; how, when and where things have changed over time.
- **Attitudes in history**. For example, retaining a critical and open-minded approach to the subject; developing empathy; appreciation of the variety of historical interpretations; cooperating and sharing ideas and information; fairness.

Forms of Assessment

Assessment may take various forms and the boundaries between these different forms are not always clearly delineated. It is entirely possible for an assessment to be criterion referenced, formative and informal simultaneously. Similarly summative assessments can be used formatively by subsequent teachers. The following section offers definitions of the various forms of assessment possible coupled with examples involving teaching and learning in history.

Formative/diagnostic assessment

Formative assessment is assessment that is used to inform the next stage in a child's learning. Its purpose is to recognize the achievements of a pupil so that these might be discussed and the appropriate next steps taken. Diagnostic assessment occurs when teachers seek to scrutinize and classify learning difficulties so that appropriate guidance can be given and intervention can take place. Failure to diagnose difficulties accurately means that effective matching of tasks and differentiation is harder to do. Formative assessment looks at where the child has progressed to, diagnostic assessment looks at why a child is not progressing; both inform the next step in terms of what the children should be learning and how to teach it. When engaged in formative/diagnostic assessment it is necessary to pay attention to the process of history as well as the outcomes. Although it is easier in some ways to make judgements about an outcome than it is to assess a child's ability to find out, for effective diagnosis and feedback in history, both the content and the process of the curriculum must be assessed.

Summative assessment

Summative assessments result in statements about what a child has achieved at a particular point in time, for example on transition from the nursery to the infant school or at the end of Key Stage 1. As such, they constitute statements about the overall achievement of a pupil in a systematic way. The outcomes of summative assessment are frequently used by the whole school and a child's subsequent school (in the case of transition) and form the basis of formal reporting to the parents. Although its primary purpose is not to inform the next step in teaching and learning, the information from summative assessment can be used in this way by subsequent teachers. A Year 3 teacher using the judgements of a previous Year 2 teacher to plan her history teaching for the Autumn Term is using the outcomes of summative assessment in a formative manner. Summative assessments have their uses as a measure of performance for children, their teachers and others. However, they are of limited use in assisting teachers who are seeking to identify and respond to the learning needs of their pupils day by day, week by week, hence the importance of ongoing formative and diagnostic assessments.

Informal and formal assessment

Informal assessment is an activity that teachers are constantly involved in. This type of assessment provides a very wide-ranging evidence base, considered over an extended period of time. It can take many forms, for example through routine discussions and observations, using a smile or a frown, spoken comments on the amount of effort being made or written comments on pieces of work as teachers move around the room. These regular interactions and observations are not planned and children's comments and actions may throw up unexpected and unanticipated evidence of learning across a wide area of the curriculum. Informal assessments are a useful way of identifying pupil success and diagnosing learning needs and act as the basis for a considerable amount of good-quality and immediate feedback to pupils. Formal assessment can be said to be taking place in those circumstances where teachers have planned beforehand for it to take place, when specific times have been identified for it and when the results will be formally recorded. Formal assessment should not be confused and conflated with summative assessment, formal assessment can also be diagnostic/formative in nature. Below, as an example of a piece of formal assessment, is a short test used at the end of a fortnight's work on the Second World War as part of a topic on Britain since 1930.

- When did the Second World War start?
- Who was the leader of the Nazi Party in Germany?
- Why did Britain declare war on Germany?
- Name two types of bomb shelter.
- What happened to pregnant women and children in large cities?
- List three of the jobs that women did during the Second World War.
- Why did Britain have rationing?

This formal and summative test was presented to the class as a fun quiz and provided the class teacher with one source of information for determining the children's historical knowledge. However, the teacher herself recognized that the limitations of this approach to assessment were fourfold. First, the test could not target more than a small amount of the historical content covered during the two weeks without becoming unwieldy. Second, the test was more a test of memory than one that allowed the children to demonstrate their historical understanding. Third, this approach did not provide the teacher with any insights into the development of the children's historical skills. Fourth, and finally, the summative nature of the assessment meant that opportunities to respond to apparent misunderstandings and errors were not available as the class was moving on to new areas of learning the following week. Consequently the teacher concerned supplemented this formal and summative approach with informal and formative approaches to her assessments.

Informal assessment

Through discussion and video material the children learned about the effects of bombing during the Second World War. The children heard how many British cities were bombed, killing and injuring thousands of civilians. Their teacher pointed out that many German cities were also bombed, killing and injuring even more civilians. The teacher asked the children what they thought about this. Their responses tended to be along the lines of 'they did it to us, so we did it to them'. Their teacher felt that this suggested limitations in the children's ability to appreciate different historical interpretations and perspectives (QCA, 1999a, p. 105, PoS 3). She therefore initiated further discussion with the children aimed at encouraging them to think about the experience of being bombed from the point of view of German civilians. She took care to encourage the children to think about the similarities between people and experiences. When she concluded her lesson, however, she realized that while many of the children were able to articulate more thoughtful views on the subject, some still persisted with their original attitudes.

Criterion and norm-referenced assessment

Assessment that is criterion referenced seeks to assess pupils' achievement against a set of standards or competences, utilizing increasingly more demanding descriptions to judge and report on attainment. The Early Learning Goals and National Curriculum level descriptions for history are examples of criterion-referenced assessment. Such criteria can be helpful for teachers in sharing the purpose of an activity with the children. Unfortunately producing criteria or descriptions that are universally understood and unambiguous is not as easy as it might sound and teachers have to engage in moderation in order to develop shared understandings about what constitutes attainment against particular statements. The example below shows a piece of writing by a Year 1 girl which arose from work on holidays past and present. The purposes of the lesson centred upon the identification of differences between ways of life at different times (QCA, 1999a, p. 104, 2b) and learning about the way of life of people in the more distant past (QCA, 1999a, p. 104, 6b). The criterion used to assess the work was drawn from the National Curriculum Attainment Targets (QCA, 1999a, p. 29, Level 1) and the work provides some written and pictorial evidence that this child has recognized a 'distinction between past and present' in this context.

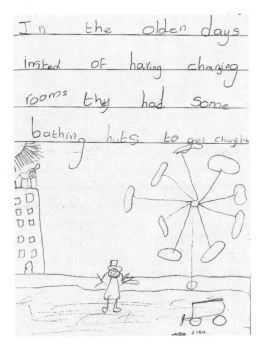

Norm-referenced assessment involves making comparisons between the achievements of one child and the achievements of others. The norms in question are intended to describe an average or typical performance, they are not intended as standards or desirable levels of attainment. The benchmarking of pupils' work in history (see page 131) is one way of utilizing norm-referenced techniques. The example below shows two pieces of Year 6 work. The children had been comparing comedy entertainment today with that of the past. The lesson introduced the children to some of the changes in entertainment between the 1930s and today. By comparing the two pieces of written work below the teacher concluded that both pupils were able to demonstrate some factual knowledge about this aspect of the history of Britain. They were able to describe some key features of film comedy past and present, identifying similarities and differences. Comparing the two pieces of work the class teacher concluded that child B was better able to describe and identify the changes and differences between film entertainment in the 1930s and similar entertainment today than child A (QCA, 1999a, p. 105).

Child A

Child B

Baseline assessment

Baseline assessments are conducted in the Reception year in preparation for the start of Key Stage 1. Baseline assessment is intended to form both a summative record of pupil attainment and a formative and diagnostic tool for future Year 1 teachers. As such it can be used to provide a benchmark against which a school can make judgements on the extent of pupils' progress at the end of Key Stage 1. It will also provide information that is useful to the school as a whole in helping it to plan and manage its provision in terms of curriculum and resources. Although baseline assessments currently lean heavily towards personal and social development, literacy and numeracy, they are also expected to consider the wider curriculum. This would include those aspects of the Early Learning Goals in Knowledge and Understanding of the World (QCA, 1999c) linked to chronological understanding, time, changes, similarities and differences.

As with initial pupil assessments in nursery, collaboration with parents and carers can be a useful feature of baseline assessment as it assists parents in becoming familiar with the nature and purpose of assessment. It also provides opportunities for them to provide information that might contribute to the assessment. Parents and carers have a considerable amount of knowledge about their children that can be invaluable in helping teachers to build up a more rounded picture of a pupil. Opportunities for structured dialogue between parents and schools on pupils' progress can take place at various intervals during a child's time in school. In reception classes, where staffing levels are often lower than those in nursery, good organization and planning are essential if a parental contribution is to be obtained in a timescale of use to the teacher. Parents need to be reassured that the information they are supplying is for positive reasons and will not be used to discriminate against their child. However, they also need to know that in instances where special educational needs are identified some of the information they give may have to be passed on to other professionals involved in the education and welfare of young children.

Possible criteria for early history learning in baseline assessment

Time and chronology

The child

- can recall past experiences/retell stories;
- can sequence familiar events;
- knows the days of the week;
- knows about the seasons and seasonal events;
- can demonstrate an understanding of past, present and future.

Skills useful in history

The child can

- seek information;
- participate in discussions and imaginary play;
- use their senses and ask and answer questions about the world;
- suggest solutions to problems;
- demonstrate an awareness of cause and effect;
- predict consequences;
- make comparisons and identify similarities and differences.

Evaluative assessment

Assessment can be used to evaluate and influence policies and planning in a school or nursery on a wider scale than merely the subsequent planning by individual teachers. Evaluative assessment is used to determine whether the goals of the teaching programme are appropriate for the pupils or whether that programme is effective in achieving those goals. Evaluation involves making a judgement of some kind, for example about the quality of resourcing for history or about the appropriateness of particular teaching and learning strategies. These judgements are based on the information obtained through other forms of assessment, as assessment provides a more valid base for policy decisions than the use of impression or anecdote. Evaluative assessment, therefore, can be used to

- keep track of the breadth and balance of the curriculum provided by the school or nursery;
- ensure progression and continuity in children's learning as they move through the school from the Foundation Stage into Key Stage 1 and on to Key Stage 2.

Evaluative assessment

With the introduction of literacy and numeracy hours School 'A' decided to review its planning and teaching across the Foundation curriculum, including history. Under the leadership of the coordinator staff considered pupil achievement and curriculum coverage. After the curriculum review it was decided to allocate one history theme to each year group to be addressed by the end of an academic year as it was felt that this would improve levels of attainment and provide better continuity, progression and curriculum coverage. This change in policy represented a change from the previous series of smaller topics arranged on a half-termly basis, some of which included history.

Methods of Assessment

When planning to assess children, a teacher needs to consider three questions. First there is the question of what is being assessed. For example, does the teacher want the pupils to demonstrate certain skills, or are they trying to assess the historical knowledge and understanding of the pupils? Second, the teacher needs to consider how they will know if the children have achieved the learning objectives. By examining National Curriculum level descriptions and Early Learning Goals teachers can gain insights into what children might do or say to demonstrate attainment. Third, teachers must decide upon a mode or method: how will they assess the children? Assessment modes in history could include:

- classroom observations (e.g. watching children's actions, listening to their conversation, listening to presentations such as reading out their stories or question-and-answer sessions);
- making judgements based on concrete outcomes, including outcomes retained from previous pupils as part of a benchmarking system (e.g. models, pieces of writing, drawings, paintings, tables, charts or ICT work).

This section examines each method in turn, suggesting strategies and raising issues for consideration.

Classroom observations

Teachers constantly check on children's progress through classroom observations involving the whole class, groups and individuals. These observations, such as an overheard conversation between children discussing an historical artefact, are an informal and often unnoticed part of the minute-by-minute interactions in the nursery or classroom. Such observation is an integral part of work with children and is essential for their continuous assessment. For example, classroom observations provide a means by which children's knowledge and skills can be checked and explored and can help to define more clearly any individual contributions to a group task. However, observation can also be used more formally in ways that are planned and focused, such as a structured observation to ascertain learning against a particular aspect of the National Curriculum. When planned observation is the chosen method of assessment it is helpful if the children are made aware of the purposes of both the task and the assessment. Explaining what you are going to be observing gives the children the chance to show if they know or can do it. Although the term observation suggests passivity on the part of the teacher, the reality is often far more active and involves more than just sitting and watching. A child's initial response to questioning is not necessarily an accurate or reliable guide to knowledge and competence (SCAA, 1997). Similarly actions and behaviour can be misinterpreted. Consequently teachers often have to check their observations through careful questioning, discussion and further observations. Discussing activities with children as part of classroom observation is a very useful device for locating evidence of a child's success, diagnosing learning difficulties, monitoring progress over a period of time and developing some insight into the ways in which a particular child learns and works.

In the Foundation Stage in particular, many of the assessments that teachers make will be based on observations. As the teacher cannot be everywhere at once, the involvement of the whole team under the guidance of the teacher makes the task of focusing on groups and individuals much more manageable in terms of creating time and opportunities to observe and talk with the children. Non-teaching colleagues (nursery nurses, non-teaching assistants [NTAs] and childcare assistants [CCAs]) can play an invaluable role in monitoring and reporting on young children's achievements and progress. All responsible staff can contribute to assessment through observation by using clipboards, post-its or notebooks.

Assessing primary aged children through observation requires good classroom organization and management skills, particularly where teachers wish to assess a small group of individuals in situations where non-teaching support is either limited or non-existent. As formal classroom observation requires attention and concentration teachers need to consider not only those children who are being observed but also the rest of the class. Failure to do this adequately could lead to constant interruptions as children request permission, mediation, instruction, advice and adjudication.

Planning to assess history by observation in primary classrooms

- Make the maximum use of non-teaching support in the classroom and plan low-intervention tasks for children not being assessed where such support is limited or unavailable.
- Assessment through formal classroom observation does not necessarily mean that you have to be with the children being assessed at all times. Planning which considers the balance between independent activity and teacher participation or group discussion may be a useful approach to take. When assessing a group of children you could visit the group at regular intervals of time through an activity, you could visit the group at fixed points in the programme of activities or you could work down a list of the children. Whichever option is chosen, it is important to ensure that there will be sufficient time to gather the necessary information without ignoring the needs of the rest of the class.
- Try to avoid becoming too close or too much of a participant in the task, as too much involvement will make disengagement difficult and complicate the task of collecting the evidence.
- Do not seek to collect evidence for large numbers of children simultaneously through observation and discussion. Trying to assess children against large numbers of learning objectives can quickly become unmanageable. It is important to have a clear and manageable set of objectives.

Assessing children's work

The concrete results of a history lesson, whether it is written work, a chart, timeline or drawing, can be a useful guide to children's learning and small collections of their work can illustrate their attainment over time very effectively. History workbooks and portfolios of this sort provide a way of displaying a range of historical work and can be used as a form of benchmarking. Benchmarking requires the teacher or the school to collect exemplar material, such as previous examples of children's work, as a way of indicating the level of work expected from a particular group of children. Benchmarking not only acts as an aid to teachers in trying to determine the *levelness* of a particular piece of work, it can also provide pupils with insights into standards and expectations and can act as a spur to greater effort and higher achievement. Below is a piece of Year 2 writing on the subject of Florence Nightingale which could provide evidence of attainment in history.

The piece of work below could be seen as evidence of the following attainment:

- this child has learnt about the life of a significant woman drawn from the history of Britain and past events from the history of Britain;
- she has recognized that people in the past did things for a reason (Florence travelled to Russia because of the war in order to help wounded soldiers);
- she is aware of some of the ways in which the past is represented (Florence kept records and the *Times* newspaper published articles about her activities).

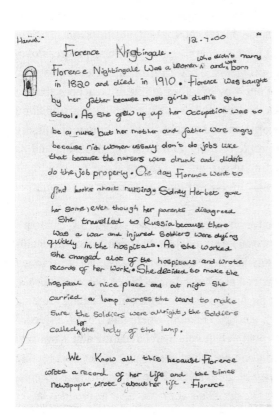

Where concrete outcomes are assessed in conjunction with teacher:pupil discussions, they can be very helpful in enabling children to become more involved and to take an active part in the process of assessment. Such an approach can help children to gain some insight into their own progress, strengths and weaknesses. It can also provide a useful starting point for setting targets for future learning. However, it is important to remember that concrete products alone may prove insufficient and inconclusive as evidence of attainment. Given the often domain-specific nature of ability, some pupils' historical knowledge and understanding could be masked by difficulties with English, mathematics or art. There are many factors that could influence the final outcome of pupils' history work. It can also be difficult to identify the features of a piece of work which indicate achievement. Consequently judgements made on the basis of outcomes may need to be supplemented by classroom observations or discussions of the work with the child.

Recording the Results of Assessment

Recording children's learning and experiences is an inevitable concomitant of assessment and evaluation. Past performance ought to be the starting point for future teaching and learning and records ought to be used to ensure that children are not repeating the same historical content at the same level in subsequent classes. Records also help teachers to monitor pupil progress over time by illuminating patterns or problems. They can inform discussions with children on target setting and are one way of informing future teachers about a child's progress, needs, interests and capabilities, thus facilitating transition within and between schools. Records should ensure that the school or nursery has an accurate and up-to-date profile of individual children's learning and as such provides the basis for reporting to parents and carers about the children's achievements and development, underpinning a teacher's summative statements.

All schools and nurseries have to keep up-to-date records of children's progress and achievements. It is impossible for any teacher to remember the details of observations and outcomes for any length of time, indeed it is possible to forget the detail of a child's remark by the end of a busy day, let alone a term. That said, recording everything is simply not practicable and would lead to teaching grinding to a halt. For teachers working with younger children, where much of the evidence of their learning and development could well be ephemeral in nature and is unlikely to result in the production of a concrete outcome, observation notes and teacher comments will form an important part of the evidence base for reporting to parents. As children get older and develop greater skills they are able to produce larger quantities of concrete evidence. In primary settings therefore there is greater scope to supplement ticks or comments from teachers concerning pupil attainment with some concrete evidence in support of these statements. Compiling portfolios is time consuming for teachers and in some circumstances could constitute duplication, especially where the children's history workbooks contain much of this evidence already. A related approach to the collection of evidence of children's learning in history could involve a more child-centred approach whereby the child selects the examples and evidence for inclusion, in discussion with the teacher. Reviewing this evidence base from time to time with children can be useful as a way of encouraging them to take greater responsibility for their own learning and get involved in self-assessment as pieces of work are superseded by subsequent and better examples. As with portfolios, compiling records of achievement and experience in this way can be a time-consuming process, however reviewing children's previous work can be an illuminating activity for both teachers and children and can provide graphic evidence of both progress and regression.

A wide range of evidence increases the chances of making accurate judgements concerning the children's capabilities. A narrow range of learning approaches in history therefore will lead to a more impoverished evidence base. Evidence collected should arise from a broad range of history activities and ought to reflect the children's achievements and learning needs. This does not mean however that teachers need to start collecting everything. There is a great deal of guidance available in the many commercially produced schemes of work for history on possible recording systems but no universally imposed one. Although this approach allows for flexibility, it has also led some schools to overestimate what is needed and, consequently, many teachers spend considerable amounts of time trying to meet the requirements of unnecessarily complicated record systems. Excessive amounts of evidence are likely to be unwieldy and teachers should therefore provide sufficient evidence to back their judgements. A minimum amount of useful evidence should be the aim in foundation and primary settings and teachers will need to decide what to collect and how long to retain it. Where the evidence base includes samples of pupils' work, selected by the teacher, these need to be reviewed and updated on a regular basis. Portfolios and records of pupil achievement ought not to be stuffed with outdated and hence inaccurate examples of children's capabilities. In the end, good records are a compromise between what is informative and what is manageable.

Evidence of children's learning in history

- Teacher notes and comments
- Drawings or sketches
- Computer printouts
- Written work
- Graphs, charts and timelines
- Photographs
- Junk models
- Clay work
- Diagrams
- Paintings
- Diaries
- Plans
- Posters

Types of record

Plans

Some of the records kept by schools and nurseries will be formed by planning documents (see Chapter 3). These documents provide information on the timing and content of history topics that the children have experienced during their time in school. Such whole school/nursery planning greatly reduces the need for individual teachers to spend time recording coverage of the curriculum. Medium-term schemes of work and short-term lesson plans are also part of this record. Lesson plans that have been modified or adjusted in the light of experience in order to respond to the learning needs of the children form a concrete record of how assessment has been used to inform future teaching.

Year 1 – History – Year Planner

Breadth of study
Stories
Houses and homes

Historical knowledge, skills and understanding
- Placing objects in chronological order (1a)
- Identifying differences between ways of life at different times (2b)
- Asking and answering questions about the past (4b)
- Communicating historical knowledge in a variety of ways (5)
- The way of life of people in the more distant past who lived in the local area (6b)

Ticklists

Ticklists enable teachers to monitor those activities and elements of the curriculum that their pupils have experienced or completed. However, although they are relatively quick to use, a tick simply means that a child has done something but does not indicate the level of performance or achievement. Ticklists also have an additional problem in that they can become very long and unwieldy. They can be made more informative, able to record not just what has been covered but also the degree of success or achievement, by using more than one symbol or by including a comments box (see page 136).

Written comments

Many teachers use notebooks, clipboards or post-its to jot down incidents and observations that are worthy of recording. It is neither possible nor desirable to note down everything and teachers need to exercise their professional judgement as to what is useful to record and what is needless paperwork. It is also likely that the level of short-term recording that teachers do may well vary depending upon the age of the pupils concerned.

Reporting and Accountability

In nurseries and primary schools where there is a high level of day-to-day contact between teachers and parents, a great deal of informal and ongoing reporting is already taking place. Regular parent–teacher contact gives considerable insight into home circumstances, needs and aptitudes. Parents can give teachers useful information on topics ranging from local events to children's learning when they arrive at the start or end of the day. This section examines three aspects of reporting and accountability. First, reporting to children by providing constructive feedback on their efforts and attainment in history. Second, reporting to parents on their child's progress in the subject. Third, accountability and communicating with parents about the history curriculum itself.

Giving constructive feedback to children

One purpose of assessment is to inform discussions between teachers and pupils intended to offer constructive feedback on their progress. Much assessment, as has already been outlined, is informal and takes place every minute of every day in most nurseries and schools. Consequently, much of the constructive feedback is also informal in the sense that it forms part of the normal exchanges between children and adults. By utilizing their

Name	Can place events and objects in chronological order	Can use common words and phrases relating to the passing of time	Can recognize why people did things, why events happened and what happened as a result	Can identify differences between ways of life at different times	Can identify different ways in which the past is represented	Can find out about the past from a range of sources	Can ask and answer questions about the past	Can communicate their knowledge of history in a variety of ways	Knows about changes in their own life, their family's life and the lives of others around them	Knows about the ways of life of British people in the more distant past	Knows about the lives of significant historical figures	Knows about past events in the history of Britain and the world

X = absent   O = not achieved/understood   Ø = partial ability/understanding   ⊗ = can do/fully understands communication skills effectively a teacher can do much to provide accurate, helpful and motivating feedback to children at a point of need. It is not just a matter of what is communicated but also how that information is communicated. Teachers need to consider the non-verbal messages they give to children as well as the oral and written feedback that they provide. Their body language, facial expressions and gestures can all be used to reinforce and emphasize the messages they give to children about their achievements and what they need to focus on in the future.

Some feedback, however, is more formal in nature and this includes marking and joint target setting and guided self-assessment by the children as even quite young children can get involved in commenting on their own successes and achievements. Marking is an important and sometimes time-consuming aspect of providing constructive feedback to pupils. It assists teachers in monitoring what the children have done and assessing where they need to go next. Marking as children are working sends a valuable message about the importance of what they are doing. Just as importantly, however, it helps teachers to pick up on learning needs and to set learning targets in an ongoing fashion, although this does require teachers to maintain sufficient mobility in the classroom to allow it to happen. Even so, in a classroom where there may be 30 or more pupils it is unreasonable to expect the teacher to be everywhere marking at once. Furthermore, if a teacher attempts to do all their marking in this way they may not leave themselves with any time to discuss the children's progress with them. As children get older and are able to cover increasing quantities of work, the task of marking as the lesson proceeds becomes increasingly difficult.

When providing constructive feedback to children on their progress in history:

- find something positive to say or write;
- try to use your feedback to support the children in improving and developing. Identify something for the child to work at during future lessons. ('I want you to try to look more closely at the artefacts next time.')
- set targets with the children at the start of an activity. ('Today we are going to be using the history books to find out about . . . and I want to see if you can use the contents and index pages successfully.')
- disseminate your feedback to the rest of the class when a child has tried especially hard or been particularly successful (praising effort and achievement at the end of the lesson or day).

Reporting on pupils' progress

Inviting parents into nursery/school to work with the children offers opportunities for shared classroom experiences which can contribute to parents' understanding of history in 3–11 settings. Equally importantly though, it offers an opportunity for

137

informal reporting on a pupil's progress and achievements. Teachers need to be professional and to adopt a partnership approach that includes making parents feel welcome in the classroom, explaining to, taking advice from and working cooperatively with parents. Although this is a time-consuming approach, it is more likely to make parents feel valued than an approach where they are in the classroom but engaged only superficially on the margins. Where more formal verbal reporting is taking place, for example at parents' evenings, the timing needs to be sensitive to the constraints many parents find themselves under, such as going out to work and caring for other children. Furthermore the numbers invited ought not to preclude meaningful dialogue with staff and the atmosphere should be conducive to positive and productive communication. Where appropriate, provide examples of the children's work in history for parents to look at while they are waiting.

In addition to parents' evenings, every parent whose child is of statutory school age is entitled to an annual written report on their child's performance and achievement during the year. Reports have to contain brief particulars on the child's achievements in the form of a series of short statements outlining successes and areas of weakness. The report should also contain information on a pupil's general educational progress that might include remarks on behaviour and attitude as well as academic attainment.

Examples of reports to parents

---

1. Baseline

Pupil name: **Helen**   School year: **1999–00 (Reception)**

Knowledge and Understanding of the World
Helen knows her days of the week and can describe and sequence seasonal changes. In conversation Helen demonstrates an understanding and awareness of the past when recalling and retelling her own experiences. Helen is very good at using all her senses to ask and answer questions about the world. She is able to make comparisons, identify similarities and differences based on first-hand experience and is beginning to understand the idea of cause and effect.

---

2. Key Stage 1

Pupil name: **Irfaan**   School year: **1998–99 (Year 2)**

History
Irfaan can recognize changes in his own and others' lives and uses appropriate vocabulary to describe the passage of time. He has used objects, books and photographs to find out more about the past, and can sequence objects and events into simple chronological order.

---

3. Key Stage 2

Pupil name: **Laura**   School year: **1999–00 (Year 4)**

History

Laura has enjoyed the 'Ancient Egypt' and 'Invaders and settlers' topics this year. She is always willing to contribute in lessons. She is learning to find out answers for herself through personal research. She now needs to start recording the results of her research in her own words and put more detail into her answers. She has worked hard on her topic books with some good results.

Reporting on the history curriculum

Schools can keep parents informed about history in the curriculum in a number of ways (see Chapter 5) both in writing and verbally. School handbooks should appear attractive to encourage parents to look at them and including examples of children's work is one way of doing this. At the same time, the description and outline of history should be clear, brief and easy to find (see example below). Overly long and complicated entries, with inappropriate, dense and badly structured text, are likely to be off-putting. When parents have English as an additional language, text in alternative languages should also be used.

History

Children are given opportunities to develop an understanding of the past and the ways in which it was different from the present. Through a range of topics such as Clothes, Houses and Homes, Shops and Shopping and Transport pupils at Key Stage 1 will be taught about everyday life in the past. They will be taught about important events, episodes and developments in the past and will have opportunities to investigate local history. Pupils in Key Stage 2 will be encouraged to develop and extend their historical skills, knowledge and understanding further. The study units introduced during Key Stage 2 include Invaders and Settlers, Ancient Egypt, Life in Tudor Times, The Victorians and Britain since 1930.

Displaying weekly planning in the classroom where it can be seen is another way in which parents and carers can be kept informed about the teaching programme and what will be happening in history lessons. The example below shows a weekly plan for a Year 1 class whose linked topic is 'Old and New'. The curriculum focus for the topic was history and design and technology. The school operated an alternating system in which pupils would experience history or geography and art or design and technology in an alternating cycle.

Letters, notices and circulars also provide a mechanism with which to keep parents informed about the curriculum and are likely to be particularly useful when

Class 7, Weekly planner 17–21 January 2000

	9–10.10	10.10–10.30	10.30 –10.45	10.45–12.00	12.00 –1.00	1.00 –2.15	2.15 –2.30	2.30–3.20
Monday	Literacy hour	Assembly	Break	Numeracy hour	Lunch	Science	Break	RE
Tuesday	Literacy hour	Assembly		Numeracy hour		Old and new toys		Old and new toys
Wednesday	Literacy hour	Class assembly		Numeracy hour		Science		PE
Thursday	Literacy hour	RE		Numeracy hour		PE		Music
Friday	Literacy hour	Assembly		Numeracy hour		D + T making toys		D + T making toys

trying to obtain historical artefacts or securing permission for visits. Children often need reminding to give letters and notices to their parents and putting their names on them helps, so too does following up and checking that delivery has actually taken place. This is especially important when working with the youngest children who may have more important things on their minds than letters. Written communication of this sort that requires parents to respond ought to include return slips and keeping copies of letters on file for future reference can save time when activities or requests are repeated in subsequent years. Finally, events such as open evenings, talks and curriculum days can enhance parents' perceptions of how and what their children learn when they are studying history and are useful venues at which parents and staff can share information and concerns.

Reflective Questions

Assessment

- Will your assessment allow pupils to demonstrate the appropriate skills, knowledge and/or attitudes? Will it recognize the process as well as the content of history?
- Do you make use of neutral and open-ended questions during teaching to explore children's historical understanding in more depth?
- How do you make your assessment an integral part of teaching and learning?
- Do you plan to assess a little bit at a time on a regular basis?
- When and where do you share the results of your assessments with pupils and parents?
- Do you ask children to report on their own progress and what they have done so far?

- Are parents able to make any contribution to the assessment of their child in history?
- How do you assess fairly children whose first language is not English?

Recording

- How do you ensure that your records are up-to-date and manageable, allowing information to be included and retrieved quickly and easily?
- Do your records show individual pupil progress and achievements and indicate areas for improvement?
- Are your records accessible for all those that need them, including colleagues, parents and other adults with a right to the information and, in the case of Primary Records of Achievement and Experience (PRAE), the pupils themselves?
- Are your records ongoing and cumulative in nature, based on regular assessment in the form of classroom observations, discussions, directed tasks and tests?
- Do your records include evidence that supports the judgements recorded?
- Do you make use of the records that are passed on to you?

Reporting and accountability

- Do you make use of the Early Learning Goals or National Curriculum when reporting on pupil attainment?
- Do you suggest areas and ways in which children can improve on their attainment to date in history?
- Do you begin your comments by referring to positive factors and ensure any subsequent criticism is constructive in nature?
- Do you maintain a professional commitment to confidentiality when reporting to parents?

REFERENCES

O'Hara, M. (2000) *Teaching 3–8: Meeting the Standards for Initital Teacher Training and Induction*, London and New York: Continuum.

Qualifications and Curriculum Authority (QCA) (1999a) *The National Curriculum: Handbook for Primary Teachers in England*, London: DfEE/QCA.

Qualifications and Curriculum Authority (QCA) (1999b) *Keeping Track: Effective Ways of Recording Pupil Achievement to Help Raise Standards*, London: QCA.

Qualifications and Curriculum Authority (QCA) (1999c) *Early Learning Goals*, London: QCA.

School Curriculum and Assessment Authority (SCAA) (1995) *Consistency in Teacher Assessment: Guidance for Schools*, Key Stages 1 to 3, London: SCAA.

School Curriculum and Assessment Authority (SCAA) (1997) *Looking at Children's Learning*, London: SCAA.

School Examinations and Assessment Council (1991) *Children's Work Assessed: Key Stage 1*, London: SEAC.

Sharman, C., Cross, W. and Vennis, D. (1995) *Observing Children: A Practical Guide*, London and New York: Cassell.

History and Equal Opportunities

History offers teachers excellent opportunities to begin to raise children's awareness and understanding of values and attitudes such as fairness, respect and equity. Those teaching pupils in foundation and primary settings play a key role in fostering positive attitudes towards diversity. The social and cultural diversity that exists in Britain today needs to be viewed as an asset for teaching and ought not to be avoided or ignored. To pretend that differences between people do not exist, that children are not exposed to ideas about these differences and to fail to encourage respect for diversity is to imply that there is something wrong. However for these ideas to be dealt with adequately teachers must themselves ensure that their message is not undermined and contradicted by their day-to-day practice in the nursery/ classroom. This chapter will outline the context within which nursery and primary teachers need to think about equality of opportunity including legislation, such as the Race Relations Act (1976) and the Sex Discrimination Act (1975), and will attempt to define some of the terms involved. Special educational needs (SEN) also raise issues of equality and entitlement which are dealt with separately in Chapter 8. The chapter then goes on to examine ways of developing an equal opportunities approach to teaching and learning in history by addressing the classroom ethos and the teaching methods selected. The chapter concludes by exploring strategies for promoting equality of opportunity through historical skills, knowledge and understanding before finally considering the development of an inclusive history curriculum by ensuring that the breadth of historical study presents positive and non-stereotypical messages about Britishness, world history and women in history.

Defining Inequality

The Race Relations Act (1976) and the Sex Discrimination Act (1975) place an onus upon schools to actively work towards the elimination of discrimination and the promotion of equal opportunities and positive relations between staff, pupils and parents. Both Acts make direct or indirect discrimination, whether on the grounds of race, colour, ethnic and national origins or gender, illegal (www.qca).[1]

Prejudice is defined as unfavourable feelings, opinions or views formed in advance and/or without knowledge or reason. People may have many reasons for being prejudiced, for example personal and cultural experiences and backgrounds, socio-economic factors, lack of information or lack of accurate information and 'different power relationships between people and groups' (Lane, 1999). Prejudice is an interpersonal matter between individuals or between individuals and groups. Prejudice is not restricted to any particular group, for example white people or men, anyone can be prejudiced. Where prejudice exists, it may result in stereo-typing in which characteristics rightly or wrongly perceived in one person are ascribed to all similar people.

Discrimination is rooted in prejudice but involves the translation of attitudes and beliefs into behaviour and action. As a result people are treated less well because they are a different colour, gender, religion or class. The treatment in question may range from verbal abuse to harassment, violence or restricted access to services. Direct discrimination is considered to have occurred in any instance where an individual is overtly treated unfavourably. Indirect discrimination relates to those instances where individuals are ostensibly being treated equally but where the outcome is actually discriminatory in nature. Racism and sexism are examples of discriminatory behaviour and can manifest themselves in institutional policies and practices as well as through personal prejudices and conduct. They are rooted in beliefs of superiority and subordination and can result in whole groups of people finding themselves kept in less powerful, less important positions in society as a result of their ethnicity or gender. Such doctrines, when expressed indirectly, can be hard to recognize or accept by those who are part of the dominant groups, as inequality becomes embedded in society and accepted as the norm (Lane, 1999). Racism and sexism can permeate the thought, speech patterns and actions of whole groups to such an extent that they are perceived as normal or natural.

Prejudice in the classroom

Direct racism
A group of young Asian girls had to be escorted into their school by the headteacher, during which time they had to suffer racist taunts and spitting from white parents (www.ofsted).

Indirect sexism
Ostensibly the history curriculum in school 'A' is the same for all pupils. However, an examination of some of the older history textbooks in use reveals the normalization of discriminatory language, such as 'men of steam' or 'stone age man'.

History is full of examples of prejudice and discrimination of all kinds. At the same time, both in terms of its content and its processes, history can be a vehicle through which children can be empowered to question discriminatory behaviour and prejudiced attitudes that have existed in the past and that they see around them today. Where issues of fairness, diversity and respect are not raised, the history curriculum runs the risk of reinforcing prejudicial beliefs by appearing to legitimize through omission, offering succour to and justification for, past discriminatory practices and attitudes. When teaching history, therefore, we need to consider how the content of the history curriculum can be used to torpedo notions of innate superiority and inferiority and how the process of studying history can equip pupils with critical skills and attitudes that are self-sustaining. There are a number of ways in which teachers can begin to build and implement a more inclusive and equitable approach to teaching and learning in history. The rest of this chapter will focus upon the ethos of the classroom and the incorporation of a commitment to equality of opportunity into the history curriculum.

Classroom Ethos

The ethos and philosophy of nursery and primary settings is informed by the Education Reform Act 1988. Under the Act, all children have a right to expect that their teachers will provide them with every opportunity to achieve their full potential irrespective of their gender, race, ability or class. They are entitled to an education that will enable them to participate fully in society, an education that prepares them for the opportunities, responsibilities, choices and experiences of adult life (NCC, 1990).

Adult Attitudes and Behaviour

Working to attain equality of opportunity is a complex and sometimes difficult challenge facing teachers. Caring and fair-minded teachers do not wish to promote any inequity in their nurseries and classes. Yet the majority of nursery and primary teachers are drawn from a relatively narrow section of society tending to originate from white, middle-class backgrounds and holding beliefs, attitudes and values based on their experiences (Marsh, 1998). What is more, teachers themselves may have experienced a history curriculum as part of their own educa- tion that gave scant attention to certain events and certain groups of people. Establishing equality of opportunity in the classroom, therefore, may necessitate reflection upon teacher beliefs, assumptions and behaviour.

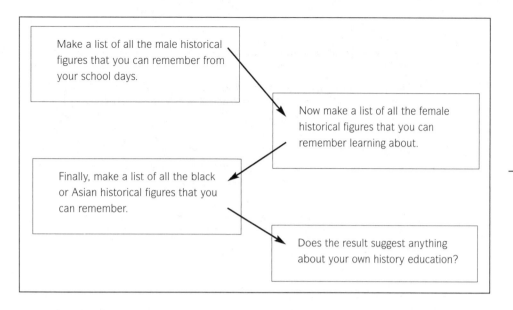

Make a list of all the male historical figures that you can remember from your school days.

Now make a list of all the female historical figures that you can remember learning about.

Finally, make a list of all the black or Asian historical figures that you can remember.

Does the result suggest anything about your own history education?

The prospect of concluding that one's historical knowledge, practices and attitudes might actually be inimical to equality of opportunity would be anathema to most teachers. One response, to pre-empt accusations of discriminatory practices, might involve 'treating everyone the same'. However, a by-product of such an approach is that it also results in the avoidance of having to confront and possibly challenge previously held truths and beliefs. A second consequence of such an approach is that far from ensuring equality of opportunity, it could well result in greater inequality, as such policies ignore and fail to tackle the individual needs and differences of children (www.ofsted). If one aspect of good practice in nursery and primary settings is to draw on the children's experiences, then clearly the children will have different experiences, including different histories.

Adult conduct is central to the task of establishing a learning environment in which the ethos is supportive of all the pupils. When working to identify and address the individual needs of children, teachers need to be careful not to fall into the trap of making stereotypical assumptions about their children concerning their intellectual, emotional, social and physical attributes (Adams, 1994). Staff expectations can have a powerful influence on children's achievement and self-esteem and establishing a positive ethos and environment in the classroom also necessitates reflection upon teachers' own ideas and behaviour. Whilst the majority of nursery and primary teachers are drawn from a relatively narrow section of society, the majority of the children in nursery and primary schools do not share this kind of background. Teacher behaviour has a powerful impact upon pupil aspirations and achievement and so teacher expectations and interactions with children need to be thought about. One way of doing this is outlined below.

- **Tolerance**: enduring rather than embracing. The first step on the road to more equal treatment. To move beyond this, Nieto advocates trying to find out about the experience of groups and peoples different from your own in order to make connections and to develop compassion.
- **Acceptance and respect**: a recognition that equality of opportunity is something to be striven for even if you don't know quite how to go about it. At this stage teachers are urged to start to reassess the curriculum and to look for multi-cultural, non-sexist approaches in teaching and learning.
- **Affirmation**: for Nieto this represents the final stage in coming to terms with diversity. At this point teachers are more self-confident and knowledgeable and are thus willing to debate and disagree openly on the issues.

(Nieto, 1992, in Lane, 1999)

Raising Confidence and Tackling Discriminatory Behaviour in Others

Discriminatory behaviour, either by other adults or by pupils, must be opposed by teachers as it creates barriers and obstacles that disadvantage and exclude children. In part, providing an entitlement curriculum concerns access; for example, ensuring that girls as well as boys gain experience of using the CD-Rom on the Tudors. However, promoting equality of opportunity also means addressing the expectations and attitudes that some pupils have acquired. It would be a mistake to think that children themselves are ignorant of the differences between them. Even the youngest pupils may have their attention drawn to these differences by others both inside and outside the school or nursery. Children are learning all the time, what they see and do not see, hear and do not hear, do and do not do, all inform their ideas about the world around them, their attitudes and their behaviour. Even quite young children can be conscious of the physical differences between themselves and others and will begin to ask questions concerning them. At the same time the attitudes and activities of other family members will have a profound impact upon the attitudes and actions that the children themselves exhibit. The wider world around them will provide still more cultural information and reinforcement on the role and place of different people in society. Images of black or ethnic minority peoples in the media and implied messages about the roles of men and women in the home, in everyday life and in employment are but two examples. Becoming increasingly effective in offering equality of opportunity in the classroom may mean therefore facing up to some uncomfortable truths about our children's, as well as our own, prejudices and assumptions.

146

Children can form strong gendered or racialized stereotypes at a very early age and as they get older these attitudes can become linked to job aspirations and life choices in a very limiting way. If some ethnic-minority pupils or girls are failing to fulfil their potential in history due to a curriculum that appears irrelevant to them, then that could constitute a form of indirect discrimination. Some children who are capable of high standards in history may be tempted to under-perform in order not to attract attention due to social pressure to conform to stereotypes that undervalue their talents. Self-confidence is an important factor in overcoming underachievement and the willingness to investigate or be creative comes from curiosity and ambition based on this self-confidence. Equally, there may be other pupils whose behaviour is overtly discriminatory. Examples of potentially discriminatory behaviour in foundation and primary settings could include

- children calling out while others put their hands up;
- children who scoff and ridicule incorrect answers to questions;
- children who engage in verbal abuse of others when they give the correct answer ('Swot!');
- children whose behaviour in practical sessions is aggressive and possessive (denying peers opportunities to handle certain historical artefacts).

At times, equality of access will require active intervention on the part of the teacher as discriminatory behaviour and attitudes need to be tackled head-on.

Strategies for raising confidence and tackling discrimination in history

- Be aware of how different ethnic and gender groups may interact in your history lessons.
- Have high expectations of all pupils in history. Teach the children that there are no gender or racially limited subjects.
- Look for ways to broaden the history curriculum to include black, Asian and female characters as positive role models and provide a variety of learning materials in order to appeal to the widest possible constituency.
- Demonstrate that you value and respect diversity and individual differences by using pupils' first language where possible and by showing respect for non-English traditions, cultures and protocols.
- Acquire and use knowledge about alternative historical backgrounds that might be present in the local community.
- Help children to recognize and challenge discriminatory practices and behaviour when they find them in history, for example historical reluctance to educate girls, stereotypical gender images in history resources which depict men as active, women as passive or black and Asian peoples as inferior to white Europeans.
- Help children to begin to understand ideas such as fairness, justice and diversity.
- Guide children in the adoption and use of non-discriminatory language and procedures.

- Give frequent, positive and encouraging feedback to both genders and children of all ethnic groups for their achievements in history and for non-discriminatory behaviour in history lessons.
- Evaluate and reflect upon your own teacher–pupil interactions. Do you treat children fairly by treating them differently on occasion?
- Seek to involve parents in your history teaching and raise and broaden parental expectations of all pupils in history.

Building Equal Opportunities into the History Curriculum

Opportunities exist throughout the Programme of Study for history and the Early Learning Goals to incorporate equal opportunities into teaching and learning. The remainder of the chapter examines ways in which teachers can seek to incorporate equality of opportunity into their planning and teaching in relation to the knowledge, skills and understanding involved in history as well as the breadth of study introduced through the study units.

Knowledge and understanding of events, people and changes in the past

The teaching and learning of history offers the chance to introduce children to some fundamental ideas about fairness and justice. Studying historical events and the actions of significant individuals enables children to test out their views and values. Group work, if properly used, can offer some children a supportive and more secure approach to developing their historical understanding and capability through the provision of analogous experiences. A key to effective group work is the establishment of conventions or ground rules, for example 'we listen to others', 'we deal with bad behaviour', 'we cooperate', 'we resolve conflicts and disagreements through discussion and reasoned debate', and 'we respect the differences between people and recognize the similarities'.

Children can find out about past people's ideas and beliefs and look for similarities and differences, for example in burial practices and historical constants such as physical needs, hopes and aspirations or experiences such as friendship, love and happiness. This aspect of the Programme of Study also offers opportunities to introduce children to concepts such as interdependence and cause and effect as they see how actions and events had historical consequences. Much of the knowledge and many of the events that children learn about involve notions of power and conflict, whether in pre-Norman Britain, interactions between civilizations or Britain since the 1930s. As power is not, and probably never has been, spread evenly conflicts have arisen in the past. People have disagreed and sometimes fought one another. Through this aspect of history, therefore, pupils can find out about and discuss ways in which certain groups of people have been able to influence world events and how, often, their actions affected the lives, welfare and freedom of others. Learning that change is normal and inevitable but not always smooth, uncomplicated or desirable is an important lesson that only history can offer.

Promoting understanding

Children can be made aware that people have come to live in new areas and countries for a variety of reasons. There may be people in the area of the school whose families originated in many different parts of the world. Children can be encouraged to explore their own histories in relation to where their parents, grandparents or ancestors came from. In this way children can also begin to explore different cultures and histories from around the world through involvement in a variety of anniversaries, celebrations and special events.

Historical interpretation and enquiry

It is quite possible that socio-cultural factors have an impact upon people's preferred learning styles (Marsh, 1998). Awareness of how these socio-cultural factors may impact on pupil learning and behaviour is a useful starting point for consideration of how curriculum delivery and teaching methods might be made more reflective of pupil experiences and expectations. A child brought up not to touch things until given permission may have difficulty adjusting to situations in nursery school in which they find themselves encouraged to handle and invest-igate historical artefacts. Children brought up not to question adults may be reluctant to seek clarification from their teachers and may need support in historical enquiry. A child used to adult instructions delivered in the imperative may feel confused by instructions featuring courtesies such as 'please' or 'would you mind . . .?', as such expressions might suggest that there is the option not to obey. At the same time a child who would be reprimanded or punished for 'eyeballing' a parent at home may be extremely reluctant to engage in eye contact with a teacher, potentially giving rise to teacher assumptions about lack of attention, disrespect, insolence or defiance. Although not all children will necessarily thrive in an enquiry environment at first, it is important not to generalize. Far better to be aware that such differences may exist and to try to evaluate individual pupils as to their preferred learning styles and start from there.

When planning for historical enquiry teachers can encourage children's interest in finding out more about different times and peoples, appreciating and respecting aspects of other times and peoples. Children can seek out links between countries and cultures from around the world, using a wide variety of techniques. They can be encouraged to be reflective and thoughtful, recognizing complexity in the past and the importance of the historical context for interpreting human behaviour. Historical enquiry is based on open-mindedness and critical thinking, exploring the distinction between fact and opinion prior to making judgements. Thinking aloud with pupils provides opportunities for reasoning, investigating and solving simple problems verbally. Children should be praised for questioning and sharing their ideas, and including work on the lives of ordinary people and women and not just famous white men helps to make diversity the norm. This aspect of the Programme of Study fosters the development of a willingness to modify views in the light of experience and additional information. It also encourages the application of logic, developing an ability to engage in rational and reasoned discussion based on evidence, in order to justify a point of view. Such attitudes and abilities constitute good preparation for the opportunities, responsibilities and experiences of adult life in a multi-cultural society.

Re-evaluating the facts

Adam (aged 8): 'My dad says women can't work in factories!'

Teacher: 'Really. Has your dad heard about what women did in the Second World War?'

If the available historical evidence gives the impression that women in the past were less likely to occupy positions of power, then that in itself is worthy of discussion and examination by pupils. Teachers could model critical thinking by reflecting upon whether this might be because the writers of history have overlooked the contributions of women, choosing instead to concentrate largely on male protagonists. They might discuss whether women did not seek important positions or whether the cultures and conventions within which they lived militated against their advancement. They could challenge ideas based on beliefs in an inherent lack of ability and ambition on the part of women by illustrating how women in past societies often experienced a lack of choice, a lack of means, a lack of education and limited career opportunities. At the same time a lack of important individuals should not be perceived as a lack of importance as a group. While many women may have been restricted in their achievements as a result of unequal social relationships, the fact still remains that past societies, both British and others, could not have functioned without the contribution of women. In history, teachers should avoid presenting women in the role of passive observers. The majority of women were still able to exercise varying degrees of decision-making over their own lives and the lives of their families even though many of them may not have held positions of power and influence in society as a whole.

Examining and evaluating artefacts can offer good opportunities to assist children in becoming more aware and respectful of diversity while simultaneously enabling them to see the similarities between the lives of people all over the world in different historical periods. Any artefact (an object designed and made by people) will be the product of a variety of factors and considerations. Children can be asked to think about the materials, skills and technologies available; economic factors such as the efficient use of energy and resources; the design, including fitness for purpose, aesthetic considerations and the potential social or religious significance. Some or all of the above factors will have been taken into account when an object was produced depending upon the purpose of the object, when, where and how it was made and who made it. By helping children to evaluate historical artefacts from different cultures and places in the light of these factors, children can be assisted in empathizing with both the maker and the user of an object. Teachers need to be alert to the danger of reinforcing evaluations that are culturally biased or negative. It can be dangerous to judge other cultures against your own values. Different cultures set greater or lesser store by different things and this does not necessarily mean that one culture is correct, the other incorrect, or one culture more advanced than another (and hence by implication superior). Finally, when seeking out sources of historical evidence for enquiry and interpretation, include sources that challenge stereotypical images of women and black and Asian people in society.

Choosing resources that promote an equal opportunities approach to history

- Select materials that present black, Asian and female characters in a positive light. Avoid stereotypical roles and seek out figures of authority. Make sure that differences are presented as normal rather than aberrant.
- Find historical characters who are presented in such a way as to encourage children from different backgrounds to identify with them.
- Avoid materials that feature discriminatory language. If such discriminatory language appears in work with pupils make sure it is the starting point for discussions on justice, fairness, right and wrong.
- Use history resources that have a non-western perspective.
- Ensure diversity in history stories
  - Accounts of experiences in Britain in the past that include black and Asian and female characters.
  - Stories, folk tales, traditional stories and myths from different countries and cultures.
  - Past accounts and biographies of people in other countries.
  - Use dual language books and tapes to give parity of esteem to languages other than English.

Communication and recording skills

Providing a wide range of communication and recording techniques and offering children the chance to describe and explain their ideas about the past in a variety of ways is one method of promoting equality of opportunity in this aspect of the history curriculum. Ensuring that displays, labels and written communication with children and their families reflect the diversity and variety of children's backgrounds and traditions is also helpful. For some, English is an additional language. While some of these children may be bilingual or even multi-lingual, they may simultaneously be at the very earliest stages of English acquisition. Failure to appreciate this could result in teachers concluding, wrongly, that these children are less intelligent than their English-speaking peers. Providing a learning environment in which children feel able to utilize the full range of their linguistic repertoire demonstrates that their first language has a legitimacy in the classroom (Barratt-Pugh, 1994). It is important to realize that recognizing and supporting the breadth of their language skills and understanding will make a positive contribution to their learning of English and their success in education generally (Marsh and Hallet, 1999). At the same time, it is essential for all children to make progress in mastering English in the interests of their future achievements in school and their future opportunities as adults. The use of bilingual teachers and support staff to facilitate the history work of pupils with English as an additional language can be a valuable way of helping these children to comprehend the spoken word. Such skilled assistance enables the children to express themselves more clearly and appropriately. Bilingual adults can provide useful models of how to use the English language appropriately, how to listen and how to respond. Such support can help children overcome feelings of isolation and frustration and avoid much of what goes on in the nursery/classroom passing them by.

Breadth of Study: Building Equal Opportunities into the Study Units

Britishness and world history

Not surprisingly an important part of history in the National Curriculum concerns British history. It is undeniably important for children growing up in Britain to know something of the country's past and to develop a sense of Britishness. One view of this Britishness is essentially a white English view in which minority cultures and groups have played little or no part historically. However, disseminating this sort of *cultural heritage* (HMI, 1988) does not do justice to the role of these groups and it can also lead to myopia concerning some of the less than glorious episodes in our past. In 1562 Sir John Hawkins stole black slaves from Portuguese colonists in Africa and sailed them across the Atlantic to Latin America where he sold them on to Spanish plantation owners. With this act, Britain began her entry into the business of slave trading. This brutal business was to continue legally in Britain and her overseas territories until 1807. Slave ownership lasted longer still, only in 1833–4 was it finally abolished. Coincidentally the period in which Britain was heavily involved in the slave trade almost exactly matches the gap in the primary history curriculum which pauses at the Tudors and does not begin again until the Victorian period. Teachers and children need to have an inclusive and accurate, rather than exclusive and partial, appreciation of what Britishness might mean and an idea of all those who have contributed to making it so. An alternative view then sees the cultural heritage of Britishness as a diverse and complex mixture resulting from thousands of years of continuous movement and interaction of peoples.

Examining the concept of 'Britishness'

The black presence in Britain did not start with the arrival of the liner Empire Windrush in 1948. Black people have been part of British society at various points in history and this involvement almost certainly became permanent three or four hundred years ago.

- c. 250 AD – Black troops were stationed on Hadrian's Wall at Burg-on-Sands near Carlisle.

⇓

- In the 16th and 17th centuries there were many black slaves in Britain but also free men and women. Although their social and economic status often means that details are hard to come by, references in documents of the time show black communities in various parts of the country (www.brixton).

⇓

- Olaudah Equiano (*ex-slave*, *traveller* and *seaman*). Olaudah played an important part in the abolitionist movement in Britain in the 18th century. As a black man Olaudah was not waiting for white people like Wilberforce to put an end to slavery, he was not a passive observer but an actor in the drama (www.bbc).

⇓

- William Cuffay (*black Chartist leader*). William was transported to Tasmania in 1848 for his political activities in support of working people.

⇓

- Mary Seacole (*nurse*). Mary was born in Jamaica and travelled to the Crimea in 1854 where she worked with the wounded, dying and sick in the front lines. She returned to Britain at the end of the conflict and wrote her autobiography (www.internurse).

⇓

- Dadabhai Noaroji (*MP*). Dadabhai was the first Indian MP to be elected to the British parliament in 1892 (www.blackpresence).

⇓

- John Archer (*local councillor*). John became the first black mayor in Britain when he was elected Mayor of Battersea in 1913 (www.blackpresence).

The history of Britain is a history that includes settlement, disputes, invasion, union and immigration by a large number of different groups from Celts and Romans to Irish, Scots, Welsh, Poles, West Indians, Travellers or Ugandan Asians. The narrow view of Britishness and British history as a history with only marginal and peripheral input from one or two recent waves of immigration is a myth. British history is replete with instances of new groups arriving and contributing in a variety of ways to British culture and society. When teaching British history, the cultural and ethnic diversity that has characterized these islands throughout recorded history ought to have its place. All pupils need to be made aware of the various contributions that new groups and cultures have made to British life and experience over the centuries. As well as making children aware of the diversity of individuals and ethnic and cultural groups in Britain's past, the history curriculum also offers opportunities to give proper consideration to the history of other nations and civilizations around the world. Many parts of the world have experienced the rise and development of great civilizations and cultures in which art, music, science, mathematics, architecture and many other fields of human endeavour have blossomed. It is important to portray these civilizations with respect and to exercise care over applying modern-day notions of right and wrong or what it is to be civilized in inappropriate ways.

Gender and History

History ought to be a study of all our pasts and that includes the 50 per cent plus of the population that are female. In history however, ordinary people and women are less likely to have their lives as well documented as powerful men. Consequently, girls could constitute a group of pupils that can easily be made to feel as though history is an area of learning with minimal relevance to them. Many history programmes on television and some of the literature could be said to give the impression that most of the important historical figures were men. Many of the key events surviving in the documentary historical record are primarily concerned with men. It can sometimes appear as though women in history (with a few notable, powerful exceptions such as queens like Elizabeth or Victoria) were virtually invisible. Where women do appear, it is often in secondary or apparently unimportant roles, and they are seemingly little more than passive observers. When the contribution of women does feature in history it is often in the context of their roles as workers, wives or mothers and just as often the crucial importance of these roles economically, socially and culturally is underestimated. There are plenty of historical examples where work both inside and outside the home has been characterized by a degree of sexual differentiation but that does not mean we should ascribe primacy to the work of men over the work of women. Similarly, family life is more than just a private matter; families play a vital part in the social and economic fabric of any society. It is important to give proper recognition to the significance of the family and the working roles that women have had throughout history.

At the same time it is certainly the case that women in the past were no more a homogeneous group than were men. The experiences of women in history, and the evidence that they were able to leave behind, was as varied as it would be today. Furthermore the position of women in societies has changed over time and space, which can further complicate the task of obtaining an accurate picture of the past. In ancient Sumer men had more legal rights than women, but women were not powerless. Women could own property and conduct business activity including the buying and selling of goods and the lending and borrowing of money. Higher-status women are also likely to have been literate and to have wielded varying amounts of administrative power. Similarly, while Viking men and women had different roles, women as well as men had rights over property, inheritances and marital status. A woman was expected to take charge and run a farm if her husband was away. All the property brought by a wife into a marriage remained her property and did not belong to her husband. Women also had the right to divorce husbands who were idle, violent or rude to her own family. When teaching history therefore we need to ensure not only that the importance of women as a group in past periods is acknowledged but that significant female characters are introduced to demonstrate that what any king could do, a queen could do just as well if not better. It is also important to introduce individuals that will challenge stereotypical views of women in history as wives, workers or hereditary monarchs. There are many women in history that can provide role models with which to undermine stereotypical views both of the past and the present.

Challenging gender stereotypes in history through the lives of significant women

Hatshepsut (1504–1482 BC) (*pharaoh*). Although ancient Egyptian society was mainly male dominated, women did have the right to own property, inherit and take a case to court. Hatshepsut began her rule as regent for the then child pharaoh, however she subsequently seized power and declared herself to be pharaoh. (www.horus)

Mary Anning (1799–1847) (*geologist*). Mary Anning was born into a poor family in Lyme Regis. As a child she accompanied her father on fossil-collecting trips. The fossils were sold to private collectors and museums. It could be a dangerous occupation as the cliffs in which the fossils were found were prone to landslides. She is thought to be the first person ever to have found an Ichthyosaur, a Plesiosaur and a Pterodactyl. As self-taught and working class, Mary had to struggle for recognition from the (male) scientific establishment and respect for her expertise both in locating and classifying fossils came only gradually. Towards the end of her life she was finally awarded a small annuity from the British Association for the Advancement of Science. (www.geocities)

Mary Kingsley (1862–1900) (*adventurer/explorer*). As a young woman Mary Kingsley sailed to the coast of West Africa in what is modern-day Nigeria. Once there she went inland and took a boat down the Congo River all the way to what is now modern-day Angola. She spent time travelling all over West Africa including Cameroon and Gabon. She visited places where very few or even no European people had ever visited before. During her travels she studied the people and places she encountered and on her return to Britain she wrote a number of books on her travels. In 1899 she planned to make a second visit to West Africa, however when the Boer War broke out she changed her plans and sailed to Cape Town where she worked as a nurse looking after Boer prisoners of war. While in Cape Town she caught typhoid fever and died. (www.netsrq)

Elizabeth Garrett Anderson (1836–1917) (*doctor/political campaigner*). Elizabeth decided she wanted to become the first qualified woman doctor in Britain. She tried to be admitted to a number of medical schools but none of them would accept her because she was a woman. Elizabeth therefore enrolled as a nurse and began to attend the lectures given for doctors. The male doctors complained and Elizabeth was prohibited from attending further lectures. She subsequently learnt that the Society of Apothecaries did not have regulations banning women from sitting their examinations and in 1865 she sat and passed the exam. As a result she was awarded a certificate which enabled her to become a doctor. The Society then changed its rules in an effort to stop any more women entering the profession in this way. Elizabeth was still determined to get her medical degree and so she learned French and went to Paris to study. She passed the required examinations but the British Medical Register refused to recognize her qualification. Eventually Elizabeth became involved in the creation of a medical school for women in London. Although she retired in 1902 she continued to fight for women's rights and became the first elected woman mayor in England in 1908. (www.spartacus)

Amy Johnson (1903–41) (*pilot*). Amy was born in Hull and went to work as a secretary for a London solicitor after finishing her degree at university. In 1928 while in London she became interested in flying and took lessons. She wanted to have a career in aviation and also to show that women were just as capable as men when it came to flying. She became the first woman in Britain to qualify as a ground engineer and she decided to fly to Australia single-handed and to try to beat the then world record of sixteen days. Her early efforts to raise the funds necessary came to nothing but in the end her father and another businessman agreed to fund the expedition. She set off on 5 May 1930 and landed in Darwin, Australia on 24 May. For the next few years she continued to set records for flying all over the world. In 1939 with the outbreak of World War II Amy joined the Air Transport Auxiliary. As a woman she was ineligible for service as a pilot in the RAF. She flew aircraft from the factories where they were produced to the RAF bases. It was while doing this in January 1941 that her plane crashed into the River Thames and she was killed. (www.ninety~nines)

Reflective Questions

- How do you ensure that the principle of equality of opportunity permeates planning and teaching and that the curriculum is enriched and enhanced by positive reference to diversity?
- Do you provide a variety of learning materials and ensure that all pupils have opportunities to develop their skills and confidence in using these materials through hands-on experience?
- Do you ensure breadth of curriculum content likely to appeal to all pupils?
- Do you challenge stereotypes of the sort sometimes found in history books by promoting positive images of women and ethnic minority peoples?
- Do you provide other history resources that actively and positively promote the diversity of culture and gender roles in society?
- Do you use attractively and professionally presented displays that incorporate objects, ideas, visual and written material from a range of cultures and geographical locations?
- Do you introduce and discuss notions of right and wrong, fairness, inequality and social justice when teaching history?

NOTE

1. Website addresses are given in full in the reference section.

REFERENCES

Adams, J. (1994) '"She'll have a go at anything": Towards an Equal Opportunities Policy', in L. Abbott and R. Rodger (eds) *Quality Education in the Early Years*, Buckingham: Open University Press.

Barratt-Pugh, C. (1994) 'We only speak English here don't we? Supporting language development in a multilingual context', in L. Abbott and R. Rodger (eds) *Quality Education in the Early Years*, Buckingham: Open University Press.

Her Majesty's Inspectors (HMI) (1988) *History from 5–16: Curriculum Matters*, London: DES.

Lane, J. (1999) *Action for Racial Equality in the Early Years*, London: The National Early Years Network.

Marsh, J. (1998) 'Schools, pupils and parents: contexts for learning', in A. Cashdan and L. Overall, *Teaching in Primary Schools*, London and New York: Cassell.

Marsh, J. and Hallett, E. (eds) (1999) *Desirable Literacies: Approaches to Language and Literacy in the Early Years*, London: Chapman.

National Curriculum Council (NCC) (1990) *Curriculum Guidance 3: The Whole Curriculum*, York: NCC.

Nieto, S. (1992) *Affirming Diversity: The Sociopolitical Context of Multicultural Education*, New York: Longman.

Race Relations Act 1976, London: HMSO (1976).

Sex Discrimination Act 1975, London: HMSO (1975).

www.bbc.co.uk/education/archive/histfile/biog.htm

www.blackpresence.co.uk

www.brixton.co.uk

www.geocities.com/capecanaveral/lab/1378/ws/manning.html

www.horus.ks.org.eg/html/queen_hatshepsut.html

www.internurse.com/marymain.htm

www.netsrq.com/~dbois/kingsley.html

www.ninety~nines.org/johnson.html

www.ofsted.gov.uk/public/docs/minority/2.htm – Raising the attainment of ethnic minority pupils

www.qca.org.uk/overview/key~principles.htm

www.spartacus.schoolnet.co.uk

History and Children with Special Educational Needs

This chapter deals with the requirement on teachers in mainstream schools and maintained nurseries to provide an entitlement curriculum that includes children with special educational needs (SEN). Dealing effectively with SEN pupils in the classroom provides an exciting challenge for teachers: 'Who can meaningfully engage with history as a subject? Realism and idealism need to be balanced' (Turner, 2000, p. 70). While the ideal of integration may be desirable it must be premised upon adequate resourcing for it. Without proper staffing and resourcing teachers are faced with the extremely difficult task of trying to respond adequately to the needs of all their pupils. This said even in situations where resourcing is not ideal there is much that teachers can do when planning and teaching history to try and make it relevant and interesting to all the children. This chapter outlines some of the special educational needs that nursery and primary teachers may encounter in the classroom including those arising from physical disability, learning difficulties, emotional and behavioural problems as well as the special needs of gifted and talented pupils. The list is intended to be indicative rather than comprehensive. The range of SEN is considerable and complex in nature. Pupils, including those with SEN, should be viewed as individuals. The only certain connection between two pupils with dyslexia is their dyslexia. We should be careful about taking one aspect of a child's life and using it to group all children with a similar impairment into an indistinguishable homogeneous whole. Furthermore, some children may experience SEN that are multiple. Although the chapter considers different areas individually the reality may be much more complicated and readers wishing to look more closely into this area should read some of the references listed at the end of this chapter. However, it is important to provide a flavour of the types of SEN possible in order to set teaching strategies and responses in history into context, as some pupils with SEN in mainstream schooling may find some aspects of the history curriculum particularly difficult to achieve in. Finally, children with SEN have the same need to develop self-esteem as other pupils and teachers have a role to play in facilitating this. In part this is a day-to-day task but it can also be added to in history. Marginalized groups need heroes and role models too and the breadth of historical study can provide some of these.

- Philip II of Spain (deaf and reputed to have possessed a hearing aid throne).
- Beethoven (deaf).
- Alexander Graham Bell (said to have accidentally invented the telephone while developing a hearing aid for his wife).
- Albert Einstein (said to have experienced learning difficulties at school).
- Julius Caesar (epileptic).

This chapter will outline some of the special needs that teachers may encounter in the nursery/classroom when teaching history and will suggest ways in which the health, welfare and progression of children with SEN can be assured. Interspersed within the various sections are suggestions on strategies designed to promote learning and academic achievement when planning and teaching those aspects of the Early Learning Goals with the potential for historical learning and the knowledge, skills and understanding elements of the National Curriculum for history.

Recognizing and Including Pupils with SEN

The publication of the Warnock Report (DES, 1978) and subsequent Education Acts (for example, DES, 1981 and DFE, 1993), in which many of its recommendations were implemented and refined, mark important points in the move towards greater integration of pupils with SEN into mainstream schooling. The Warnock Report suggested that as many as 20 per cent of children could have some form of special educational need during their education that would merit additional provision of some kind. Not only did the report envisage a move of some pupils with SEN out of special schools but also suggested that many SEN pupils already existed in mainstream education (Stirton and Glover, 1998) and that these children would benefit from identification and support. Since 1978 the number of children in mainstream education identified as having SEN of some description has increased both in terms of numbers and in terms of the range of needs. Special educational needs might involve social, emotional, sensory, physical or intellectual factors or a combination of these factors. Where the need is based on a difficulty or disability, rather than on a particular gift or talent, then this can range from mild to severe. This trend and its implications for teachers and teaching was further elaborated upon in *Excellence in Schools* (DfEE, 1997). Underlying all these developments is a belief that integration will greatly benefit all pupils, those with SEN and those without, both in terms of personal and social development and academic achievement.

Special educational needs are considered to exist in circumstances where special provision has to be made for a child because

- he/she is affected by a disability which precludes or hampers his/her efforts to avail himself/herself of the educational facilities on offer;
- he/she is experiencing learning difficulties. A learning difficulty in the context of SEN implies a significantly greater difficulty in learning than that experienced by the majority of children of the same age;
- he/she is gifted or talented.

Identifying children with SEN is not always an easy or straightforward activity. Some children will experience a form of physical or sensory impairment that is easily identified, while others are much harder to discern. Some pupils, for example, may experience hearing impairments which are not immediately obvious to a teacher or which are intermittent, while another child may be clearly identified as suffering from a medical condition such as cerebral palsy. Similarly, some children have learning difficulties, the nature of which is not instantly apparent; all that may be evident is the fact that a child finds it noticeably harder to achieve in certain areas of the curriculum than their peers. At the same time, other children will have been diagnosed as having quite specific learning disabilities such as dyslexia and, in some instances, the difficulties encountered by children may be rooted in emotional and behavioural problems. Irrespective of the needs and their origins, failure to recognize the signs and to take steps to adapt the educational provision for these children can result in low self-esteem, frustration, anger, cycles of underachievement and alienation. Nursery and primary teachers can play an important part in identifying and assessing children with special educational needs and their subsequent role in addressing SEN includes providing support to enable SEN children to have equal access to the curriculum and providing opportunities for appropriate learning experiences, including social experiences. In order to do this effectively, teachers would be well advised to elicit knowledge of children's conditions and needs from parents, carers and other professionals concerned with the education and welfare of children. Assessments of SEN, for example, may involve collaboration with external agencies and experts such as medical practitioners, support teachers or educational psychologists. It is important as teachers not to oversimplify or make inaccurate and sweeping generalizations about children with special educational needs. Teachers need to know about the implications of a range of conditions in order to work for full involvement in the activities of the nursery/class and to facilitate pupil learning. Effective teaching practices are those which offer children 'the maximum opportunity to learn' (Westwood, 1997) and liaison and discussion with these groups is likely to be an important part of planning and delivering learning programmes that will best meet the specific needs of the children.

The revised National Curriculum outlines three principles through which to facilitate the inclusion of children with SEN. First, teachers need to set suitable learning challenges. Second, they need to respond to pupils' diverse needs and third they must overcome potential barriers to learning and assessment for individuals and groups of individuals (QCA, 1999a). The aim is to keep children on task as much as possible in part through establishing a clear structure in which pupils with SEN are encouraged to review previous work and learning, while new skills and concepts are presented in clear, unambiguous ways and are sometimes modelled by the teacher. Guided pupil practice should help to ensure higher success rates, offering more opportunities for positive feedback to individual children. Finally, teachers need to find ways to facilitate independent pupil practice, whereby children with SEN have the chance to apply new knowledge and skills appropriately (Westwood, 1997). The remainder of the chapter, therefore, considers some different manifestations of SEN in the classroom and uses these as the starting point for comments on how children's learning in history can be enhanced for SEN pupils.

Physical Disabilities

There are a great many physical disabilities that teachers may encounter in nursery and primary schools. This chapter can only give an overview of some of the more common conditions. Students and teachers wishing to gain more detailed knowledge in this field should, therefore, consult some of the texts indicated in the list of references at the end of the chapter. Children with some of the conditions below are no more likely to have learning difficulties than some of those children without the same conditions. However, the impact of hospitalization, absences from nursery/ school and occasional reluctance to avail themselves of available aids may impede their educational progress and, as a result, some areas of the history curriculum may need careful consideration, adaptation and supervision by the teacher.

Key characteristics of some physical disabilities

Arthritis	Although this might be thought to be a disease of the elderly, some children do suffer from a form of rheumatoid arthritis. In such cases the children may be under medication or have to have physiotherapy. Although a reasonable and sensible amount of physical activity is desirable, excessive physical activity could result in the condition being exacerbated, causing the child considerable discomfort and anxiety.
Asthma	Asthma appears to be becoming increasingly common in children and is caused by a narrowing of air passages in the lungs which makes breathing difficult. While some children have only mild attacks, for others it can be far more serious and even life threatening. Triggers for attacks range from temperature changes and allergic reactions, to infections and excessive physical exertion. Serious cases may result in frequent or extended absences from nursery/school, interrupting a child's progress, and could restrict their involvement in some activities such as PE or out of school work. Once again, where pupils feel self-conscious about their difference teachers may need to remind children about using their inhalers.

Cerebral palsy	Cerebral palsy results from brain damage. Movement from 'a' to 'b' in the nursery/classroom may be awkward and jerky in nature, while at rest, the body may experience irregular and uncoordinated motion. This condition can also produce problems with balance and coordination. Depending on the seriousness of the condition some pupils may need wheelchairs, others may find fine motor control impaired or experience difficulties in speech and articulation. As with serious asthma, some children may find themselves absent from school resulting in them having to try to catch up with their peers. They may also experience a lower self-image as a result of their condition.

Cystic fibrosis	Cystic fibrosis is a genetic disorder that results in the appearance of thick mucus in the child's lungs. The consequences for the child include infections of the lungs and stomach and daily treatment including physiotherapy, medicines and special diets, all of which are necessary to ameliorate the effects of what is an incurable condition.
Diabetes	Diabetes results from difficulties with the body's production of insulin and a consequent inability to make use of sugar, causing it to build up in the body. Undiagnosed diabetes can result in • excessive thirst; • excessive urination; • weight loss; • fatigue. Children with diabetes often have to have insulin injections and they may also be placed on a diet that strictly controls their intake of carbohydrates. Meals have to be eaten at regular times in order to balance insulin with sugar. Where the balance breaks down children may find they have either too much or too little sugar in their bodies. Falls in blood sugar as a result of lack of food (hypo attack) can happen quite quickly and the results can include headaches, bad-temperedness, lack of colour, sweating, palpitations or anxiety. Biscuits or sweets are sometimes used to rectify the situation. Excessive blood sugar levels can be far more serious, the onset is slower and if not dealt with can result in vomiting and diabetic coma. This is rare but hospitalization is essential when it occurs. Older children are often capable of recognizing when a problem is arising.
Epilepsy	Epilepsy is an unpredictable cerebral disorder caused by temporary changes in the brain's electrical activity. It can require control through drugs. Fits (sometimes referred to as seizures or convulsions) can be brought on as a result of illness, emotional and physical stresses or a lack of medication. Minor fits (absence attacks) often appear as momentary lapses of attention. Major fits (tonic-clonic seizures) can result in facial or whole body spasms, loss of consciousness and loss of bowel or bladder control. Although frightening for the observer, teachers need to remain calm, reassure the rest of the class, loosen clothing around the child's neck but must not put anything in the child's mouth. Place the child in the recovery position, check breathing and pallor and monitor the length of the attack. If the situation persists for more than five minutes teachers are advised to seek medical help.
Hearing impairment	Some children experience hearing loss as a result of blockages that stop or impede vibrations in the air from reaching the inner ear, known as conductive hearing loss. Such blockages can be caused by a number of factors, even heavy colds, and they are often susceptible to medication and other treatments. Other hearing problems, however, may result from faulty nerve connections to the ear (sensori-neural hearing loss) and this can be both irreversible and profound in its effect. Hearing aids can be used to amplify sounds for children with sensori-neural problems but they will not cure the problem and can also distort the sounds a child hears. There can also be problems with children who feel self-conscious about having to wear a hearing aid and who consequently lose it or forget to bring it to school.

HISTORY AND CHILDREN WITH SEN

Signs of hearing loss can include
- poor listening abilities (difficulties in comprehending spoken language);
- slow in learning to talk, limited vocabulary;
- speech problems (articulation, discriminating and sequencing sounds);
- confused in class over instructions and tasks;
- watching for cues from peers;
- hearing some sounds better than others (higher frequencies can be a problem).   (Dean, 1993)

Muscular dystrophy	Muscular dystrophy is an incurable wasting disease that affects motor skills rather than the brain. The condition is genetic and certain forms affect boys only. As the condition worsens the child may not be able to attend school. Working with families may be difficult and it needs to be done with sensitivity, as ultimately the condition is fatal.
Spina bifida	Spina bifida and other malfunctions of the spinal cord can range in their seriousness. For some children there may be only slight mobility problems. For some, the condition can result in specific learning difficulties, for example judging size, direction, shape, fine motor control and personal organization.
Visual impairment	Visual impairment can have a range of causes and can result in moderate or severe problems with vision. It is also important for teachers to recognize that a child's eyesight may improve or deteriorate. As with hearing aids, children can be reluctant to wear glasses as a result of the stigma sometimes attached.

Signs of visual impairment can include
- clumsiness;
- pulling faces and squinting;
- poor handwriting;
- bringing text up close to the face;
- poor coordination;
- headaches and dizziness;
- trouble seeing white/blackboard;
- tiredness.

Supporting the historical learning of children with physical disabilities

It is clear from the list above that history activities such as handling artefacts, visiting historical sites and accessing audio-visual and documentary evidence may present difficulties for some pupils with physical disabilities. In addition to the mobility question for some children on out of school visits, such as those with rheumatoid arthritis, it would also be necessary to give consideration to issues such as likely triggers for asthma attacks, or the need for diabetic pupils to keep their blood sugar levels stable. When reconnoitring such sites, it is advisable to look for places where pupils could sit or rest if necessary. Adult supervisors need to be properly briefed about supporting both the children's health and their education, for example an adult with an epileptic pupil who experiences an absence attack during a visit may need to repeat or check on information and instructions given. A teacher supervising a visually impaired child may need to think of ways in which they can encourage the child to use their other senses such as touch, smell or hearing, in order to find out about the site. Some children may need additional time or alternative ways to complete history tasks such as recording their findings. Making the most of educational technology (video, ICT, concept keyboard) is one possible response to this. Resources may need to be carefully chosen to ensure participation by all including those pupils who may experience difficulties with gross or fine motor skills. A further strategy may involve the establishment of a buddy system for some activities.

When teaching history to hearing-impaired pupils the use of visual clues to back up verbal ones may be helpful, as may rephrasing and emphasizing key words or phrases. If new vocabulary or phrases are to be introduced then write these down clearly so children can see them and general noise levels should be kept down when giving instructions or initiating discussions in history lessons. Minimizing background noise might involve cutting down on chatter or instituting supportive classroom conventions, such as lifting furniture and not dragging chairs. Facing the child during such discussions will aid attempts to lip read and teachers need to be careful of moving around too much as this can make it difficult for a hearing-impaired child to keep track of them and the cues that they are giving. Finally when using text-based resources such as historical fiction it is important not to obscure the teacher's face either with the book or by moving around too much.

When teaching history to visually impaired pupils limit the visual demands made on children, for example having to look at the white board, then the teacher, then a book and then back again to the board in quick succession or trying to follow the teacher's movements. Where such activities are taking place, try to position the child in such a way as to support vision, for example placing them nearer to the white board in a well-lit area. Where written or visual resources are being used, such as photographs or documentary evidence, try to avoid reflective papers and make use of larger print sizes, wider lines and magnifiers. Where history lessons will require a degree of mobility either around the classroom or on a site visit try to minimize potential obstructions.

Learning Difficulties

While some physical disabilities can cause learning difficulties for some pupils, there are other children who, although they do not have a physical impairment, will still experience learning difficulties. Learning difficulties can range from mild to severe and from specific to complex. In some cases the difficulties are rooted in problems located elsewhere, such as in their social and emotional development. Other learning difficulties are cognitive and often result in problems with core elements in the curriculum, namely literacy and numeracy. As it is the acquisition of skills and knowledge in these areas that can open doors to learning in other areas like history, special needs relating to literacy and numeracy can have very severe consequences for pupils if not identified or tackled properly. Language acquisition in particular is both a precursor and co-requisite for learning in many other areas of the curriculum and communication problems, like a physical impairment, can mask children's real potential and intelligence. Furthermore, an inability to make oneself understood is likely to result in considerable frustration and could lead to aberrant behaviour such as withdrawal or aggression. The list below shows some of the indicators that teachers can look out for which may suggest a child is experiencing a learning difficulty of some kind. It needs to be stated straight away that just because a child is frequently involved in off-task chatter or has difficulty in following instructions does not mean that he/she has a learning difficulty, it is more likely just to mean that he/she is a child. However, if a child displayed a significant number of the characteristics below these would be grounds for concern and teachers would probably wish to seek advice from the Special Educational Needs Coordinator (SENCO).

Some possible indicators of learning difficulties are listed below

- little apparent awareness of, interest in or knowledge about the world around him/her;
- draws on very limited previous experience in lessons;
- struggles with imaginative and creative approaches to history;
- few interests;
- has difficulty in following instructions;
- has difficulty in relating learning in one area to work in another;
- poor vocabulary/speech (for example, limited sentence use);
- reluctance to contribute to group/class discussions;
- limited concentration span, easily distracted and often involved in off-task chatter;
- hyperactive and constantly involved in activities other than the one they should be doing;
- struggles with literacy and numeracy;
- seeking recognition or work avoidance through housekeeping activities such as tidying or washing up;
- prefers practical activities;
- lack of interest in books and reading;
- constantly requests adult help, alternatively never asks for adult help;
- slow finisher/never finishes anything;
- finishes quickly, carelessly or incompletely, pretending to have finished;
- propensity for losing things;
- poor personal organizational skills.

Aphasia	Children with aphasia experience difficulties in understanding the meaning of words or difficulties in expressing themselves. Other pupils with aphasia know perfectly well what they want to say but have problems in producing and articulating the words, in some cases speech may be so garbled as to be almost unintelligible.

Attention-deficit (Hyperactivity) Disorder, AD(H)D

Attention-deficit (Hyperactivity) Disorder ought not to be confused with EBD. While AD(H)D may also present teachers with challenging behaviour, its origins are biological, whereas environmental factors play a significant part in EBD. Not all children with Attention-deficit Disorder are necessarily hyperactive. The absence of attention and disruptive behaviour can be particularly challenging for teachers and it is important to remember that AD(H)D is a disability and that consequently care needs to be taken over punishing children for a disability. Teachers, therefore, are faced with trying to initiate strategies that will support the children in modifying their behaviour.

Indicators of an attention deficit
- failure to give close attention, being careless and making regular mistakes;
- forgetful of regular activities, such as going to assembly or PE;
- problems in sustaining enthusiasm, will avoid tasks requiring extended effort;
- appears not to listen when addressed verbally;
- appears unable to follow instructions, regularly fails to complete work/tasks;
- difficulties in organizing self, often loses the tools necessary for the task (e.g. pencils, books, rubbers) thus avoiding work;
- very easily distracted.

Indicators of hyperactivity
- constant fidgeting with hands and feet;
- often unable to stay seated;
- will move in an inappropriate fashion around the room, for example running, climbing over/under tables;
- difficulties in playing without excessive noise;
- will interrupt and intrude upon the activities of peers;
- talks incessantly, blurting out answers to questions without observing classroom conventions and often without waiting for the questioner to finish the question;
- difficulties in waiting for a turn.

Autism

Autism is a lifelong disability, usually appearing by the age of three, in which a child will experience difficulties in communication and social skills, imagination and problem-solving. Autism can occur by itself or it may be in association with other disabilities, such as epilepsy. It is important to realize that some children with autism may combine their areas of difficulty with areas in which they are just as capable as and, sometimes, even more capable than their peers, for example when it comes to drawing, musical ability, arithmetic or memory tasks.

Communication difficulties may include
- difficulties with non-verbal communication behaviour such as eye contact, expression and gestures;
- delays in or inability to develop spoken language;
- stereotyped and repetitive use of language.

Social skills difficulties may include
- difficulties in developing relationships with peers;

167

- preferring solitary activities to ones involving reciprocal relationships with peers and others;
- treating people as inanimate;
- difficulties in sustaining conversations with others, can be stilted and halting;
- lack of spontaneous need to share experiences, interests and pleasures;
- dislike of being touched.

Problem-solving, symbolic and imaginative play difficulties may include
- lack of varied and spontaneous imaginative play, socio-dramatic role play;
- lack of interest in toys;
- inflexibility in the face of changes to routines and conventions;
- restricted and repetitive patterns of behaviour;
- all-consuming preoccupation with restricted area of interest (intensity and focus);
- extreme dislike of sounds, textures, tastes;
- repetitive mannerisms. *(Autism: Fact Sheets for Health Professionals)*

| **Dyslexia** | Dyslexia is a specific learning difficulty related to literacy that can inhibit children's ability to read, write and spell. Dyslexic children often confuse words and letters but then so too do many children when they are learning to read and write. In dyslexic children, however, these difficulties persist in the face of good teaching. Although primarily impairing children's written work and reading, dyslexia can also impact upon numeracy, coordination, behaviour and a child's ability to deal with time. Dyslexic pupils sometimes |

- have difficulty learning to tell the time;
- show poor time keeping and general awareness;
- have poor personal organization skills;
- have difficulty remembering, for example days of the week, birthdays, years;
- have difficulty with concepts such as yesterday, today and tomorrow.

(www.dfee.gov.uk/sen/hints.htm)

| **Dyspraxia** | Dyspraxia is an impairment that affects motor coordination. Children with dyspraxia experience movement difficulties associated with correctly gauging their surroundings, working out what to do and executing particular movements. As this impairment affects muscle control it can impact upon speech resulting in poor articulation. |

(Macintyre, 2000)

| **Emotional and behavioural difficulties (EBD)** | Children with EBD may exhibit a wide range of signs from extreme withdrawal to highly volatile, aggressive and disruptive behaviour. The causes of these patterns of behaviour are far from simple and may involve multiple factors including |

- divorce/separation;
- parental unemployment and poverty (resulting in the provision of free school meals, few holidays, outings, clothing);
- being placed in care, lack of contact with natural parents;
- overly anxious parent(s);
- being compared negatively with sibling(s);
- affected by other sibling(s), previous school record and self-fulfilling prophecies;
- frustration due to another impairment or learning difficulty;
- physical or sexual abuse;
- neglect.

Dealing with EBD can be particularly 'intractable and frustrating for teachers' (DFE, 1994) as the learning difficulties are caused by emotional and behavioural factors that are beyond their control. Teachers need to exercise extreme care in identifying children as suffering from EBD as statistically there is a higher chance of some children being more prone to EBD than others but EBD is not restricted to poor or working-class children. Indicators that may suggest a child has emotional and behavioural difficulties can include

- loners/staying on the fringes or margins of activities;
- seeking friendships with other age groups;
- aggressive towards peers;
- clingy/precocious;
- disruptive;
- spoiling other children's play;
- immaturity;
- poor self image ('I can't do this', 'My drawing's rubbish!', 'Boring!')
- high anxiety;
- attention seeking;
- restless and easily distracted;
- tearful/irritable/moody;
- capable of tantrums;
- distant, 'off with the fairies'.

Supporting the historical learning of children with learning difficulties

Context – Year 4 class, children coming into the classroom after lunchtime break.

Teacher: 'Come in, that's right. Put your indoor shoes on, get your topic books and sit down please. Please don't mess around with the coins on the tables, you'll have a chance in a minute, we're going to look at old money. Hurry up now. If you're already sitting down you can put today's date in your books. Who are we waiting for?'

By this time the majority of the class are seated and attentive. However, Michael, a child with learning difficulties, is still looking for his topic book and as a result he has not been listening to anything else the teacher has said since that point.

Where a teacher has suspicions that a child is experiencing learning difficulties advice and guidance ought to be sought from those with relevant expertise and experience, such as parents, speech therapists and the school's SENCO, as any strategies employed will need to fit with the school's SEN policy and procedures. Breaking a history lesson down into shorter, more manageable tasks in which the opportunities for success are increased and the requirement for sustained concentration is decreased, is one option. Pupils with learning difficulties are more likely to work best and stay on task longer in situations where routines are clearly understood, where they are able to exercise some control over their work with support and where work is set at an appropriate level. Similarly taking care to avoid overly long strings of instructions during history lessons and activities is useful as the example above shows. Teacher-centred or high pupil autonomy approaches to history (for example, *chalk and talk*, dictation, note-taking from books or unstructured/free writing) are the least effective teaching methods to employ.

Children with language difficulties will need plenty of opportunity for reinforcement and repetition and using and applying similar vocabulary and ideas in different contexts. Teachers may need to keep referring to previous work and experience to help children make links and sense of what is going on. Scaffolding the development of children's observational skills through careful questioning, introduction to artefacts and site visits which foster description, attention to detail, asking their own questions and looking at similarities and differences are effective in supporting pupils' gradual progress. Some children with language and communication difficulties, such as dyslexia, can find concepts such as chronology difficult to grasp. Children with autism may also find particular aspects of history especially challenging such as the use of empathy, group tasks and, once again, the concepts of chronology. Using personal life stories is one way of introducing the passage of time. Other useful strategies include simple sequencing tasks using 'hands-on' experience with historical artefacts and avoiding traditional approaches in which dates predominate. Story too can be a useful way of helping children to be aware of other times but teachers should not be surprised to find the Victorians and the dinosaurs coexisting on occasion. Other approaches to the task of developing a more inclusive history curriculum for pupils with learning difficulties include

- the use of computers which can act as a stimulus to children who lack confidence in their literacy skills or who are autistic (Siddles, 1999);
- developing readings that are more appropriate by adapting, simplifying and translating historical texts and documents into language that is easier for the children to understand.
- precising documents into single paragraphs or short sentences;
- teachers reading with or for a child and teachers acting as scribe;
- long-winded or difficult documentation can be tape-recorded and the children allowed to listen to it as they read;
- marking pages in reference books to enable children to find the information they want more easily;
- key words can be employed to help children structure their findings, organize information and express themselves, rather than asking them to *write about it;*
- written tasks and questions can be put on a white/blackboard or onto worksheets and writing frames;
- using shorter, less complex sentences that draw on concrete, first-hand experience;
- utilizing a range of non-text-based teaching methods. Class discussion means no writing but it cannot be sustained for too long, especially with younger pupils. Participation needs to be encouraged so teachers work around, rather than shoot down, incorrect or partial answers. Teachers also foster discussion of what other children have said in order to develop partial into more complete answers. Non-text-based activities could also include drama and socio-dramatic play, historical visits, guest speakers, oral history, story telling, work with a range of artefacts, producing replica artefacts or the use of visual prompts such as pictorial timetables.

Classroom support for a child with learning difficulties

Paul, a Year 5 pupil, experienced learning difficulties at school. He struggled with literacy and had great difficulty in organizing himself effectively. Paul often spent significant amounts of time searching for lost items and was usually the last to finish, if he finished at all. He found following instructions a challenge and often displayed a very limited concentration span, especially when reading or writing was involved. Paul's teacher discussed ways of supporting Paul with the SENCO who sat down with Paul one lunchtime and talked to him about how to get ready for work. In collaboration with Paul the SENCO drew up a checklist which Paul could use at the start of lessons to help him get off to a prompt start. Paul's teacher made sure that Paul used his checklist in her history lesson and amended the list in order to include the history materials and equipment necessary for the task. She also produced a key word list and some abridged information that Paul could use.

As the table on pages 167–9 shows, some learning difficulties can result in disruptive behaviour. Children with emotional and behavioural difficulties or AD(H)D may struggle to concentrate and focus on a task for the same length of time as their peers. It is often assumed that children with behavioural problems are seeking attention and that they obtain satisfaction from that attention. However, children with EBD or AD(H)D may not be enjoying their behaviour any more than their teachers. Some of the difficulties that these pupils present may therefore be susceptible to some modification and improvement over time by examining and altering the setting in which the children's behaviour manifests itself. Looking at when and where disruption occurs is the first step in this process.

Children may become difficult for a teacher to manage

- during particular sorts of lessons (such as sessions in which there is little structure and direction);
- at particular times of the day;
- when particular methods of classroom organization are chosen;
- when the teacher is doing certain things;
- when the child is asked to do certain things.

The situation may be exacerbated when

- teachers respond in certain ways;
- other children do certain things.

Where difficulties do occur with, for example, EBD, AD(H)D or autistic pupils, it is important to try to remain as calm as possible and there will be times when this will require near superhuman self-control on the part of the teacher. Trying to keep the child productively engaged and on task is the aim and liaison with non-teaching support staff on the best ways of providing extra support in group settings can be helpful. Autistic pupils, for example, may respond better to statements, instructions and directions rather than asking questions and demanding choices. Appropriate pacing of lessons too can make a big difference to children with learning difficulties.

The need for appropriate strategies

Simon (Year 2) experienced emotional and behavioural difficulties. Simon's teacher had alerted her student teacher to this fact and had made recommendations about how lessons should be organized and managed, particularly in terms of pacing and timing and what could be expected of Simon and his ability to stay on task. During an afternoon lesson on the Vikings Simon presented himself to the student teacher and made it clear that he had had enough. The student did not realize what was about to happen and instead of trying to divert the impending crisis or offering additional support, he told Simon that he would be the judge of when Simon had had enough. A few seconds later chairs started to fly around the room as children scattered for cover. The student teacher realizing his mistake held on to Simon's arms and tried to calm him down by talking to him. He then told Simon that he was going to stop holding Simon's hands and that he wanted him to take a deep breath and then they could talk about how he could help Simon. He let go and Simon grabbed a pair of scissors from the desk and lunged at the student's face.

The following strategies can be effective in supporting the learning of pupils with learning difficulties and in lowering the incidence of disruption

- Develop a clear and logical progression through a task. A lack of structure to lessons, coupled with deadtime and a lack of supervision are likely to encourage pupils to misbehave.
- Establish conventions and routines that reduce the need for constant teacher instruction at key points during the day such as transition times. Structured approaches, which involve routines and clear expectations, are important.
- Class discussion can be particularly challenging for some children with learning difficulties as it requires pupils to be patient and to listen to each other as well as to the teacher. Commit yourself to a long-term investment of teacher time and energy in order to persuade some children to observe conventions associated with whole-class speaking and listening.
- Develop your ability to anticipate events. Classroom layouts that create blindspots are likely to exacerbate problems of disruption and task avoidance.
- Unwanted behaviour, such as aggression, may result from frustration and alienation or may be because the child has never learned or been taught strategies for resolving conflict and confrontation. There may be ways in which the child can be assisted in modifying their behaviour and developing new strategies for coping with school. Teach children to verbalize anger, for example by asking for artefacts or reference materials to be returned or expressing their feelings, and then praise and reward them for doing it.
- Monitor pupil progress, provide positive feedback and include children with learning difficulties in setting simple goals and targets that can be achieved within a short period.
- Give specific targeted historical tasks such as a practical sequencing activity, short pieces of writing or illustration/drawing tasks.
- Offer an easy task to do, stay with the pupil while the task is completed and make sure positive feedback is given. Success in one area can transfer to other areas.
- Find out what a child with EBD or AD(H)D sees as a reward and ensure that they are rewarded when they show determination and perseverance.

- Be prepared to step in quickly once you have spotted the build up of disruptive behaviour. Capitalize on the impact that your presence as the teacher can have. It is sometimes possible to head off, divert or defuse an imminent outburst. On occasion the use of humour (although not at the expense of the child) is an effective strategy for easing the tension. Similarly teachers can attempt to distract a child before a crisis is reached by asking questions, offering a change of task, a change of location or a simple housekeeping chore that they enjoy and which confers responsibility on them for which they can receive praise and recognition.

173

The demands of behavioural difficulties

Philip, a Year 3 child, came to Miss B in September with a reputation. She had been told that Philip had emotional and behavioural difficulties and, amongst other things, had a claim to fame for saying, 'F**k off. I hate you all. I'm going to cut myself' to his previous teacher and her class. Miss B soon realized that Philip would often make provocative remarks just loud enough for other children to hear, resulting in their reporting it and thus Philip gained Miss B's attention and the lesson would be disrupted. After liaising with the SENCO, Miss B instituted a series of measures to try and reduce the incidence of disruptive outbursts. During her history lesson on Roman soldiers she made sure that Philip received praise for making constructive contributions to the class discussion and for putting his hand up and not calling out. Philip was a bright child and had no difficulty in understanding or keeping up with the pace of the lesson. When she realized that Philip was starting to put his hand up at every opportunity, simply to attract her attention or gain positive recognition, she moved the lesson on. The children were going to produce child-size figures of Roman soldiers that they would label. Miss B made sure that Philip played an active part in drawing round one of the 'legionaries'. While the children were working in groups she ensured that he had access to a reference book in which he could locate information on the various items of a Roman soldier's kit. She also made sure that she was able to monitor the group dynamics and stepped in quickly at one point to defuse a disagreement and mediate in Philip's relationships with the other children. During the plenary session at the end of the afternoon Philip was one of those selected to come to the front to address the class and answer a question. Philip seemed to appreciate the public recognition and Miss B made clear the linkage between his selection and his behaviour during the lesson. During the clearing up period she asked Philip to take responsibility for collecting up the reference books and putting them back on her desk as Philip often responded well to such special tasks. Just before the bell went Miss B praised the class for their hard work singling out one or two children in particular, including Philip, and awarded each of the groups a merit point. As usual Philip was reluctant to go home at the end of the day and wanted to talk about 'his' soldier. When he had finally gone Miss B sat down wearily and began to think about the following day!

Gifted and Talented Pupils

Exact definitions of what constitutes giftedness are hard to produce. All teachers encounter pupils who are bright but giftedness suggests abilities that exceed those of even their very able peers. It is important to be aware of the wider curriculum when considering gifted and talented pupils; a child might be an average reader but an outstanding artist or technologist, they might be quick thinking and creative but have writing skills that are less well developed. There is considerable debate over the concept of giftedness and singling out children as gifted has been seen by some as potentially damaging (i.e. parental pressure, raising of expectations that put undue pressure on a child). The arguments can be further complicated by the suggestion that singling out pupils as gifted is an elitist approach to education. However, if there are children in mainstream education who are very able then ensuring that their needs are met ought to be seen as an equal opportunities issue rather than elitism (Ofsted, 1994).

Children who are considered gifted in a particular area are likely to be capable of pursuing their learning in greater depth and at a faster pace than their peers. Such abilities can themselves cause difficulties. Pupils can easily become bored and disruptive, can dominate their more average peers and be intolerant, they may be hypersensitive to criticism and rejection, they can become troubled by their difference and be tempted to underachieve to conform. Gifted children may also frighten or annoy their teachers. The speed and pace at which these children often work as well as the high levels of autonomy and independence of which they are capable can make great demands on already overloaded professionals. It is possible to feel intimidated by the level of questioning that gifted pupils may engage in during history lessons as teachers may worry about their own lack of historical knowledge and about whether they will be able to keep pace with the additional workload.

Gifted and talented pupils often

- demonstrate a thirst for knowledge;
- learn easily;
- are original, imaginative, creative;
- are persistent, resourceful, self-directed, determined and single-minded;
- are informed in unusual areas, often beyond their years;
- have an outstanding vocabulary, are verbally fluent;
- are artistic/musical;
- are sceptical/logical;
- have numerical fluency;
- are independent workers, show and take initiative;
- are versatile, have many interests;
- show unusual insight;
- exhibit unusually extroverted or introverted behaviour in a group;
- show speed and agility of thought and a preference for verbal rather than written expression;
- show leadership qualities.

(Advisory Services Unit, 1995)

Supporting the historical learning of gifted and talented children

Making room for extra ability

Katie was an extremely able Year 4 child. Although very able it was sometimes difficult to motivate her and she often *cruised*, doing just enough to meet the requirements of a lesson but no more. During a linked history and English topic on the Tudors Katie became very interested in accounts of Shakespeare and the Globe Theatre. She initiated her own research at home. She questioned her parents and her mother was able to give her some copies of Shakespeare's plays, which Katie brought into school one morning to show her teacher. Katie's teacher decided to capitalize on this sudden burst of enthusiasm and suggested to Katie that she might like to tell the class what she had found out at the end of the day. She offered Katie some time at lunchtime to work out what she would talk about and spent ten minutes reviewing Katie's plan with her. A quarter of an hour before the final bell Katie's teacher stopped the class and explained how Katie had brought some things to show and then introduced Katie's talk. Katie spoke for a few minutes showing her mother's plays and telling her peers what she had done and found out. Katie's teacher then chaired a short question-and-answer session.

Gifted and talented children can find that history offers them the sorts of intellectual and practical challenges that they need and trainee and newly qualified teachers may wish to access the National Association for Gifted Children website (www.rmplc.co.uk/orgs/nagc) for more information on this group of pupils. It is essential to maintain the interest and motivation of gifted and talented pupils by presenting curriculum content in clear and exciting ways. Furthermore, effective differentiation is a vital prerequisite for supporting the learning of gifted pupils as it ensures that the history curriculum that they encounter is more complex and challenging. If the special needs of gifted and talented pupils are not addressed then this potential is being ignored, risking the onset of underachievement, boredom and even disruptive behaviour. Although able to complete teacher-set tasks quickly, gifted pupils may benefit from opportunities to have additional time and being asked to study history in much greater depth than their peers. Teachers should not hesitate to use more challenging vocabulary and language with gifted pupils, as well as offering them a wider variety in methods of finding out. Research skills can be a particularly productive area in which gifted children can be challenged and this area fits well with their characteristic thirst for knowledge. Providing gifted children with the chance to use and apply historical ideas and skills in a range of different contexts puts gifted children in the position of having to make deductions, develop and test hypotheses and take their research into new areas. Gifted pupils can also be encouraged to share their historical learning and findings with others as a way of raising the historical knowledge and understanding of the whole class. Gifted and talented pupils therefore benefit from

- extension work and enrichment activities in history with greater depth and variety (some of which may be extra-curricular);
- encouragement to think at a higher level;
- the chance to solve demanding problems;
- project work with carefully prepared briefs;
- opportunities for autonomous work;
- opportunities to work at their own pace and cover the normal curriculum more quickly combined with opportunities to engage in sustained work without timetable interruptions;
- an enabling culture, in which there is a positive attitude from teachers towards high achievement;
- contact with non-gifted peers;
- contact with gifted peers;
- contact with adults;
- thoughtful teacher intervention, including inspiration, challenge and constructive criticism;
- opportunities for divergent thinking.

(Advisory Services Unit, 1995)

Reflective Questions

- Do you have clear and appropriate learning objectives for pupils with SEN when teaching history?
- Have you allowed sufficient time for pupils to complete tasks in history?
- Has the lesson been structured into a clear sequence of manageable chunks for pupils who may experience learning difficulties?
- Do you modify your exposition or instruction on the basis of the responses received?
- Do you use historical vocabulary and language at an appropriate level?
- Do you adjust your questions according to ability?
- Do you present tasks in history at an appropriate level of difficulty?
- Do you encourage children to set their own learning goals with support?
- Do you ensure that there are opportunities for success for all and do you provide regular and immediate feedback for pupils?
- Do you monitor the attainment of children with special educational needs and use the information to inform your decisions about progression?

(Westwood, 1997)

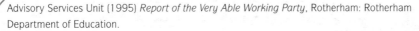

REFERENCES

Advisory Services Unit (1995) *Report of the Very Able Working Party*, Rotherham: Rotherham Department of Education.

Autism: Fact Sheets for Health Professionals, http://hna.ffh.vic.gov.au/yafs/cis/facts/autism

Autism-UK: Advice and Information, www.autism-uk.ed.ac.uk/advice.htm

Dean, J. (1993) *Managing Special Needs in the Primary School*, London and New York: Routledge.

Department for Education (DFE) (1993) *Education Act*, London: HMSO.

Department for Education (DFE) (1994) *Circular Number 9/94: The Education of Children with Emotional and Behavioural Difficulties*, London: DFE.

Department for Education and Science (DES) (1978) *Special Educational Needs (The Warnock Report)*, London: HMSO.

Department for Education and Science (DES) (1981) *Education Act*, London: HMSO.

DfEE (1997) *Excellence in Schools*, London: DfEE.

DfEE SEN website, www.dfee.gov.uk/sen

Gerland, G. (1997) *Finding out about Asperger Syndrome, High Functioning Autism and PDD*, London: Jessica Kingsley Publishers.

Macintyre, C. (2000) *Dyspraxia in the Early Years*, London: David Fulton Publishers.

Office for Standards in Education (Ofsted) (1994) *Exceptionally Able Children: October 1993 Report of Conferences*, London: DFE.

Qualifications and Curriculum Authority (QCA) (1999a) *The National Curriculum: Handbook for Primary Teachers in England*, London: DfEE/QCA.

Qualifications and Curriculum Authority (QCA) (1999b) *Circular 44/99 Shared World – Different Experiences: Designing the Curriculum for Pupils who are Deafblind*, London: QCA Publications.

Siddles, R. (1999) 'Teaching children with autistic spectrum disorders in mainstream primary schools', in L. Smeardon (ed.) *The Autistic Spectrum – A Handbook 1999*, London: National Autistic Society.

Stirton, J. and Glover, C. (1998) 'A code in the head: special educational needs in the mainstream classroom', in A. Cashdan and L. Overall *Teaching in Primary Schools*, London and New York: Cassell.

Turner, A. (2000) 'Redefining the past: Ofsted, SLD schools and the teaching of history', *British Journal of Special Education*, Vol. 27, No. 2, June 2000.

Westwood, P. (1997) *Commonsense Methods for Children with Special Needs*, 3rd edition, London and New York: Routledge.

www.rmplc.co.uk/orgs/nagc

9 Coordinating History Across the School

The introduction of the National Curriculum in England and Wales in 1989 placed new pressures on primary school teachers in terms of their subject expertise. Teachers were faced with the task of developing their understanding and capabilities across a broad range of subjects. Subsequent developments in the Foundation Stage may have a similar impact on teachers of the 3–5 age range. In many primary schools the response to these developments since 1989 has been to appoint curriculum coordinators for specific areas including subjects such as history. The idea of curriculum coordinators was not new in 1989–90. It had, however, been an underdeveloped idea (Bentley and Watts, 1994) and developments in primary education since 1989 have done much to accelerate the process of reappraising what the role involves. This reappraisal has resulted in a move away from seeing coordination posts as rewards for general competence, resulting from long service and experience, towards much more precise definitions of the role involving specific curriculum responsibilities. The intention is to enable nurseries and schools to capitalize upon the collective subject strengths amongst their staff (Alexander *et al.*, 1992, p. 21) by giving coordinators responsibility for curriculum planning in their subject areas, for the organization of resources and for leading staff development. All teachers are now expected to shoulder some degree of curriculum responsibility. Titles vary and include curriculum coordinator, post holder and subject leader. In addition team leaders may also find that history or the early ideas about history contained in the Early Learning Goals are also part of their concern. This chapter will use the term coordinator to encompass all these titles.

For many primary school teachers the skills and knowledge associated with curriculum coordination would appear to have been caught not taught (Webb, 1994, p. 64). If the potential of curriculum coordinators for enhancing the quality of teaching and learning within history is to be realized fully this state of affairs must be altered. Many newly qualified teachers have to take on the increasingly complex and accountable role of curriculum coordination early on in their careers and preparation for it is needed during ITT (Initial Teacher

Training). In small schools staff often have to take a lead in more than one subject area and in other situations staff are asked to take on subject areas for which they have only a minimal subject background even though they may be very experienced as coordinators in other contexts. This chapter is aimed at supporting teacher training students with a subject specialism in history and newly qualified teachers for whom history was a non-core, non-specialist subject to take a lead in the development of the subject across a school.

The chapter begins with an overview of the role of a history coordinator in supporting teaching and learning across a school and continues with a discussion of some of the challenges facing any coordinator who is attempting to introduce changes in the history curriculum. The chapter then takes a situation faced by a history coordinator following receipt of an Ofsted (Office for Standards in Education) inspection report and uses her responses to this report to introduce some of the key skills that history coordinators need in order to be successful. The chapter includes an analysis of the issues raised in the report and illustrates the importance of effective organizational and planning skills. The areas for improvement are raised at a staff meeting and the coordinator, therefore, has to be an effective communicator. Finally, the school decides to make use of some inservice training time to begin to tackle one of the areas for improvement requiring the coordinator to be effective in motivating colleagues, as well as leading and facilitating team work with other staff. The chapter concludes with the outcome of this process in the form of a revised policy statement and a set of guidelines for history across the school.

Roles and Responsibilities of History Coordinators

 . . . . *Nursery/Infant/Junior School*

Job description

Class teacher/History Coordinator, CPS (Common Pay Spine)

General duties
- To take responsibility for a Year 2 class. This responsibility includes:
  - the planning, preparation, delivery and assessment of a varied and relevant curriculum;
  - ensuring a stimulating, active learning environment for pupils through good classroom organization and display;
  - motivating children by personal influence and by awareness of needs.

- To work as part of the staff team, adhering to the school's behaviour policy, showing consideration to colleagues, assisting in curriculum development and involvement in extra-curricular activities.

Specific responsibilities
- To be responsible for the development of the history curriculum across the school to ensure breadth and balance, progression and continuity.
- To develop and maintain the history policy, guidelines and schemes of work.
- To keep up to date with local and national developments in the history curriculum.
- To liaise where appropriate with other curriculum coordinators.
- To lead staff development in history.
- To support teaching and learning in history across the school.
- To be responsible for monitoring and purchasing resources for history across the school.

Although at first glance the job description above may appear straightforward the reality can be very different. Some subjects, like history, had not been well defined in primary schools prior to 1989–90, or had been part of something else; in the case of history this often involved being subsumed into broader environmental and/or local studies topics. Nor has the appearance of documentation outlining the content and nature of history (DFE, 1995; QCA, 1999a) led to a sudden and coherent upsurge of teaching in this area. The introduction of literacy and numeracy strategies has had a significant impact on the opportunities for teaching and learning in the foundation subjects generally. Similarly, parallel changes to the priorities for initial teacher training (DfEE, 1998a) are also likely to impact upon the preparedness of some newly qualified teachers to deliver quality teaching in history and other Foundation subjects in years to come. The introduction of the Desirable Outcomes for Children's Learning (SCAA, 1996) and the Early Learning Goals (QCA, 1999b) have added a further dimension to the need to develop progression and continuity in this area. National documentation alone cannot overcome the varied preconceptions concerning the nature of a subject like history, although it may go some way towards addressing the lack of subject knowledge amongst some teachers. Overcoming this problem is likely to constitute one aspect of the history coordinator's role.

Managing resources and the production of school documentation for the subject (e.g. policy statements, schemes of work and guidance for colleagues) are two more areas which are the responsibility of the coordinator. These are also areas where curriculum coordinators have already made an impact in primary schools (Alexander *et al.*, 1992, p. 37; Webb, 1994, pp. 59–61). Such work is important in laying some of the foundations for good practice in teaching history. The establishment of Ofsted in 1992 and the stated intention to inspect all primary schools on a four-yearly basis have given an added impetus to ensuring that school documentation is in place. Curriculum organization and delivery also form part of the coordinator's management and planning responsibilities. Alexander *et al.* (1992, pp. 16–19) drew a distinction between curriculum conception and curriculum organization and the history coordinator will be expected therefore to take a lead in discussions over the integration of subjects, as well as teaching approaches, techniques and methods.

Central to the role of the history coordinator is their responsibility to improve the quality of teaching and learning within the subject area across the whole school. The work of Alexander and others (1992, pp. 20–1) emphasized the importance of 'curricular expertise' as a precursor to quality in teaching and stressed the need for coordinators to possess such expertise. Curricular expertise includes a knowledge and an understanding of the subject, an understanding of the factors which promote effective learning and the possession of the skills needed to teach a subject successfully. Subject expertise needs to be developed across two broad areas. The first should relate to knowledge and practice within the school; the second should relate to knowledge and practice outside the school, at local, national and, at times, international levels (Bentley and Watts, 1994, p. 160). History specialists will have a degree of expertise upon which to build when becoming practising teachers. Once in post there will be the opportunity to develop expertise in the first area, within their own schools, through practical experiences gained while working with pupils and alongside other colleagues. Support in developing the second, wider area of expertise might be offered through local in-service provision but such opportunities are limited and may not be available in some authorities.

History coordinators charged with promoting quality teaching and learning across the school not only have to update their own subject expertise but also have to be capable of disseminating such expertise to others. School-based dissemination could involve working alongside colleagues in their classrooms or conducting curriculum development meetings. Such dissemination ought to be based, at least in part, upon the coordinator's own school-based assessments and evaluation. Coordinators, therefore, need to consider their role as educators, advisors and facilitators (Bentley and Watts, 1994) as the educating, advising and facilitating component of the coordinator's role brings interpersonal skills into sharp relief alongside subject expertise.

- As an educator you will have to help your colleagues to develop their own subject knowledge and understanding in history. Inspiring and motivating colleagues has to be underpinned by an ability to empower and enskill those colleagues. Insufficient attention to the latter can undermine attempts to inspire and motivate by reinforcing feelings of inadequacy, both real and imagined, amongst staff.
- As an advisor you will need to have an eye to future developments in the teaching of history and be able to communicate not only with colleagues but also with parents and governors and the headteacher in the school.
- As a facilitator you will need to create a climate of trust and openness in which change can occur. To be effective as a leader you have to become effective as a supporter.

(Bentley and Watts, 1994, pp. 159–60)

181

Curriculum coordination, therefore, has become an increasingly complex task. It requires the incumbent not only to concentrate on their subject expertise but also, and crucially, upon their interpersonal skills and their ability to motivate and lead colleagues. Inservice training can only go part way towards developing subject expertise. Curriculum coordinators will have to underpin such training opportunities that do exist by developing autonomous strategies to promote and enhance their subject expertise through self-directed research. In addition, curriculum coordinators are becoming increasingly accountable as a result of parallel developments in education (Webb, 1994, p. 59); not least teacher appraisal and Ofsted inspections. The remainder of the chapter seeks to identify some of the key issues facing history coordinators and to highlight some of the key skills that such a task requires.

The Impact of Curriculum Change and Development

Dear Lord,
Give me the serenity to accept what I cannot change,
Give me the courage to change what I can,
And give me the wisdom to distinguish between the two.
                                        Notice above a Sheffield headteacher's desk

To varying degrees and at different times, history coordinators will be engaged in planned change and they need to recognize the feelings that such change may inspire in some of their colleagues. Many nursery and primary teachers could be forgiven for concluding that the only certainty in their professional lives currently is change. Even a cursory glance at just some of the curriculum changes experienced by teachers in the ten years prior to 2000 illustrates the point: Desirable Learning Outcomes (SCAA, 1996); Early Learning Goals and the Foundation Stage (QCA, 1999b); National Curriculum and Key Stages 1 and 2 (DES, 1989; DFE, 1995; QCA, 1999a); National Literacy Strategy (DfEE, 1998b); National Numeracy Strategy (DfEE, 1999). Many assumptions are made about change and those who support or oppose it. For some, change always has to justify itself while the *status quo* never does, 'if it ain't broke, don't fix it'. For others, supporters of change are portrayed as progressive, positive and forward looking, while critics of change are characterized as reactionary, negative, backward looking or 'the forces of conservatism'. Both positions are flawed. The first can foster complacency while the second is both arrogant and simplistic.

Everyone can find themselves supporting or opposing change depending upon their circumstances and the changes proposed. The feelings of those affected by change and the extent to which they are acknowledged will affect the success or otherwise of a coordinator in achieving their goals. This section will therefore outline some of the reactions that history coordinators may encounter while trying to develop their subject across the 3–11 age range.

Factors both external and internal to the nursery/school can be involved in initiating change. Some changes prove more long lasting than others, for example those that originate nationally and are backed by the force of legislation clearly have considerable impetus. Partly as a result of national developments, changes that are internally inspired may have a much less certain future even though they may be more in tune with the development needs of the nursery/school. It can be a daunting prospect for a history coordinator to try to make a case for history to be a priority across the school in the face of core curriculum pressures and the everyday strains and pressures placed on teachers. It can be equally difficult to argue the case for externally imposed changes that few teachers have had any say in devising and external pressures can be used as reasons for not taking on internal changes.

Change in a nursery, school or educational system implies corresponding changes in the individuals working in that organization. Although the changes demanded of individuals may range from major to trifling, most people are concerned by change to a greater or lesser extent and some people will actively resist it. Whilst these situations can offer teachers opportunities to do things differently and be creative, they can also be uncomfortable and worrying experiences for those affected, particularly when colleagues feel as though they are being asked to make alterations to their practice on a number of fronts simultaneously. History coordinators need only to reflect on their own feelings about changes in areas of their work where they are not the expert in order to appreciate the feelings of their colleagues. Curriculum change, therefore, can threaten the stability of teachers, causing anxiety about the new skills and knowledge needed. In some cases the concerns may be rational and based on a professional assessment of the proposals. In other instances the concerns, worries and consequent resistance may be more emotional in nature. Proposed changes to the history curriculum across a school could result in

- the disruption of established routines and practices established in the old documentation for the subject;
- the loss of existing benefits, such as possible redundancy of old resources;
- perceived threats to teacher status through the loss of confidence and self-esteem in situations where the changes proposed require historical knowledge and skills from staff who do not feel equipped;
- loss of previously held beliefs and ideas, for example colleagues who feel history is an inappropriate concern for those working with the younger children;

• anxiety for staff whose own history experiences at school were less than satisfactory and who as a result do not 'like' history.

History coordinators need to take both forms of concern seriously, as both are interrelated. Taking some time to try to understand why colleagues feel as they do about history as a subject is worthwhile as they may well have very valid reasons for their reactions. If a coordinator is to be successful in bringing about curriculum development in history, they will need to reassure colleagues about their fears, ensure that they feel empowered rather than deskilled and persuade them of the potential benefits of any change. For example, how will proposed changes to the history curriculum improve teaching and pupil attainment and learning? Making change happen is hard work and history coordinators have to accept that change is a process, not an event. It takes time and trying to ensure that changes and improvements to the teaching and learning of history are successful means of making the most of some key skills.

Responding to colleagues' concerns about change

- Your style matters. Offer leadership and set an example. Take care over focusing on the task and forgetting about the people. Your colleagues are more likely to respond positively to initiatives that are led by a coordinator who is well prepared, enthusiastic, caring and aware of group dynamics.
- You need to be clear in your own mind on why you wish to change. What problem will be overcome? What improvements on existing practice and achievements will be gained?
- You will need to be well organized. *Planning and preparation prevent poor performance.*
- Set some short-term achievable goals as nothing succeeds and motivates like success.
- Communicate like never before and that means listening as well as talking. It may be therapeutic, cathartic and even an essential part of the process of change to give your colleagues the opportunity to have a good moan before they can begin to face up to the need for change.
- Think about what you will need to do to reduce the amount of resistance and increase the amount of commitment to the changes proposed. Ensuring early involvement can help to ensure 'all hands on deck'.
- Think about what sort of help and support you will need to provide:

  - **Empowerment and enskilling**: increasing knowledge and skills, reinforcing current thinking, encouraging issues to be viewed from different perspectives.
  - **Relevance**: offer support that is focused and specific to the age range(s) concerned, as colleagues can see direct curriculum development benefits and application to their classroom practice. Offer a balance of approaches, such as working with colleagues, sharing experiences or well-structured workshops.
  - **Realism**: think about the timing and the energy levels of staff when planning the support that you can offer.

Responding to an Ofsted Report: Key Skills for History Coordinators

The remaining sections of the chapter will use a history coordinator's attempts to respond to an Ofsted inspection report (below) as a way of highlighting some of the skills and strategies that coordinators need to develop if they are to be successful in improving teaching and learning in the subject.

Ofsted inspection comments for teaching and learning in history

107. Attainment in history in both Key Stage 1 and 2 is in line with national expectations. In Key Stage 1 pupils are developing a sense of chronology. They can also give some valid reasons for people's actions and past events. By the end of Key Stage 2 most pupils are able to combine information from a variety of sources and make inferences and deductions. They have a sound general knowledge of the Tudors, Vikings and Ancient Egypt. Progress in both Key Stages is good.

108. Pupils' attitudes to learning history are good. They are interested in the topics and study units, answer questions with enthusiasm and concentrate well.

109. In the small number of lessons observed, the quality of teaching was sound. Teachers' subject knowledge is secure. Individual lessons are well planned with clear learning objectives. More precise references to the programmes of study would aid both progression and assessment of pupils' attainment and progress.

110. The new coordinator has not yet had time to make a significant impact, nor has she had the opportunity to benefit from inservice training. The policy and guidelines for the subject need updating to bring them into line with the rest of the school's documentation. The role of the coordinator in monitoring curriculum development and the quality of teaching is not yet in place. The subject is adequately resourced and pupils' work is displayed well. The history curriculum is significantly enriched by school visits.

Preparing for Change: Planning and Organizing

The above report highlights the need for effective organization and planning if the history coordinator is to be successful in responding to the areas identified for improvement and to build on those aspects in which standards were already satisfactory. The overwhelming majority of coordinators in nursery and primary settings receive little or no non-contact time in which to pursue their coordination responsibilities. The job has to be done in addition to all the other tasks facing them as class teachers. Effective personal organization and time management are therefore clearly essential precursors to success in the role of history coordinator.

Like any valuable resource time needs to be budgeted and coordinators need to be efficient at getting the most out of it.

Strategies for improving your organization and efficiency as a coordinator

- Do not try to keep everything in your head. Use a diary.
- Draw up work plans on a daily, weekly or termly basis that distinguish between tasks that must be done, those that should be done, those that would be pleasant to do and those that other people could do.
- Make sure that longer-term work plans give an indication of the time scales and deadlines involved.
- Be realistic about the amount of time that can be devoted to any one task.
- Review how your time is spent and look for ways in which more time could be made available for completing your tasks as a coordinator.
- Do not allow yourself to become overloaded or deflected from your objectives. If necessary learn how to say '*No*' from time to time, alternatively '*I can do it but not until . . .*', or '*I can do it but only if . . .*'.

Miss N., the coordinator for history, had the job of leading the school's efforts to respond to the areas in history identified for improvement by the inspectors. For Miss N. to be successful in responding to the report she had to manage her time effectively in order to be able to think and plan ahead. Miss N.'s first task was to analyse and summarize the Ofsted findings. Having done this and drawn up a draft plan of action for eventual inclusion in the school's development plan she then needed to consider the best way of communicating her ideas to her colleagues and eliciting their thoughts and reactions. Having drawn up her draft response to the inspection report Miss N. discussed the best way of keeping colleagues informed and getting feedback and suggestions from them with her headteacher. The headteacher agreed to make some time available during one of the weekly staff meetings at which Miss N. would be able to present her action plan for discussion.

Below is a copy of the draft action plan which was produced in response to inspection findings.

Targets	Criteria for success	Action	Member(s) of staff responsible	By when	Completed on
To improve documenta-tion for history in the school	• Produce policy and guidelines for history • Produce scheme of work for history	• Draft action plan to be drawn up by Coordinator	Coordinator	End of Autumn Term	
		• Draft action plan to be reviewed/adapted/approved by staff	All staff		
		• Draft documentation to be produced by coordinator	Coordinator		
		• Draft documentation to be reviewed/adapted/approved by staff	All staff		

Targets	Criteria for success	Action	Member(s) of staff responsible	By when	Completed on
To enhance subject expertise of history coordinator	• Attend LEA training courses for history	• Agree funding for staff training with governors • Obtain copy of LEA Inset provision and apply	Headteacher Coordinator	By end of academic year	
To institute monitoring of the history curriculum	• Planning for history is reviewed • History teaching is observed in classrooms • History resources are recorded	• Arrange staff meeting to discuss and agree systems for coordinator to review history planning • Draw up timetable for classroom observations • Conduct audit of history resources across the school	All staff Headteacher/ Coordinator in consultation with staff Coordinator	By end of academic year	
To make increased use of National Curriculum documenta-tion in planning for history	• Long-term plans clearly state relevant PoS • Medium and short-term planning is based on whole-school plans	• Use new policy and guidelines and map out history coverage across the year groups • Check that reference to relevant PoS appears in planning • Check that lesson objectives are informed by the National Curriculum during peer observation	Coordinator All staff Coordinator Coordinator	By end of Spring Term	
To improve assessment and recording of pupil attainment in history	• Class records to include history • Agreement amongst staff about levels at Key Stages 1 and 2 • Informative reporting to parents	• Create resource of benchmarked history work • Organize moderation meetings • Develop exemplar material to support report writing	All Staff Coordinator Coordinator	By end of Summer Term	

Communication Skills

People learn about communication from their earliest days, a significant proportion of early school experiences are aimed at improving communication skills and almost everything teachers do in the classroom involves communication of one sort or another. As a result teachers should be experts. Yet effective communication can present coordinators with a challenge given the nature of teaching and an oft-made error concerning communication is the assumption that it has actually taken place.

In some cases the situations in which communication takes place are poorly chosen, for example in a corridor or during a lesson in which there is too much noise and staff are too busy to take things in properly or to respond. In others there may be a history of poor communication and relationships resulting in mistrust of any message, for example colleagues may feel that they only ever receive the bare minimum of information and that they are being kept only partially in the picture. Communication that takes place at too short notice, so that by the time staff are involved messages are late or worse, out of date, does little to dispel feelings of being the last to know. Communication that is too one-sided has a similar impact as staff feel that they are not included or asked for their views and opinions and the message is simply delivered as a *fait accompli.* A further impediment to effective communication involves excessive use of jargon in education and unfamiliar acronyms that can intimidate the listener while ambiguity can creep in where words have more than one meaning and no clarification is possible or allowed. Finally, coordinators need to exercise care over bringing about information overload in which the timescale involved is too short and too many topics are involved.

At the core of some of the problems that face coordinators in nurseries and schools is a communications breakdown. Where communication is poor, rumours are rife, information is inaccurate, fear and uncertainty thrive and there can be a breakdown in trust. A history coordinator who fails to communicate effectively with his/her colleagues may create considerable resistance to change. Involvement is crucial and colleagues should be regarded as active participants in the development of

Technique	Advantages	Disadvantages
Informal conversation	Fast, less intimidating, free ranging	Inconsistent and unreliable leading to a 'Chinese whispers' effect, often forgettable
Meetings	Consistent, provide good feedback	Require planning and chairing skills Can reduce input from less confident colleagues
Noticeboards	Good for communicating simple information such as dates and times	Have to be maintained and kept up-to-date, may not be referred to, no immediate feedback
Documentation	Consistent, available for future reference	May not be followed or read
Peer review	Offers scope for in-depth discussion and exchange of views	Can be intimidating or threatening, needs a sensitive as well as professional approach

the history curriculum even though the coordinator carries the responsibility and must take the lead. This is true even in situations where the changes proposed are radical and far-reaching. While it is possible that other staff may not be as familiar or knowledgeable about the history curriculum as the coordinator, they are still experienced professional practitioners who will be well able to think intelligently about the implications. Consequently coordinators need to get their colleagues involved early, listen to their thoughts and concerns and discuss what they think should be done, when and by whom. This early involvement in formulating proposals for change helps to reduce resistance and without some degree of commitment on the part of staff to the need for change, the history coordinator is unlikely to be successful in his/her attempts to develop and improve teaching and learning across the school. The table on page 188 shows some of the communication methods open to coordinators.

Verbal communication

Confusing or conflating information and communication is risky, only one of them suggests a two-way process involving listening as well as speaking. This two-way traffic helps to make people feel involved, it also helps in checking that people understand one another and share an agreed view of what is required. Face-to-face communication in its various forms is a valuable strategy for coordinators as it offers good opportunities to give praise and recognition, as well as providing feedback to coordinators on their own performance and effectiveness. Being accessible and visible as the person responsible for developments in teaching and learning across the school is an effective way of 'taking the temperature' of colleagues on the topic of history and much of this type of communication is informal in nature. In more formal circumstances, such as staff meetings, coordinators need to acquire a sense of audience and use this to inform what they say. This is true not only in terms of content but also in terms of style and delivery. Parents, for example, may not be as concerned with the minutiae of alterations to the history curriculum as staff who will have to implement them. Similarly, reporting to governors on progress in implementing action contained in a school's development plan is likely to require a different style from that needed for a thirty-minute peer review meeting with a colleague at lunchtime.

A number of elements play a part in getting the message across to listeners who will interpret not just the words but also the tone and the accompanying non-verbal body language. The latter two elements may well be at least as influential as the words themselves. When disseminating information in this way it is a good idea to avoid the assumption that once will be enough. Communication needs to be consistent and continuous and history coordinators will need to check back on occasion to confirm that there is a shared understanding about what has been said. Timing too is important and colleagues need information and opportunities to communicate in good time, when they are in a position to listen and ask questions and not at the last minute or while a dozen other things are happening around them simultaneously.

Listening is an important part of communication

Appear interested

- Make eye contact
- Face the speaker
- Maintain a relaxed and open posture (avoid folded arms and stern expressions)
- Make interested and encouraging noises and gestures (Hmmm, yes, nod, smile)

Be interested

- Analyse what your colleagues are saying, for example, what is not being said?
- Avoid interrupting except in the interests of democracy, for example to give other colleagues a chance to contribute to a discussion.
- Listen to the tone of voice.
- Note the non-verbal signs.
- Clarify any points that you are not clear on by asking questions. Use
  - focused questions aimed at ascertaining specific details, for example, 'Did you . . .?', 'When did . . .?', 'How many . . .?', 'How long . . .?';
  - exploratory questions that allow people to provide general information and outline their views, positions, ideas and opinions, for example, 'What do you think about . . .?', 'Tell me about . . .';
  - clarification questions designed to demonstrate interest, elicit further information and investigate attitudes and ideas in more detail, for example, 'How do you mean?', 'Why do you say that?', 'Are you saying . . .?';
  - emotional questions, for example, 'How did you feel about . . .?';
  - behavioural questions, for example, 'How would you . . .?', 'What have you . . .?'.

Written communication

When engaged in written communication precision is particularly important as the dialogue and scope for questioning and clarification present in verbal discussion is absent. Coordinators need to aim for clarity and to try to avoid potential ambiguity in the text, anticipating and addressing any possible scope for misinterpretation. It is important not to be tempted to make things more complicated than they need to be in an attempt to appear wise. Using shorter sentences to avoid excessive punctuation and overblown paragraphs, coupled with a minimum use of jargon can all help to make things clear and unambiguous. Where the audience is not employed in education, for example parents or governors, they may have a very limited familiarity with the terms and acronyms in everyday use by teachers. Where jargon does have to be employed in the interests of brevity then some form of succinct explanation or glossary may be necessary. Coordinators should exercise great care contemplating the use of humour, as flippancy or forced jokiness can create an unprofessional impression and run the risk of offending some people. Any written communication should also be thoroughly checked for misspelled or misused vocabulary. Finally, relevance is extremely important. People are far more likely to read written material if they perceive the subject matter as something of relevance to them. Anything that proposes changes, no matter how small, to the way in which they do their job, is likely to be read carefully and should be drafted to reduce the incidence of misinterpretation to a minimum.

Taking a Lead: Chairing Staff Meetings

Organizing and leading meetings about the history curriculum will mean managing other people's time. Meetings can be a very useful forum for the exchange of ideas and are an effective method of communicating complicated information. They can also provide a venue for establishing a degree of agreement and consensus and can help to foster a commitment to a particular course of action or decision. Yet many people, including teachers and coordinators, find themselves uninspired and unenthusiastic at the prospect of a meeting either as an attendee or as the person running it. Meetings are sometimes regarded as a waste of time or worse as a distraction from the real task of the teacher which is to teach. Effective meetings are those where the person leading the meeting can balance the need to consider the task in hand, the group involved and the individuals making up the group. Coordinators leading meetings have to get the job done but they also have to make sure that the group functions as a team and that the individuals in the group feel valued. Failure to succeed in the task denies the group the feeling of satisfaction that comes with achievement. At the same time overemphasis on the task can lead to members of staff feeling undervalued.

How to make sure that your staff meetings are a disaster	How to encourage colleagues to see your staff meetings as useful and productive activities
Have a meeting for everything.	Ask yourself if a meeting is necessary. In some cases an alternative method of communication may be faster and more efficient. When trying to decide if you need a meeting ask yourself what the consequences would be if you did not hold the meeting.
Invite everyone to every meeting even if it's not relevant for them.	
Don't tell anyone what the meeting is for.	Have a clear objective or purpose for the meeting and share this with your colleagues.
Don't use an agenda.	
Don't worry about the venue, for example having insufficient space.	Ask yourself who needs/has to be there? Smaller groups tend to be more efficient when it comes to achieving the objectives/purposes set out. However, smaller groups do not necessarily think of everything or make the best decisions.
Arrive late, hot and bothered.	

continued

How to make sure that your staff meetings are a disaster	How to encourage colleagues to see your staff meetings as useful and productive activities
Try to cover too many items in the meeting. Dominate the discussion. Shoot down other people's ideas and contributions whenever you can. Be sarcastic. Carry on a private conversation while someone else is speaking. Don't say anything. Let the meeting go on and on and on . . . Never take minutes. Never summarize the discussion and decisions in order to check on agreement. Never evaluate the success or otherwise of your meetings.	Enable colleagues to become active participants rather than passive recipients. Circulate the agenda beforehand (the agenda should show start time and duration), if documentation is under discussion make sure that those involved have a copy in advance and request that they read it prior to the meeting. Remember to chair the meeting, seek to involve and listen to everyone, seek clarification, note the time, keep the meeting on track (watch out for people sidetracking, getting off the point, introducing their pet topic). Move the process forward using non-verbal gestures or statements that draw people back to the original agenda, referee the discussion (argument and disagreement can be productive but it can also be hurtful if debate becomes aggression or bullying), try to avoid taking sides. Summarize the discussions; where necessary seek a decision and repeat the decision to all present as a check on understanding and agreement. Ensure that minutes are taken if you wish to avoid future arguments about who said what, when and what people did or did not agree to do. This is particularly important where the topic of the meeting involves detailed action planning and decision-making of any kind.

Miss N. made sure that she carefully planned her input to the weekly staff meeting, taking into account the fact that people were likely to be tired at the end of a day's teaching. Copies of her draft plan were circulated to colleagues beforehand and she timed her input to ensure that it did not drag on. During the staff meeting Miss N.'s draft proposals were agreed with minor modifications. The staff decided that the documentation for history would be the best place to start. It was agreed that a half-day would be made available during an inservice training day in October to review the school policy and guidelines.

Making Change Happen

Motivating colleagues

While being paid may motivate people to go to work, it does not necessarily result in people working hard or working well. Certainly, there can be few teachers who entered the profession because of the financial rewards. This is probably just as well from the point of view of history coordinators, many of whom will find themselves fulfilling their leadership role unpaid and at the same time having to find ways of motivating their colleagues in ways other than financial. Fortunately, motivation is a measure of the extent to which people will commit themselves to achieving things in order to satisfy their own needs and needs are complex things. They can be fulfilled in a variety of ways, both inside and outside the context of work. For example, we all have a need to feel safe and secure in our jobs but when our jobs are threatened in some way these needs become much more important and higher levels of needs, such as the need for recognition and achievement, diminish relatively in importance. Teachers can be motivated by

- their sense of vocation, dedication and commitment to the children;
- belonging to a supportive team;
- achievement and success;
- a sense of self-worth;
- external reward of some kind, such as allowances or holiday entitlement;
- a combination of these or other factors.

The factors that motivate teachers, therefore, could be seen as falling into two categories, extrinsic and intrinsic. Extrinsic factors do not necessarily improve a teacher's performance but if withdrawn or undermined they can certainly demotivate people. Extrinsic motivators can include pay, positive relationships with colleagues, high-quality leadership in the school, a high-quality working environment in which there is plenty of storage space, the roof does not leak and the heating systems work in the winter. Intrinsic motivators tend to result in moving people on, impelling them to want to do different things or the same things in different ways. Intrinsic motivators include factors such as feeling a sense of achievement, receiving recognition from your colleagues, parents or pupils, being given responsibility and some opportunity to be creative, having variety and interest in your job, or career advancement. It is possible that intrinsic motivators satisfy deeper needs relating to self-esteem and the realization of potential and as such they may be longer lasting. That said, extrinsic and intrinsic factors should not be seen as mutually exclusive or that one is inherently better than another.

There is little that a history coordinator can do directly to alter many of the extrinsic factors that contribute to staff morale. Consequently the focus tends to be upon the intrinsic factors. One strategy is to model motivated behaviour. If the history coordinator is not motivated about developments in the history curriculum, why should anyone else be? Other techniques include using praise in direct and focused ways and not taking credit for the efforts of others. Coordinators need to be alert to the warning signs that indicate a lack of motivation, for example absence, avoidance, lack of punctuality or poor per-formance. It is also important to remember that teachers have lives outside of the nursery/school and that these may impact upon their motivation at work. Trying to promote involvement in developments in the teaching and learning of history can also be effective in promoting a sense of ownership and motivation amongst colleagues. Involvement means keeping colleagues informed, seeking their ideas and suggestions and ensuring that people are clear on their roles and responsibilities. Coordinators need to set targets with colleagues which are realistic and attainable but that also stretch ability as this will develop a greater sense of achievement when they are met. Once agreed coordinators ought not to alter targets without consulting the staff concerned. They must also be prepared to show leadership as good leadership is an important factor in motivating people. Similarly, communicating with colleagues in a clear and honest fashion, for example expressing your thoughts and feelings as they really are, gives people confidence and promotes trust.

Working with others

Activities such as working alongside other teachers in their classrooms, developing whole-school initiatives or delivering inservice training to colleagues bring to the fore potential tensions in the coordinator's role. As a class teacher a coordinator is part of an essentially collegial ethos (Webb, 1994), one of the team. In their role as coordinator they are trying to influence the classroom practice of colleagues and, as such, find themselves placed in a semi-inspectorial position, one of the management. This tension can be exacerbated when the coordinator in question is newly or recently qualified and the colleague being educated, advised or monitored is an experienced member of staff. Working with colleagues in this way, therefore, places coordinators in a very different and highly visible position in comparison to classroom teaching (Campbell, 1985, p. 76). Subject expertise alone will not enable history coordinators to bring about curriculum change. An understanding of interpersonal relationships is crucial for success and one of the skills required of coordinators in foundation and primary settings is the ability to work effectively as part of a team or group. It is neither possible nor desirable for coordinators to work alone and in isolation. Effective team work in schools and nurseries can contribute to the more rapid implementation of new ideas, promote better use of a wider range of individual experience, skills and attributes and offer greater security and motivation for all members of staff.

Clearly, any attempt to work effectively as a group will take place within the overall ethos and climate that pervades the whole nursery/school and this atmosphere is very much a product of the impact of external changes and the activities of senior management. Although not necessarily directly related to a history coordinator's attempts to implement changes in the history curriculum, factors such as National Curriculum modifications, SATs, Local Management of Schools, inspection, appraisal or performance-related pay can all impact indirectly upon their efforts to foster collaborative work. Coordinators may find themselves trying to manage and overcome resistance to change that is an inevitable concomitant of a top-down approach in which those who have to implement the changes have had little or no input into the process. That said, coordinators need to practise what they preach, show consistency and lead by example. Colleagues who feel respected and valued are more likely to contribute positively in group situations. The ability to work well with others is particularly pronounced in early years settings such as nurseries where the majority of staff, teaching and non-teaching, are likely to be involved in every aspect of the pupils' learning. The irony for many primary teachers is that although educational developments such as the National Curriculum, SATs and Ofsted inspections have compelled staff to work more collaboratively at certain points, an individualistic approach to teaching is still discernible. Coordinators can, therefore, be faced with trying to square the circle by showing that working collaboratively is not inimical to professional independence but can actually be supportive of it. One possible approach to this task is to remember that any group is made up of individuals. While team work can be good for offering companionship and support, colleagues may also welcome recognition for their individual contributions. If the group is to remain motivated it needs to offer the individuals in it a sense of personal achievement and a degree of challenge and responsibility consistent with their abilities.

The role of the history coordinator in leading collaborative work with colleagues

- Mediate the relationships within the group to facilitate a degree of cohesion and common purpose. Everyone has a right to contribute, including younger, less experienced, less high status staff.
- Encourage other members of staff to take a professional approach to teamwork by recognizing the different and complementary strengths that they bring to collaborative work.
- Be positive, energetic, enthusiastic and creative.
- Be caring and considerate, offer praise, recognition and practical support to the group. Allow others to take the credit for their own efforts.
- Share information and responsibility.
- Be open and honest, accept constructive criticism with good grace (not easy when you are feeling highly visible and vulnerable).
- Give yourself permission not to know everything and to seek advice when necessary.
- Show confidence in front of others and demonstrate a reluctance to 'flap'. Be prepared to represent your colleagues, for example in discussions with the headteacher and governors about developments in the teaching and learning of history across the school.

Delegation

Although the history coordinator is responsible for the subject, there will be occasions when they need to draw on the expertise and experience of their colleagues. Delegation is one means of doing this. Effective delegation can be a useful way of ensuring involvement and encouraging commitment to curriculum change and development by offering opportunities to colleagues to have their say and influence the final outcome. To delegate is to get something done through the efforts of others. A coordinator who delegates part of their job is attempting to achieve results by empowering and motivating other members of staff to carry out tasks that they are ultimately accountable for. Delegation is not *passing the buck* or *dumping* unpleasant or tedious tasks onto other people. It is giving the right people the right task at the right time for the right reasons. Such participation can lead to increased levels of motivation by offering more variety, responsibility and wider experience. Delegation can also be a useful mechanism in developing a flexible, multi-skilled staff team, resulting in a wider reservoir of talent, experience and expertise for the nursery or school. Finally, delegation can produce time for the coordinator to engage in the managerial and leadership aspect of their role. Quality teaching and learning in history cannot be achieved by the coordinator alone, such provision across a nursery or school is only possible when everyone is involved and included to a greater or lesser extent. Clearly coordinators have to think carefully about when, what and how they might delegate, particularly as every other member of staff also has curriculum responsibilities.

When to delegate

- The coordinator does not have time to do something. There might be someone who can do the task today whereas the coordinator cannot do it until much later.

    Three teacher training students were placed with Miss N., the history coordinator, for a week. They were all history specialists and the focus of the placement was on the role of the history coordinator. One of the tasks delegated to the students by Miss N. was to conduct an audit of the resources for history at Key Stage 2.

- The coordinator wants to create an opportunity for staff development. There may be someone on the staff who would benefit from doing a task in terms of their personal or professional development.

    In addition to her role as history coordinator Miss N. is also the mentor for a newly qualified teacher (NQT). Both teachers will be accompanying the Y3 pupils on a forthcoming visit to The Jorvik Centre in York to support the history topic 'Invaders and settlers'. The NQT is given the task of organizing the visit with guidance from Miss N.

- The task can be done better by another member of staff.

    Miss N. decided to compile samples of pupils' history work across Key Stages 1 and 2 in order to create a benchmarking resource that would facilitate assessment and moderation in the subject. Rather than go individually to every teacher throughout the school, she asked the Key Stage 1 and 2 team leaders to organize the collection of material and to pass the work on to her.

Routine jobs, chores and one-off tasks can all be delegated from time to time. So too can certain activities that will allow colleagues to employ special skills or aptitudes that the coordinator does not have. In some cases colleagues may have developed a particular enthusiasm for developing an aspect of the history curriculum in which case they could be encouraged to take their ideas forward. However, coordinators ought not to delegate major tasks, the handling of crises or policy-making decisions. In nursery and primary schools teachers are used to delegating tasks to other adults in the classroom, whether supervising groups or producing resources. Teachers are less likely to spot the opportunities for delegating to fellow teachers, partly because most teaching staff have a curriculum responsibility. Yet delegation is a possibility and a useful strategy for coordinators to consider in certain situations, for example during staff meetings and inservice days. Having decided what can and cannot be delegated and to whom, the history coordinator will need to think about the level of decision-making involved. Although a colleague may be doing the task, the coordinator is still accountable. They need therefore to have a mechanism for monitoring and controlling the process that enables them to be aware of progress, to guide and coach where necessary and to ensure the project is on track. Coordinators have to

- consider the levels of direction that colleagues are likely to need and the level of support;
- make sure that the person delegated understands what is being asked of them, by communicating the nature and purpose of the task clearly, the timescale involved and the desired outcomes or results;
- make clear the level of responsibility and the resources available to those delegated;
- check back to ensure that there is a shared understanding of what is involved;
- establish the right climate by listening to the thoughts and ideas of the delegate: they might bring a fresh perspective to the situation;
- be available and approachable so that the delegate can approach for help in resolving problems;
- review progress on a regular basis and build in praise and feedback along the way so that the delegate feels appreciated for what he/she is doing and so that credit is given where it is due. Intervention must not become interference, it is important to show that individuals are trusted;
- build in support and guidance such as coaching and development opportunities where necessary so the individual has the skills and abilities to complete the task;
- review the eventual outcomes against the original targets. What learning has taken place? What new skills and competencies have been developed? What future targets might there be? How effective were they at delegating?

Miss N. was asked to prepare a programme for the inservice day and produce draft materials on the policy and guidelines for history. Using the Local Authority model to provide headings for inclusion Miss N. produced a first draft of the updated policy and guidelines for history and circulated them to colleagues prior to the inservice day. She realized that she would need to balance involvement with manageability. Writing a school policy and guidelines by committee was likely to prove difficult. However, without the involvement of the staff in the process the documentation was unlikely to be used. Consequently she opted for an approach in which staff would be delegated to work in small groups to discuss and review the draft documentation and Miss N. planned to work with the different groups. This would be followed by a plenary session in which the various groups would be asked to feed back to the whole staff their thoughts and ideas on the proposed new documentation. Miss N. felt that this approach would create a degree of involvement and a sense of a team approach. Miss N. decided that she would minute the comments and suggestions and use the feedback to redraft a final version for approval by the school governors.

Producing Whole-school Documentation

The production of documentation for history is a good example of a coordinator's task that draws in contributions from the whole staff team. Such documentation is composed of policies, guidelines and schemes and team work in their production is essential if teachers are to feel a sense of ownership and confidence in their ability to deliver. Policies are succinct descriptions, outlining the nursery's/school's overall rationale for teaching a subject or tackling an educational issue. A policy statement should be to the point and written in plain English. A policy consists of broad principles which underpin the way in which a subject or issue is approached in a nursery/school. In effect it answers the questions, *What is it?* and *Why do we do/teach it?* Guidelines set out how the nursery/school expects staff to approach a subject or issue with their pupils and they are often attached to the policy statements. Guidelines provide a general framework and deal with a range of issues including organization and management, cross-curricular links and assessment. Schemes of work are based on national documentation and set out the detail of the history curriculum, showing where progression and continuity exist in the teaching of history during a child's time in the school (see Chapter 3). Below is the final draft of Miss N.'s policy and guidelines for history following the inservice day.

. . . . Primary School

Draft policy statement and guidelines

Subject: History   **Coordinator**: Miss N.

Date of publication: **Date of next revision:**

1. The aims of history teaching

Through the teaching of history pupils will develop an awareness of the past and an understanding of the changes that have taken place over time. Children should appreciate the social, political, economic, cultural and religious development of their society and other societies in Europe and the world over time. They will gain a greater understanding of their own world through being introduced to the events and personalities of the past.

We aim to teach the children
- historical skills;
- historical knowledge;
- to apply knowledge and skills from other curriculum areas in history.

2. Contribution to cross-curricular skills

Communication – communicating historical knowledge and understanding in a variety of ways.
– acquiring vocabulary and phrases relating to the passing of time.

Observation – describing and identifying reasons for and results of historical events and changes.

Study skills – in-depth study of particular periods.
– using a wide range of sources of historical information.

Problem solving – appreciation of different interpretations of historical events.

Numerical – the chronology of the main events within a Programme of Study.

Personal and social – historical features of particular periods including religious, social and cultural diversity of the societies studied.
– arouse interest in the past and realize that it can be enjoyable and exciting.

3. Planning for history

The National Curriculum and the Early Learning Goals provide the basic framework for our programme of teaching and assessment in history throughout the school. Schemes of work are planned over a two-year cycle and are linked to the QCA history documentation. This programme incorporates a mixed approach to the planning and teaching of history. It may be delivered in three ways during each year:

a. Linked work – thematically linked topics integrated with one or two other areas of the curriculum.

b. Blocked work – history units providing a series of linked history lessons that develop particular skills and knowledge.

c. History events or single lessons – in response to current events.

Medium-term planning is based on this programme and the weekly planning of teachers shows how each teacher undertakes these activities within their class.

4. Links with other subjects

History has the potential to be linked with a number of different subject areas. The main ongoing links identified are

Language and literacy/
English – speaking and listening, drama, socio-dramatic role play,
– reading and writing, essential for finding out about the past and communicating an understanding of history;

Numeracy/
mathematics – measures and chronology, ordering and sequencing, counting;
ICT – handling and communicating information, simulations.

Links with other curriculum areas are made explicit in medium-term planning sheets.

5. Classroom organization and management

Children are taught by class teachers and non-teaching colleagues using a range of whole-class, group and individual work. History can be a collaborative subject and pupils will be taught the skills required to work both as individuals and as members of a team.

6. Teaching methods

Staff will use a variety of teaching methods that include evidence-based approaches using documentation, artefacts and audio-visual materials as well as imaginative and creative approaches including the use of historical fiction and socio-dramatic role play.

7. Assessment, recording and reporting

Staff will make individual assessments of pupils based upon National Curriculum Programmes of Study, Early Learning Goals and the learning outcomes contained in the relevant QCA medium-term planning sheets.

  Annual reports to parents coupled with termly parents' meetings enable teachers to provide detailed information of pupils' progress and achievement in history.

8. Use of ICT in history

This is in line with the school's ICT policy.

Pupils will use ICT in history to
• handle historical information, including the use of the Internet;
• communicate historical information;
• work with programmes involving historical simulations.

9. Meeting the needs of pupils in the Foundation Stage

Young children are learning continuously and do not necessarily make subject distinctions. Learning objectives for nursery and reception pupils are based on the Early Learning Goals with particular reference to Knowledge and Understanding of the World. Staff are encouraged to use pupil observations and questions and familiar experiences as starting points for early historical discussions. Play and talk are central to the 3–5 curriculum and every opportunity is used to encourage young children's mastery of literacy as well as promoting their personal and social development.

10. Resources for history

A selection of resources is kept in a central store. The appropriate resources should be readily available to the children in order that they might exercise some responsibility for their own learning in history. We expect these resources to be kept in good condition and to be replaced when worn or used up. Staff will be responsible for returning resources to the central store when they have finished using them. In addition the school makes full use of the local museum loans service for providing historical artefacts.

11. Links with the cross-curricular elements

Links will be made between history and appropriate cross-curricular elements, such as Economic and Industrial Understanding; Citizenship; Environmental Education and Health Education. These links will be identified on the school's scheme of work for the subject.

Equal opportunities and multicultural education have a high priority in the school. In selecting curriculum materials staff should aim to raise children's awareness of the fact that history is not the preserve of any nation, culture or gender and to examine events from a wide variety of cultures and civilizations.

12. Links with the wider community

Opportunities are provided for the children to look at history locally through links with local businesses and organizations, through visits to historical sites and by inviting parents and other adults into school.

13. The role of the history coordinator

The coordinator, working alongside the headteacher, has the responsibility for ensuring quality in the teaching and learning of history in the school. He/She will take the lead role in the production of whole-school documentation and in addition will support colleagues in the production of short-term planning. He/She has responsibility for the maintenance of existing resources and equipment and for the ordering and purchase of new equipment and materials. He/She will attend courses, be a source of subject knowledge and provide inservice training for his/her colleagues.

14. The role of the headteacher

The headteacher will support the history coordinator in encouraging colleagues to teach history effectively. He/She will be responsible, through the history coordinator, for ensuring that the policy and guidelines are used and for bringing the policy and guidelines to staff for periodic updating. This policy will be reviewed every two years. The next review will begin in . . . . and the revised policy will be in place by . . . . The headteacher will ensure that the school's policy is in line with national policy and that of the LEA.

Summary

In the early stages of your career as a history coordinator, try to work with colleagues who are supportive and constructively critical. Devoting large amounts of time and effort to staff who are sceptical, suspicious or hostile may be draining and deflect you from success. Target your limited resources of time and energy carefully by concentrating your efforts on those who are at least willing to work with you. Make sure they get your support and any resources they need. At the same time make sure that you involve key people on the staff including the headteacher as you will need their support to be effective. Finally, remember that to a certain extent at least, when working as a history coordinator, 'Tain't what you do (it's the way that you do it), Tain't what you say (it's the way that you say it)' ('Fats' Waller, 1939).

Reflective Questions

Change

- What do your colleagues think history is/involves?
- How would you respond to colleagues who:
  - appear to enjoy the excitement of change?
  - may be open to persuasion but wish to be convinced before taking on the changes proposed?
  - are open opponents of change and whose criticisms are rational, well thought out, and well articulated?
  - may support something verbally, or at least make no overt opposition, but will avoid taking action to implement the changes required?
  - seem to lack both the will and the ability to change, doing nothing in the apparent hope that it will all just go away?

Motivation

How will you provide opportunities for colleagues to:

- experience a sense of achievement?
- feel that good work is recognized?
- participate in decision-making?
- take on some responsibilities and ownership for developments in the history curriculum?
- have some freedom to plan and organize their own work?
- grow in confidence and competence in history teaching?

Working with others

Experience of team membership can inform approaches to team leadership. Treat members of a team in the same way that you yourself would wish to be treated. Think about instances of team work that have been positive experiences. Add your own examples to the list below:

- Colleagues listened to what I had to say.
- I was asked for my views.
- I was made to feel that my contribution was equally valuable.
- I felt supported in an unfamiliar area.

- _____
- _____
- _____

Think about instances of team work that have been negative experiences. Add your own examples to the list below:

- I was interrupted and denied the opportunity to contribute properly.
- My views were not wanted or valued.
- I was put down and harried.
- The activities of the team were totally dominated by one or two individuals.

- _____

- _____

- _____

REFERENCES

Alexander, R., Rose, J. and Woodhead, C. (1992) *Curriculum Organisation and Classroom Practice in Primary Schools: A Discussion Paper*, London: DES.

Bentley, D. and Watts, M. (1994) *Teaching and Learning in Primary Science and Technology*, Buckingham: Open University Press.

Campbell, R. J. (1985) *Developing the Primary School Curriculum*, London: Holt, Rinehart and Winston.

Department for Education (DFE) (1995) *Key Stages 1 and 2 of the National Curriculum*, London: DFE.

Department for Education and Employment (DfEE) (1998a) *Circular 4/98: Teaching: High Status, High Standards*, London: DfEE.

Department for Education and Employment (DfEE) (1998b) *The National Literarcy Strategy*, Sudbury: DfEE.

Department for Education and Employment (DfEE) (1999) *The National Numeracy Strategy*, Sudbury: DfEE.

Department of Education and Science (DES) (1989) *National Curriculum: From Policy to Practice*, London: DES.

Qualifications and Curriculum Authority (QCA) (1999a) *The National Curriculum: Handbook for Primary Teachers in England*, London: DfEE/QCA.

Qualifications and Curriculum Authority (QCA) (1999b) *Early Learning Goals*, London: DfEE/QCA.

School Curriculum and Assessment Authority (SCAA) (1996) *Nursery Education: Desirable Outcomes for Children's Learning on Entering Compulsory Education*, London: DfEE/SCAA.

Waller, F. (1939) 'Tain't what you do', on *Fats Waller and his Rhythm, Complete Recordings* (vol. 16), Paris: RCA Black and White Series.

Webb, R. (1994) *After the Deluge: Changing Roles and Responsibilities in the Primary School*, London: Association of Teachers and Lecturers (ATL).

Index

206